THE
Baseball ⟨27⟩ Research
JOURNAL

Editor: Mark Alvarez
Designated Reader: Dick Thompson
Copy Editor: A.D. Suehsdorf

THE BASEBALL RESEARCH JOURNAL (ISSN 0734-6891, ISBN 0-910137-78-1), Number 28. Published by The Society for American Baseball Research, Inc. P.O. Box 93183, Cleveland, OH, 44101. Postage paid at Birmingham, AL. Copyright 1999 by The Society for American Baseball Research, Inc. All rights reserved. Reproduction in whole or in part without written permission is prohibited. Printed by EBSCO Media, Birmingham, AL.

The Society for American Baseball Research

History

The Society for American Baseball Research (SABR) was founded on August 10, 1971, by L. Robert "Bob" Davids and fifteen other baseball researchers at Cooperstown, New York, and now boasts more than 7,100 members worldwide. The Society's objectives are

- ◆ to foster the study of baseball as a significant American institution,
- ◆ to establish an accurate historical account of baseball through the years,
- ◆ to facilitate the dissemination of baseball research information,
- ◆ to stimulate the best interest of baseball as our national pastime, and
- ◆ to cooperate in safeguarding proprietary interests of individual research efforts of members of the Society.

Baseball Research Journal

The Society published its first annual *Baseball Research Journal* in January 1972. The present volume is the twenty-eighth. Most of the previous volumes are still available for purchase (see inside back cover). The editorial policy is to publish a cross section of research articles by our members which reflect their interest in history, biography, statistics and other aspects of baseball not previously published.

Interested in Joining the Society?

SABR membership is open to all those interested in baseball research, statistics or history. The 2000 membership dues are $50 US, $60 Canada & Mexico and $65 overseas (US funds only) and are based on the calendar year. Members receive the *Baseball Research Journal*, *The National Pastime*, *The SABR Bulletin*, and other special publications. Senior, Student and family options are available. To join SABR, mail the form (or a photocopy) below to SABR, 812 Huron Rd E #719, Cleveland OH 44115 or check www.sabr.org.

- -

SABR Membership Form: 2000

Name: _____

Address: _____

_____

Home Phone: _____

E-Mail/Fax: _____

Birthdate: _____ Application Date: _____

__ How I Found Out About SABR
__ SABR member who referred me
__ Gift from:

_____

2000 Annual Dues:	US	Canada/Mexico	Overseas
	$50	$60 US$	$65 US$
Three-Year	$140	$170 US$	$185 US$
Students	$30	$40 US$	$45 US$
Seniors	$30	$40 US$	$45 US$

Family Membership: Additional family members living at the same address may join SABR for $15 per year per person. Family membership entitles one to full member benefits except the publications. One set of publications will be sent to each household

Students are under 18 years of age or full-time college student (Copy of college ID required).
Seniors are 65 years or older
SABR membership is based on the calendar year.

Will you allow SABR to sell your name to baseball-related companies who rent SABR's mailing list?

	YES	NO
Are you interested in regional meetings?	YES	NO
Are you willing to research?	YES	NO

Areas of Interest:

1. Minor Leagues	12. Collegiate Baseball
2. Negro Leagues	13. Latin America
3. Baseball Records	14. Umpire/Rules
4. Biographical Research	15. Computerization
5. Statistical Analysis	16. Women in Baseball
6. Ballparks	17. Oral History
7. Hall of Fame	18. Baseball Education
8. 19th Century	19. Scouts
9. Socio-Economic Aspects	20. Pictorial History
10. Bibliography	21. Baseball Music and Poetry

Rogers Hornsby

Sure, modern offense is great, but let's not forget this guy

Paul Warburton

To many St. Louis fans Mark McGwire's fabulous seventy-homer 1998 campaign must seem like the best season ever enjoyed by a Cardinal player. Yet back in 1922 a guy by the name of Rogers Hornsby in many ways turned in a superior performance while playing for the Redbirds. In 1998, McGwire blasted seventy homers with 152 hits, 130 runs scored, 147 RBIs, twenty-one doubles, 162 walks, 383 total bases and a .299 batting average. In 1922, Hornsby rang up 250 hits, 141 runs scored, 152 RBIs, forty-two homers, forty-six doubles, fourteen triples, sixty-five walks, 450 total bases and a .401 batting average. The Mighty Rajah's offensive statistics top Big Mac's numbers in every category except home runs and walks. McGwire's awesome accomplishments are fresh in the minds of baseball fans, but a visit back to 1922 will add a little perspective.

Unlike the free-living Babe Ruth, Hornsby took care of himself. He would not attend movies because he feared they might damage his eyesight and he even avoided reading to any extent. He believed religiously in the benefits of a good sirloin steak and would search out visiting cities for the best places to get one. The formula seemed to work. In the five years from 1921 to 1925, the amazing hitter who grew up playing ball against grown men in the stockyards of Fort Worth, Texas, went to bat 2,679 times and made

1,078 hits for an average of .402.

No other batter has put up a better record of sustained hitting and it is doubtful anyone ever will. Of the five seasons, 1922 was Hornsby's best, despite the fact that he hit the modern-day record .424 in 1924. Ty Cobb hit for a higher lifetime batting average and Ruth was a more powerful home run threat, but Hornsby for a time combined the ability to hit for a stratospheric average with the ability to drive the ball over the fence better than anyone who ever played the game.

Before the 1921 World Series between the New York Giants and the New York Yankees, John McGraw was asked if his Giants were worried by Babe Ruth's bat. McGraw replied, "Why should I worry about Ruth. My pitchers have been throwing to a better hitter all summer." He was referring, of course, to Hornsby. McGraw coveted Hornsby's tremendous hitting ability, and rumors circulated before the 1922 season that the Giants were offering $200,000 (a lot of money in those days) and four players to get him. Hornsby, however, said he didn't want to play in New York and promised Cardinal fans that he wouldn't leave St. Louis as long as Branch Rickey was his manager. *The Sporting News* invented a name for the Hornsby trade rumors that seemed to pop up each spring during the 1920s: "hornsbyitis."

Hornsby kept his batting eye sharp after the 1921 season ended by playing in a four-team league in California. The teams played a late-autumn ten-week schedule. Hornsby played for the Los Angeles entry

Paul Warburton *is a former sportswriter for Wilson Publishing who now works for Metropolitan Insurance Company. His cousin, Robbie Derksen, managed the Australian Olympic Baseball Team in 1996.*

while Ty Cobb, Harry Heilmann, and George Sisler were the featured stars on the three other teams. Cobb led the league in batting average, but Hornsby hit .390 in sixty-one games and led in home runs with thirteen. When the short season ended Cobb declared that Hornsby was the best hitter he had ever seen. Sisler added that Hornsby possessed a better sense of the strike zone than anyone in baseball.

The basics—Hornsby batted from the right side. He stood at the far rear corner of the batter's box, feet close together, but pitchers who thought they could get him out by pitching to the outside corner of the plate discoverd he had tremendous power to the opposite field. He said he never tried for home runs but that he did try to hit every pitch as hard as he could. He was renowned among opposing catchers as one of the two hitters of his era who would not shorten their grip with two strikes. The other was Ruth.

While the Babe thrilled crowds with skyscraping home runs that sometimes traveled 500 feet, Hornsby wielded his thirty-five-inch bat to rocket line drives. His swing was a thing of beauty to fans and players alike: perfectly balanced, powerful, and smooth, with a gorgeous followthrough.

All the same, Hornsby was not popular. He was aloof, austere, single-minded, arrogant, and tactless. His main acknowledged diversions from baseball were sitting in hotel lobbies and betting on the horses. When he was told that the public didn't consider him a colorful ballplayer, Hornsby responded, "I am told that I lack color. I don't fight with umpires and I'm not going to. I don't run wild on the base paths spiking other players. If I had to play dirty baseball, I would rather not play at all. Color, in the popular eye seems to consist of just these things. I'll go along doing my best, letting my work speak for me."

Beginning the great season—On April 12, opening day at Sportsman's Park in 1922, 17,000 fans saw the Cards humble the Pirates, 10-1, as Hornsby socked a single and belted a homer. A then franchise record 550,000 fans would see the Cardinals at home in 1922. They battled the Giants for the league lead until falling in mid-August and September into a tie for third place eight games off the pace. The Cardinals hit .301, but ranked seventh in the league in pitching with a 4.44 ERA, and last in fielding with 239 errors.

Hornsby hit safely through his first eight games, tagging two homers and four doubles along the way. His streak was stopped in Cincinnati by four walks.

On April 28 in Chicago, Hornsby walloped a three-run homer in the first inning and smashed a titanic solo shot over the dead center field fence in the ninth inning. The second blast was reported to be the longest ball yet hit at Wrigley Field. The Cards won the game, 11-3, and were banging the ball consistently, but their 8-7 record at the end of April was nothing to get excited about. Hornsby was hitting .389. Unlike most .400 hitters in baseball history he would stay under .400 most of the season before going three-for-five on the final day to finish at .401—.402 at Sportsman's Park, notoriously friendly to hitters, and .400 on the road.

On May 15, the Cards routed the Phils, 19-7, slashing twenty-three hits. Hornsby ripped two singles and a triple. Two days later the Cards shelled Brooklyn's spitballer Burleigh Grimes, 11-0, as Hornsby singled twice, homered, and swiped two bases. He stole seventeen bases in 1922, as he had in three previous seasons. It was his top mark. Though he wasn't known as a base stealer, Hornsby, like DiMaggio later, went from first to third like an impala. Christy Mathewson, picking his all-time team in 1926 called Hornsby "the fastest man in baseball."

Manhandling the NL—On May 19, during a 10-6 win over Brooklyn, Hornsby lined a rocket into the center field bleachers at Sportsman's Park that newspapermen said was easily the longest drive ever hit in the city of St. Louis. On May 22, his seventh-inning three-run homer against Boston tied the score at 6-6, but the Braves went on to win in thirteen innings, 8-6. The next day Hornsby belted another three-run homer in the seventh inning, but the Braves won again by the same score. Boston and Cincinnati were the only teams that held Hornsby under .400 in 1922. He hit a mere .348 against the Braves.

(Oldtimers used to tell a story about Hornsby's 1928 season with the Braves. A decade after that season, one of the Braves came into the dugout complaining to manager Casey Stengel about the configuration and prevailing winds at Braves Field. "How the hell can they expect anybody to hit up there," he wanted to know. "The wind is always with the pitcher. Nobody can hit up there." Stengel answered mildly, "All I know is that Hornsby played here one whole season and batted .387." [.372 at Braves Field and .401 on the road.])

On May 25, a special day to benefit the St. Louis playgrounds, brought a capacity crowd including Judge Kenesaw Mountain Landis to Sportsman's Park. The Pirates topped the Cards, 7-3, but Hornsby was perfect at three-for-three with his tenth homer. He homered again the next day as the Cards rebounded to win, 6-2, and lined two more homers in a 4-3 victory over the Bucs two days later, propelling him past St. Louis Browns slugger Ken Williams and into the major league lead.

At the end of May, *The Sporting News* said of the Cardinals, "The team would be in a sad way without Hornsby. He's not the most showy or the noisiest player in the game, but his quiet thoroughness can't be equaled anywhere." *The Sporting News* added, "Rogers is about two-thirds of the Cardinal infield when it comes to defense and everybody knows what he is on offense." This comment flies in the face of the general belief that Hornsby was a poor fielder, especially at going back for pop flies. (Lefty Gomez once famously quipped, "He never hit any so how would he know how to catch them.") The rap on his fielding may have been, at least partially, a result of his long fade after the 1930 injury that ended his real productivity, and his bitter unpopularity with his peers. They sure couldn't criticize his hitting.

On June 12, in Philadelphia, the Cards ripped ten hits in a row during the sixth inning of a 14-7 thrashing of the Phils. Hornsby enjoyed another perfect day with four of the Cards' twenty-three hits, including a three-run homer. He hit .522 at Baker Bowl in 1922. What might he have hit for the season if he'd been a Phil?

On June 15, Hornsby's tenth-inning RBI double beat Brooklyn, 4-3. He added two singles and homer number fifteen the succeeding day, but the Cards lost in Flatbush, 12-2. On June 22, he was hitting .397. His closest competitor in the league was Pittsburgh's Carson Bigbee at .363. On June 29, his first inning homer in an 8-5 win at Pittsburgh was called one of the longest balls ever hit at Forbes Field. On July 1, he boomed two doubles, a triple, and a home run in a doubleheader against the Pirates.

On the Fourth of July, the Cards split a doubleheader with the Reds in St. Louis. The Reds won the morning game, 11-9. Hornsby was ejected from the contest for disputing a close call at first base. The fans and newspaper reporters thought that he had clearly beaten out an infield bouncer in the fourth inning, but rookie umpire Charles Pfirman didn't see it that way. Hornsby angrily pointed a finger at Pfirman, eventually poking him in the nose with it. That was his ticket to the clubhouse. Such occurrences were rare for Hornsby. As long as his base hits kept coming he paid little attention to umpires.

The ejection seemed to spark the team, however.

The Redbirds went on a rampage, winning seventeen of their next twenty games, including ten by one run. They won the afternoon game, 6-5, as Hornsby returned to slam his nineteenth homer. He hit his twentieth homer the following day as the Cards routed the Reds, 11-4. Brooklyn was the next unfortunate visitor to Sportsman's Park. A twenty-hit attack, including two by Hornsby crushed Uncle Robbie's ballclub, 14-2, in the opener. On July 7, Hornsby slashed three hits and won the game, 6-5, with a ninth-inning home run off Dazzy Vance. He had four hits and two stolen bases on July 8 as the Cards beat Brooklyn again, 10-7. The Cards then won their sixth straight, 6-5, as Hornsby doubled, tripled, and threw a Robins runner out at the plate to save the game. On July 10, his three-run homer in the seventh inning was the difference in a 4-1 win, as St. Louis completed their sweep of the Robins. In 1922, Hornsby hit .533 against Brooklyn pitchers in St. Louis.

Even Hornsby's foul balls seemed to be doing damage. A professional singer named Eleanor McLaughlin filed suit against him for $15,000. She claimed that the shock of being struck by a foul ball from his bat on July 10 ruined her voice.

"The greatest batsman of all time"—Hornsby tied Gavvy Cravath's post-1900 National League home run record on July 14, with his twenty-fourth blast, against Cravath's old team, the Phils. The Cards had cut New York's lead to 2-1/2 games, and the Giants were due in town for a four-game series. A record total of 75,000 fans jammed the ballpark for the four games. The Cards won three of them. In the final game, Hornsby doubled twice and singled to spark a 9-8 victory. He hit .409 against the Giants in 1922—.395 in St. Louis and .422 at the Polo Grounds—with eight home runs. (Hornsby always hit well against the Giants. During a series in 1924 he made thirteen hits in fourteen at bats against them, prompting National League President John Heydler, who was in attendance, to proclaim Hornsby "the greatest batsman of all-time." No wonder McGraw wanted him so badly.)

The Boston Braves followed the Giants into baseball-crazy St. Louis. Hornsby won the first game, 7-6, with a dramatic ninth-inning, three-run homer. An overflow crowd of 25,000 fans ran out on the field and mobbed him. He was carried off the diamond on their shoulders. Thousands waited for him at the clubhouse door while he dressed and gave him another huge ovation as he left the park.

Twenty-four hours later he was back, slugging a

two-run homer off Rube Marquard in the sixth inning as the Cards beat the Braves in ten innings, 5-4. The Cards took over first place two days later. Hornsby contributed a single and two doubles in a 9-8 triumph over the cellar-dwelling Braves. Hundreds of straw hats sailed onto the field at the game's conclusion.

On July 23, the Cards left cozy Sportsman's Park and boarded a train to New York for a five-game series. The Giants scored forty-two runs to win four of them. Hornsby was "held" to eight hits in twenty-two at bats. Three of his hits were doubles and he homered once.

July proved to be Hornsby's best month for power in 1922. He slammed sixteen doubles, three triples, and ten home runs and drove in forty-two runs in thirty-five games. Ballplayers commonly got worn down by the sizzling summer heat in St. Louis. Not Hornsby. As a youngster in the Lone Star State he played ball from dawn to sundown. He carried that same endurance into the major leagues. In 1924, he hit .509 in August.

St. Louis rallied to enjoy its last day in first place on August 10 by topping the Braves in Boston, 7-3. From then on their fortunes slid downhill. Not so for Hornsby. On August 13, his homer in a 16-5 loss to the Cubs started him on a thirty-three-game hitting streak.

On August 25, the Giants visited St. Louis for the final time and swept the Cards three straight. St. Louis pennant hopes were dead. Hornsby went nine-for-twelve in the series with two triples and three homers. He finished August hitting .389.

The season was winding down, but Hornsby's bat was still white hot. In a five-game series at Redland Park in Cincinnati, the St. Louis hitting machine sprayed ten hits in twenty-four at bats including a double, two triples off Eppa Rixey, and an inside-the-park homer that rebounded off the facing of the right field bleachers. His next stop was Philadelphia, where he rattled Baker Bowl for twelve hits in nineteen at-bats including four doubles and two homers. He had hit in thirty straight games.

His streak was stopped in Brooklyn by Burleigh Grimes's moist delivery in the first game of a double-header on September 20. In the second game of the day Hornsby homered in the first and ninth innings sandwiched around a single as the Cards won, 13-7.

Hornsby's last New York trip of the season was memorable. The Giants again took three of four games, but Hornsby ripped nine more hits including three homers. One of the homers was a bomb that kited deep into the upper right-field stands, while another was a towering fly to left center that Hornsby beat out for an inside-the-parker with a terrific sprint between third base and home. In the final game, Jesse Haines seemed to express the frustration of the entire St. Louis pitching staff, hurling the ball over the grandstand roof when he was relieved in the fifth.

In 1921, Hornsby had been above .400 before going hitless in his last two games to finish at .397. In 1922, shortly before the Cards took the field for their final game in Chicago, James M. Gould of the St. Louis *Dispatch* told Hornsby that he needed three hits to finish over .400. He got them. He had saved his best hitting for September, when he wore out opposing hurlers for a .438 average.

Fade—Hornsby managed the Cardinals to a world championship over Babe Ruth and the Yankees in 1926, then moved on to New York, Boston, and Chicago in successive years. He was still productive, leading the league in batting and slugging as Boston's player-manager in 1928, and in slugging in 1929 with pennant-winning Chicago.

But after an operation on his right heel following the 1929 season Hornsby's days as a full-time player ended. He tried to play in 1930, but limped noticeably and was benched. He fractured his left ankle while sliding into third base in May, and became a virtual baseball cripple at the age of thirty-four—just too early to take advantage of that all-time offensive year.

During the 1920s Hornsby hit .382 in 5,451 at bats. He led the league in batting seven times, slugging nine times, on-base percentage eight times, runs scored five times, RBIs four times, home runs twice, hits four times, doubles four times, triples twice, walks three times, and total bases seven times. Lifetime, in his shortened career, he had 2,930 hits (thirty-five percent of which went for extra bases), 301 home runs, and a .358 batting average.

Hornsby managed the Cubs and the St. Louis Browns during the '30s, and in that role managed to hit .313 in 719 at bats through 1937. He came back for another year with the Browns and a season plus with the Reds in the early '50s. As a manager Hornsby was harsh and unpopular. He often expressed disdain for players who couldn't play the game as well as he had. But when he held a bat in his hands it was said that he still had nothing but admirers.

Hornsby is a fascinating transitional character who was already an established star when Ruth came along to showcase the power game. As a result, he is often misremembered today as a Dead Ball Era figure. He was anything but. He was his league's premier slugger—as well as its finest pure batsman—for a decade. As an all-around offensive force, he was on the same level as DiMaggio, Williams, Musial, Mays, Aaron, Mantle—even Ruth himself.

Let's relish the wonderful Mark McGwire, but let's not forget that other Cardinal of seven decades ago, whose 1922 season was merely the best of a decade of great performances. In St. Louis, in baseball, Rogers Hornsby takes a back seat to nobody.

Stahl's Suicide

Chick Stahl's suicide is a well-known piece of baseball lore. The two accepted theories about why Stahl took his own life are first, that the pressure of managing a big league team, the Boston Red Sox, was too much for him, and second, that his prowess as a ladies man had finally caught up with him. These factors may have played a role in Stahl's death, but the sadder truth can be found in the March 30, 1907 edition of the Fort Wayne Journal-Gazette, Stahl's hometown paper. The following condensed version carried the headlines, MEDITATED SELF-SLAYING, CHICK STAHL HAD OFTEN TALKED ABOUT SUICIDE, *and* BALL PLAYER HAD ENTERTAINED DANGEROUS IDEAS ABOUT SELF-DESTRUCTION.

Close friends of Chick Stahl were not surprised at his suicide, although there was universal regret over his tragic death.

"I looked for it when I heard he was worrying about the management of his team," said a friend of Stahl's since his boyhood. "Chick talked about killing himself several times, when he was discouraged about his affairs, and I recall one time when he was in a barber's chair, about five years ago. I heard him tell the barber who was shaving him that it would be a good thing for him to put the razor through his neck.

"Of you would just push that blade in a cut my head about half off, so I would never feel it I'd be rid of my trouble," said Stahl to the barber. But more than once before that time and more than once afterwards he was heard to say things that indicated a suicidal tendency.

To his friends Chick Stahl always seemed the soul of joviality but there was ever to his ready laughter a sort of half-repressed melancholy.

Years ago, when Stahl was playing amateur ball, he had periods of mental depression, and when the future looked dark he used to talk about taking his own life. Sometimes the slightest disappointment would sink him into almost a stupor of depression.

Even when he was playing in the city league he once, in a time of discouragement, expressed a wish for death. And but a few months ago he told a friend that he should never be found playing in a minor baseball league.

It is not unlikely that his own worst realization of his inability to manage the Boston team increased his depression to the point that led to his suicide. He realized his downfall, and he knew he was not to blame, for he said, before he accepted the management of the team that he was a ball player and not a manager. He told his friends that the managership interfered with his playing. He foresaw his failure as a player, and the old promise that he would not play in a minor league was made good when he put an end to his life.

—Dick Thompson

Twenty-Game Losers

Many are winners, too

Steve Charak

In his only winning season, Steve Arlin logged a 1-0 record in two appearances with the San Diego Padres in 1970. Arlin went 9-19 in 1971, then 10-21 in 1972. His winning percentage in 1972 may have been lower than that of the rest of the team, but so was his earned run average.

Roger Craig pitched in two World Series for the Dodgers. He became famous for his 10-24 and 5-22 seasons with the expansion Mets. After being traded to the Cardinals, he once again appeared in the World Series. Like Arlin, he was a good pitcher hurling for a bad team.

Most SABR members can answer the question, "Who was the last pitcher to lose twenty games in a season?" Every time someone closes in on Brian Kingman's 8-20 "achievement," he is mentioned or interviewed. Oakland A's manager Billy Martin used a five-man rotation in 1980 (and virtually no bullpen). The other four starters compiled winning records, and the team finished 83-79. Despite Kingman's record, Martin felt confident enough to put him out there every fifth game.

Arlin, Craig, and Kingman show that it takes a decent pitcher to be a twenty-game loser. This is pretty common wisdom, but I didn't know just how elite a group of pitchers these "losers" were until I studied them. Some of the surprises I uncovered:

1. The number of seasons before 1980 when no one lost twenty games.
2. The number of Hall of Fame pitchers who had twenty-loss seasons in their careers.
3. The number of twenty-game losers who were also twenty-game winners at some time in their careers.
4. The number of twenty-win seasons that followed twenty-loss seasons and vice versa.

Thirteen seasons before 1980 had no twenty-game losers. The American League went from 1946 to 1953 without one. If the 1918 season hadn't been shortened by World War I, Eddie Cicotte, who won more than twenty in 1917 and 1919, would have lost twenty.

Counting the two from the Federal League, the major leagues have had 171 twenty-game losers since 1901. Twenty-three of those seasons were accumulated by players now in the Hall of Fame. In addition, two Hall of Famers who never lost twenty each led their league in losses once. Forty-eight other twenty-loss seasons were "accomplished" by players who were also twenty-game winners at some time during their careers. The Hall of Famers noted won at least twenty games eighty-two times. The non-Hall pitchers won twenty games seventy-three times. These were quality pitchers.

It makes sense that many of the twenty-loss seasons happened in the Dead Ball Era, when pitchers were asked to pitch more innings. Sixty-three of the twenty-loss seasons occurred between 1901 and 1910.

Few major league teams had four twenty-game win-

Steve Charak *is a writer, publisher, educator, and musician who lives in Olympia, Washington. His first CD or original songs,* Come Here, Go Away, *was recently released.*

ners in one season. Only one major league team has had four twenty-game losers in one year, and they did twice—in consecutive years. The Boston Nationals, led by Vic Willis's record twenty-nine losses did it in 1905. (Kaiser Wilhelm went 4-23 that year.) They repeated in 1906. Vic Willis had gone to Pittsburgh, where he went 22-13 for a third-place team. His replacement, Gus Dorner, who joined the team from Cincinnati early in the season, led the league in losses with twenty-six. The 1905 team managed to avoid last place, since their 51-103 was better than Brooklyn's 48-104.

Since 1920, no league has had four twenty-game losers in one year.

One might not have suspected that Walter Johnson, with his 13-25 in 1909, would win over 400 games in his career. Yet he followed that season with ten consecutive twenty-win seasons. (Including 36-7 in 1913.)

Red Ruffing becomes Exhibit A in the argument that the team's play helped determine a pitcher's won-lost record. With the Red Sox, he went 39-93, with two twenty-loss seasons. After being traded to the Yankees, he became a winning pitcher. Ruffing won twenty or more each year, 1936-39.

Bullet Joe Bush was the ace of the 1916 Philadelphia A's. His 15-24 record led a team that went 36-117. (Bush and Elmer Myers combined for 29-47. The rest of the team went 7-70.) For the 1922 pennant-winning Yankees, Bush went 26-7.

His team's performance doesn't explain Steve Carlton's record, however. Carlton went 27-10 with the 1972 Phillies, who won 59 games. In 1973, the Phillies improved to 71-91, but Carlton slipped to 13-20.

Dolf Luque's 1922 record is also a puzzle. He went 13-23 with a Reds team that went 86-66 (and included twenty-five-game winner Eppa Rixey). In 1923, when Luque posted a 27-8 record, the Reds improved to 91-63.

No pennant-winning team has had a twenty-game

Twenty Wins and Losses in the Same Season

Joe McGinnity	
1901	26-20
1903	31-20
Vic Willis	
1902	27-20
Bill Dinneen	
1902	21-21
George Mullin	
1905	21-21
1907	20-20
Jim Scott	
1913	20-20
Walter Johnson	
1916	25-20
Wilbur Wood	
1973	24-20
Phil Niekro	
1979	21-20

loser since George Mullin went 20-20 for the Tigers in 1907. (He also won two games in the World Series.) He also managed to go 21-21 in 1905. Mullin must have liked being a .500 pitcher.

Seven other pitchers won twenty and lost twenty in the same season. Iron Man McGinnity went 31-20 and 26-20 in his two twenty-loss seasons. Phil Niekro put together a 21-20 season after his manager decided to copy Chuck Tanner's strategy of using knuckleballer Wilbur Wood every fourth day. Wood put together four twenty-win seasons. One of those was a 24-20. Togie Pittinger tried. He went 19-23 in 1903, after going 27-16 in 1902. Walter Johnson's 25-20 in 1916 made him one of four Hall of Fame pitchers in this group.

If your name was Sad Sam Jones and you pitched in the major leagues, you belong to the élite group. Sad Sam I lost twenty in 1919 and twenty-one in 1925. In between those years, he won twenty twice. Sad Sam II lost twenty with the Cubs in 1955 and won twenty-one with the Giants in 1959. Looks as though he, too, was at the mercy of the team for which he played.

Again, it takes a good pitcher to lose twenty. Even Milt Gaston, who went 97-164 as a pitcher "only" lost twenty once. Ned Garver, with his 129-157 lifetime record, never lost twenty. Ken Raffensberger, 119-154 as a pitcher, lost twenty but once. Pedro Ramos led the American League in losses 1958-1961, yet he was able to lose twenty "only" one time.

Once upon a time, this year's twenty-game winner could be next year's twenty-game loser. Or, more pleasantly for the pitcher, the reverse could happen. While most of twenty-four instances since 1901 occurred early in the century, six of them happened to pitchers in the '60s and '70s. Again, these were good pitchers, including Cy Young winner Randy Jones. Hall of Famer Phil Niekro belonged to this group. Wilbur Wood posted 160 decisions 1972-1975, an average of forty a year. We may never see that again.

Bill James once criticized Chuck Tanner for sparing one of his pitchers the stigma of losing twenty games in a season. These day, managers are likely to go quickly to one of their five middle relievers. Then again, with rich teams getting richer and poor teams getting poorer, some managers may be forced to stay with pitchers longer. Maybe we'll see the return of the twenty-game loser.

Number of Twenty Game Losers in Each League, 1901-1980

Year	AL	NL	FL	Year	AL	NL
1901	3	2		1941	0	0
1902	1	2		1942	1	1
1903	3	2		1943	1	1
1904	6	6		1944	0	1
1905	4	7		1945	1	1
1906	2	6		1946	0	0
1907	3	2		1947	0	0
1908	1	4		1948	2	0
1909	2	3		1949	0	0
1910	1	3		1950	1	0
1911	0	0		1951	0	0
1912	1	2		1952	1	0
1913	2	2		1953	1	0
1914	0	2	1	1954	1	1
1915	1	0	1	1955	0	1
1916	2	1		1956	1	0
1917	0	2		1957	1	1
1918	0	0		1958	0	0
1919	1	0		1959	0	0
1920	3	4		1960	0	1
1921	2	1		1961	1	0
1922	1	2		1962	0	3
1923	0	0		1963	1	1
1924	0	1		1964	0	1
1925	2	0		1965	0	3
1926	0	0		1966	1	1
1927	1	1		1967	0	0
1928	1	1		1968	0	0
1929	2	0		1969	1	1
1930	2	0		1970	0	0
1931	2	0		1971	1	0
1932	1	0		1972	0	1
1933	2	2		1973	2	1
1934	1	1		1974	2	3
1935	0	1		1975	1	0
1936	1	2		1976	0	0
1937	1	0		1977	0	2
1938	1	1		1978	0	0
1939	1	0		1979	0	1
1940	0	1		1980	1	0

20 Wins (or Losses) in a Year Followed by 20 Losses (or Wins) the Next

Steve Carlton
1972   27-9
1973   13-20

Paul Derringer
1934   15-21
1935   22-13

Russ Ford
1911   22-11
1912   13-21

Larry Jackson
1964   24-11
1965   14-21

Walter Johnson
1909   13-25
1910   25-17

Oscar Jones
1903   20-16
1904   17-25

Randy Jones
1974   8-22
1975   20-12

Alex Kellner
1949   20-12
1950   8-20

Jerry Koosman
1976   21-10
1977   8-20

Dolf Luque
1922   13-23
1923   27-8

Ted Lyons
1929   14-20
1930   22-15

Joe McGinnity
1901   26-20
1902   21-18
1903   31-20
1904   35-8

George Mullin
1904   17-23
1905   21-21

1906   21-18
1907   20-20

Bobo Newsom
1940   21-5
1941   12-20

Al Orth
1906   27-17
1907   14-21

Togie Pittinger
1902   27-16
1903   19-23
1904   15-21
1905   23-14

Jack Quinn
1914   26-14
1915   9-22

Eddie Rommel
1931   16-23
1932   27-13

Mel Stottlemyre
1965   20-9
1966   12-20

Luis Tiant
1968   21-9
1969   9-20

Ed Walsh
1910   18-20
1911   27-18

Vic Willis
1901   20-17
1902   27-20
1905   12-29
1906   22-13

Wilbur Wood
1972   24-17
1973   24-20
1974   20-19
1975   16-20

Cy Young
1906   13-21
1907   21-15

Hall of Fame Pitchers
Who Lost at Least
Twenty in One Year

Name	No. 20-loss seasons	No. 20-win seasons	Notes
Carlton	1	6	
Chesbro	1	5	
Grimes	0*	4	Led league, 1925 (19)
Haines	3	1	
W. Johnson	2	12	
Lemon	0*	7	Led league, 1951 (14)
Lyons	2	3	
Marquard	1	3	
McGinnity	2	8	26-20, 31-20 in 20-loss seasons
P. Niekro	2	3	
Rixey	2	4	
Roberts	1	6	
Ruffing	2	4	
Walsh	1	4	
Willis	2	6	
Young	1	6	From 1901 on

Non-Hall of Fame Pitchers Who Lost Twenty
at Least Once and Won Twenty at Least Once

Name	No. 20-loss seasons	No. 20-win seasons	Notes	Name	No. 20-loss seasons	No. 20-win seasons	Notes
Jesse Barnes	2	2		Kellner	1	1	
Joe Bush	1	1		V. Kennedy	1	1	
Camnitz	1	2		Koosman	1	2	
Cantwell	1	1		Lolich	1	2	
Cicotte	*	3	*lost 19 - short 1918	Luque	1	1	
Derringer	2	4		McLain	1	3	
Dickson	2	1		Meadows	1	2	
Dinneen	1	3		Mullin	3	5	
Doak	1	2		Newsom	3	2	
Ehmke	1	1		Orth	2	2	
Ellsworth	1	1		Quinn	1	1	Both Federal League
Falkenberg	1	2		Pittinger	1	2	
Russ Ford	1	3		Rommel	1	2	
Fraser	3	1		Jim Scott	1	2	
Gray	1	1		M. Stottlemyre	1	3	
Larry Jackson	1	1		Tiant	1	4	
Oscar Jones	1	1		Walters	1	3	
Sad Sam Jones I	1	2		Doc White	1	1	
Sad Sam Jones II	1	1		Wilbur Wood	2	4	

Baseball and the Law

In defense of Justice Oliver Wendell Holmes and good baseball

Monte R. Hess

There are strong grumblings these days by many baseball fans concerning the direction the game has taken. A growing number of fans believe good, traditional baseball has been taken away from them and a very poor-quality product has been left in its place. Yes, last season had its moments, but a souped-up baseball and a narrow strike zone can't make up for tight pennant races...or players truly representing the communities they play for in the tradition of Ted Williams, Joe DiMaggio, and Ernie Banks...or prices a family can afford...or games played in privately financed ballparks.

It is remarkable that all the negatives we hear about professional baseball can be traced directly to a very good law—the Sherman Antitrust Act of 1890.

Baseball's Problems—In the new world of professional baseball many players become free agents each season. The good ones are quickly gobbled up by large-market clubs. And once the season begins the poorer "small market" clubs are left in the dust. Last year the richer guys ran away with the pennants by an average of 12.5 games over the second-place finishers. The average last-place finish was 34.5 games out. The situation is not exactly what Alexander Cartwright and the old Knickerbockers of New York had in mind when they drafted that first set of rules back in 1845. Rule number 3 stressed fairness: "Players opposite

each other should be as nearly equal as possible." That's the way fans would like to see the game played. Each club should have the same opportunity as any other to put together a winning team.

In the 1940s, '50s, and '60s many teams had eight or even nine players in the starting lineup who were brought up from the farm system. Teams averaged seven "homegrown" starters. Now, fans are lucky to have three. According to USA Today, this past season only 111 of 838 players on opening-day rosters played for the same team four years earlier. The revolving players of today can hardly be considered representatives of the communities they play for. "Hired Hessians" might be a more fitting term. Lost is the rapport and loyalty between players and fans of days gone by.

The going price for star free-agent players is some $10,000,000 per season. The ordinary player brings in about $3,000,000. Even reserves can top $1,000,000. The high price of signing free agents, of course, is passed on to the consumer. So much so, that many families are being priced out of the ballparks. More and more, it is the purchase of blocks of tickets by local businessmen and corporations (and used as a tax write-off) that the baseball owners must now count on to pay salaries. Last season salaries totaled more than $1,200,000,000.

Free agency has led to another problem. It gives the baseball owners an excuse for pushing the lion's share of the costs of enormous stadiums off on the public. Owners claim that after competing for the services of

---

Monte R. Hess *is a recently retired city planner. He has researched the relationship between baseball and antitrust law for over ten years.*

free-agent players there is little money left for such things as building their own ballparks. These extravagant, state-of-the-art facilities typically cost in the $300,000,000 to $500,000,000 range. "Pass a bond issue or we'll move our team to where we're appreciated," the owners threaten. The return on any money the owners might contribute comes right off the top from personal-seat license fees, luxury suite revenues, and increased ticket prices. Luxury suite income alone can net the owners as much as $10,000,000 per annum. And owners need not pay any taxes on those stadiums that are publicly owned. After the owners' money is recaptured they have no real investment in the ballpark or the community. They too become "free agents" and can look elsewhere, pitting community against community for their services. The thought that maybe a portion of the $2,000,000,000 the owners and players collect each year should go into building funds doesn't seem to enter the minds of either group.

Justice Holmes' 1922 Opinion—The reason good baseball has been taken away is due in no uncertain terms to the overturning of the Supreme Court ruling in *Federal Baseball Club v. National League* (1922) and a reinterpretation by judges and congressmen of the problem the Sherman Antitrust Act of 1890 was intended to fix. The Act was supposed to protect the public from poor-quality, high-priced goods and services. Today it is being used to bring about the opposite affect in the instance of professional baseball.

The Federal Baseball Club case was an offshoot of the "war" between Organized Baseball and the upstart Federal League, which came into existence in 1914 and competed directly with the American and National leagues for two years.

By the end of the second season most of the baseball magnates on both sides were losing large sums of money and wanted to stop the competition. The owners of seven of the Federal League teams agreed to be bought out in one way or another, leaving the Baltimore club as the sole holdout. The Baltimore club owners then claimed they had been run out of the baseball business. "No single club can operate without the other members of the circuit," attorneys for the plaintiff argued, and they filed suit under the Sherman Antitrust Act, charging Organized Baseball with conspiracy to monopolize professional baseball.

The Sherman Act is a federal law and applies only to interstate commerce. The Court of Appeals of the District of Columbia ruled that professional baseball was not interstate commerce, directing the judgment in favor of the defendant. The case finally came before the United States Supreme Court on appeal in 1922. Justice Oliver Wendell Holmes spoke for the Court. His opinion included the following:

> The defendants are the American League … and the National League … unincorporated associations, composed respectively of groups of eight incorporated baseball clubs, joined as defendants; the presidents of the two Leagues and a third person, constituting what is known as the National Commission, having considerable powers in carrying out an agreement between the two Leagues.
>
> The decision of the Court of Appeals went to the root of the case and if correct makes it unnecessary to consider other serious difficulties in the way of the plaintiff's recovery.
>
> We are of the opinion that the Court of Appeals was right. The business is giving exhibitions of baseball which are purely state affairs. It is true that in order to attain for these exhibitions the great popularity that they have achieved, competitions must be arranged between clubs from different cities and states. But the fact that in order to give the exhibitions the League must induce free persons to cross state lines and must pay for their doing so is not enough to change the character of the business. According to the distinction insisted upon in *Hooper v. California* (1894), the transport is a mere incident, not the essential thing.

Holmes is personally crucified these days by lawyers, legislators, and just about everyone else for rendering what they feel is a terrible opinion. Various judges have denounced the opinion as: "a mistake;" "unrealistic, inconsistent, and illogical;" "an impotent zombie," and "not made on one of Mr. Justice Holmes' happiest days."

The criticisms hit at both of Holmes' findings: that professional baseball did not involve interstate commerce and that, even if it did, Organized Baseball was not the type of business combination prohibited by the Sherman Act. Today, Holmes' critics believe that Major League Baseball, unfettered by the Sherman Act, is a combination in restraint of trade—a sinister monopoly. They believe that this conclusion is obvious, and that Holmes ought to have come to it quite readily. No one mentions that the eight other members of the Supreme Court agreed with Holmes' findings and that all the judges on the Court of Appeals had come to the same conclusion.

Recent Rulings—Efforts by baseball owners to have Congress pass a bill aimed specifically at exempting it from the Sherman Antitrust Act have failed. Moreover, recent court opinions pertaining to other professional sports point out that professional football, basketball, and hockey are no longer simply state affairs. This finding should be conceded by all. Today the sale of television and radio broadcasting rights puts all major professional sports in the interstate business.

However, from there the courts found that the reserve systems of the National Football League, the National Basketball Association, and the National Hockey League were illegal as conspiracies in restraint of trade under the Sherman Act. The outlawed reserve systems were similar to baseball's: they tied players to one club for "life," and they included the amateur draft and the right to assign a player's contract to another team.

Baseball itself has been dealt a couple of severe blows. Two arbitration cases—the Messersmith Case (1975) and the Baseball Collusion Case (1985)—rang in the era of free agency. Also, the Curt Flood Act was signed into law in October, 1998, allowing baseball players to bring federal antitrust suits against the owners.

Any "exemption" the 1922 Federal Baseball Club case may have provided the owners has been diluted to the point of extinction. The owners know they are now vulnerable to federal antitrust suits by almost anyone. The direction judges and congressmen have given to the owners is to iron out their differences with the players' union on matters of reservation and parity, and fit them into a collective bargaining agreement. The result of this advice is the watered down parity agreements we have today, which promote lousy baseball.

Baseball owners also understand, especially since the ruling in the 1981 Raider case (*LA Memorial Coliseum v. NFL*), that judges and congressmen will not support any united effort of owners to enforce rules that prevent individual club owners from relocating their teams to wherever they please, whether or not the move is necessary.

So judges and congressmen have spoken. Imposed parity rules restrain the trade of players; rules restricting the relocation of teams restrain the trade of individual club owners; and both types of agreements are per se violations of the Sherman Act.

But there is a big hitch in this line of thinking.

Unanswered Questions—Parity measures and relocation rules aside, major league baseball clubs are still united through hundreds of agreements perhaps as complex as those that held together the oil, steel, meat, and tobacco trusts of old. Clubs share revenues, limit production, divide territories, deal exclusively with one another, agree on how, when, and where their product will be sold, and so on and so on.

Unlawful combinations can't do those things. Lawful combinations can.

So the question becomes, do the owners have the right to combine their several corporations into a single association or partnership? This question has not been addressed to a conclusion by either the courts or Congress. To be sure, the issue has been bandied about, but it's also been skirted and left to drift, perhaps purposely.

If it were to be determined that Major League Baseball does not have the right of combination and falls under the head of an indictable conspiracy *in restraint of trade*, it must be because the owners harm the public in general by preventing others from engaging in fair competition with them, and gaining the power to extort unreasonable prices from consumers. If this is the case, Major League Baseball is a monopolistic menace to society and ought to be obliterated. The owners should be fined and the business partnership dissolved into one-team leagues, each at war with all the rest, just as readily as the courts are wont to do with illegal combinations in other fields of commerce. Then, of course, there would be no professional baseball as we know it. Nor any jobs for baseball players. And judges and congressmen know this.

As to the advice given by authorities that owners and players negotiate their differences in a collective bargaining agreement—well, it would have amazed the world if the Supreme Court had ruled in 1911 that the Standard Oil monopoly was not a combination in restraint of trade as long as John D. Rockefeller kept his employees happy; that an employer-employee agreement on certain working conditions somehow eliminates the evils of monopoly aimed at by the Sherman Act. Yet that is the precise answer to one of the baseball antitrust issues we get up to now from the courts and Congress. And pretending that Major League Baseball becomes an illegal combination only in respect to player reservation and club relocation agreements, while being blind to the hundreds of other tying agreements, is tantamount to saying the Standard Oil monopoly of 1911 was illegal only in northeastern Kansas.

On the other hand, if the owners of Major League Baseball have the *right* to unite as a single entity or partnership under the Sherman Act and form a nationwide league of teams—say, to the same extent that Sears, Roebuck and Company has the right to build and operate hundreds of stores in every part of the country—they then, certainly, may enter into agreements which partially unite their clubs. In other words, the right to integrate fully as a single entity gives the owners the right to make all the tying agreements they do indeed make. And it would give them the right to make agreements concerning policies on the hiring and placement of employees (the reserve system) and the location of the clubs.

If baseball were judged to be a lawful combination, with the owners entitled to make all the agreements allowed a normal partnership, fans would not have to accept inferior, costly baseball as a given required by law. They could protest directly to the owners and players and probably would be able to bring about the desired changes. There is enough money in the baseball business to compensate those engaged in it and, at the same time, provide fans with good, traditional baseball.

Baseball's Right of Combination—There are compelling reasons to support the belief that Major League Baseball should be allowed to function as a single entity. The reasons are based upon the premises that there is no professional baseball without combination and no public injury with it.

First, one baseball team produces nothing. There is no marketable product without clubs uniting as a business unit. A league of teams is a prerequisite to the business. This was readily admitted by the plaintiff's attorneys in the Federal Baseball Club case. Only through combination can owners present fans with what they desire: a fair match between representatives of one community against those of other communities across the nation. It is irrelevant that clubs are divided into two or more "leagues" for marketing purposes.

Second, the right of one person or several persons in partnership to produce the whole of a commodity has never been questioned. Major League Soccer is allowed to function as a single-corporation partnership. The Supreme Court has said:

"The disintegration aimed at by the statute (Sherman Antitrust Act) does not extend to reducing all manufacture to isolated units of the lowest degree.

It is as lawful for one corporation to make every part of a steam engine and to put the machine together as it would be for one to make the boilers and another to make the wheels." *United States v. Winslow* (1912).

"If various corporations owning railroad lines determine in the public interest to so combine as to make a continuous line, such agreement or combination would not be repugnant to the Act." *Standard Oil v. United States* (1911).

Third, the fact that the baseball owners have not integrated the clubs into a single corporation has no bearing on the issue. The Supreme Court has so reasoned:

"We agree that there is no ground for holding defendant's plan illegal merely because they have not integrated their properties and have chosen to maintain their independent plants…We know of no public policy, and none is suggested by the terms of the Sherman Act, that, in order to comply with the law, those engaging in industry should be driven to unify their properties and businesses…The question is whether there is an unreasonable restraint of trade or attempt to monopolize. If there is, the combination cannot escape because it has chosen corporate form; and if there is not, it is not to be condemned because of the absence of corporate integration." *Appalachian Coal v. United States* (1933).

Finally, the test of the lawfulness of a combination at the common law was its effect upon the public in general. Did the combination prevent competition or in any other way tend to bring about unreasonable prices or poor-quality goods? Justice Holmes, who literally wrote the book on the common law, pointed out the rule concerning restraints of trade:

"But in all such cases the ground of decision is policy, and the advantages to the community on the one side and the other, are the only matters really entitled to be weighed." *Harvard Law Review* (1894).

The Sherman Antitrust Act is acknowledged to be but a reflection of the common law:

"This bill does not seek to cripple combinations of capital or labor, but only to prevent and control combinations made with a view to prevent competition, or for the restraint of trade, or to increase the profits of the producer at the cost of the consumer. It is the unlawful combination, tested by the rules of common law and human experience aimed at by this bill. They can combine provided they do not do so to prevent competition…I feel the best effect of the bill will be a warning that all trade and commerce, all struggles for money or property, must be governed by the universal law that the public good must be the test of all." *Senator John Sherman, Congressional Record* (1890).

The Supreme Court has backed this principle of antitrust law many times. A good example is *Wilder v. Corn Products* (1914):

"The prohibitions of the Antitrust Act were enacted to prevent not the mere injury to an individual which would arise from the doing of the prohibited acts but from the harm to the general public. The purpose of the statute was where a combination was found to be illegally existing to put an end to such illegal existence for all purposes and thus protect the whole public."

The right that people have to form a business partnership that is clearly in the public interest should not be a wrong to others, whether the "other" is an employee (player), a partner (individual club owner), a business rival, or anyone else—even when the business combination happens to be alone in its field. Judges who ruled against the reserve systems of the NFL, the NBA, and the NHL did not show that the systems in some way prevented others from entering the field as competitors, or were a means of exacting extortionate prices from the public, or lowered the quality of the product. The judges simply took the position that the restraint the reserve systems placed upon the players was enough. Even though players are employees, not competitors. Even though, as employees, players can join together in the form of a union and push collectively for more money and better working conditions. Even though they may strike to attain their goals. And even though they may go en masse to others with capital who might be willing to help them financially in the creation of their own league.

The most hypocritical aspect of the whole issue is that everyone knows that the business of professional baseball cannot be carried on at all without clubs combining in league form through hundreds of tying agreements which, in effect, constitute a single entity. If players or individual club owners have allusions that they are harmed by some of the actions taken by the owners as a whole, they ought to visualize the harm that could occur to them if the owners had no right to combine in any respect.

Justice Oliver Wendell Holmes' conclusions were not illogical. Those who have reasoned otherwise now give us poor-quality, expensive baseball. And John Sherman most certainly turns over in his grave.

Stadium Agreements—There is one aspect of professional baseball that appears to be a real offense under the Sherman Act. The stadium financing agreements made between individual club owners and local governments absolutely prevent competition.

As long as agreements to publicly finance stadiums are in place, any would-be competitor to the established club stands no chance. Once city or county officials agree to give away hundreds of millions of taxpayer dollars for the construction of a ballpark, they certainly will not attempt to exact another similar amount from the same taxpayers to finance a second stadium to house a club of a rival league.

Those attempting to establish a rival club in the area must first acquire a large piece of land without the power of eminent domain. Then they would start the costly process of drafting documents for public hearings regarding general plan revisions and environmental impact studies, fighting the city, which would want to protect its investment, all the way. If for some remarkable reason the new club owners succeeded with that phase of their effort they'd be faced with financing a $300,000,000 stadium without the help of tax-exempt bonds. Only then, after several years of ballpark construction, could they begin the bidding war for the services of players. And the new club owners, unlike their established rivals, would also be saddled each year with huge property taxes on their privately owned facility.

Granted that prior to publicly financed ballparks competition was not often attempted. Granted that fans have never cared for the bidding wars of rival baseball leagues that led only to massive player movement and franchise instability. Still, it is hard to deny that the stadium agreements have effectively forestalled the possibility of any competition and amount to combinations in restraint of trade.

Billy McGunnigle

Baseball's forgotten pioneer

Robert A. Kane

Tall, slim, and handsome," said his daughter, Mrs. Doris (McGunnigle) Caputo. Added his son, William E. McGunnigle: "A remarkable man in many respects: practical joker, story teller, good singing voice, and a hearty appreciation of friendship. His family cherished him and numerous friends took delight in his company. In dress he was a Beau Brummell."

On September 20, 1959, Frank Leary, Boston *Globe* sportswriter, wrote a feature story on this Brockton, Massachusetts, man who, in the minds of many, was a natural choice, as a pioneer in baseball, for the Hall of Fame. Leary raised the oft-asked question: "Why hasn't Billy McGunnigle been chosen for the Hall of Fame?" Today, few of us hearing that could say anything but, "Who's Billy McGunnigle?"

In a career that spanned twenty-two years during the infancy of baseball, few men did as much as Billy McGunnigle to "encourage, foster and elevate the game of baseball," as the National League constitution stated as part of its purpose. He caught, he pitched, and as an outfielder he had few peers. He was an exceptional manager and field captain, and was credited with being the innovator and first user of a catcher's mitt. He was also a showman, a drawing card wherever he played.

William Henry McGunnigle, better known as "Billy," "Mac," or "Cap," althought the encyclopedias

Robert A. Kane *is a city historian, a sports historian, and an Irish historian. He is the author of over fifty articles that have appeared in various publications.*

list his nickname as "Gunner," was born in Boston's North End on January 1, 1855, to James F. and Hannah McGunnigle. As a young man he came to Brockton by way of Avon (now East Stoughton) and found employment at a shoe factory.

Irish-born Owen F. Canary, an early teammate of McGunnigle, told at a February, 1915, Knights of Columbus sports night how Mac broke into the game in 1873. "I remember the first game he played. We needed a catcher for our game with the Graftons. Mac, a young fellow of eighteen, came out of the woods with a gun on his shoulder and asked for a chance to catch the pitching of Joe Hallett, local twirler for the Brockton nine. I gave it to him and he made good."

He made good all right—so good he quickly decided that there was a better future in baseball than in the shoe shop. In 1874, Brockton won the Junior Championship of Massachusetts with Mac as captain and catcher of the Howard Juniors. He left the Juniors in 1875 and signed a contract with the Troy club of Fall River, the first professional to play for that nine. When that club folded Mac helped form the Fall River Baseball Club, which finished second in 1875 and first in 1876, with Mac pitching, catching, playing every position on the field and making himself widely known throughout the New England League as an all-round player.

Much has been written about the evolution of the catcher's mitt and mask. Credit has been given to Fred Thayer, Charles G. Waite, and James Tyng. Yet,

Transcendental Graphics

Billy McGunnigle

strangely enough, although these men were associated with Harvard University baseball, the "H" book of Harvard gives credit to McGunnigle. Another source favoring Mac is Irving Leitner's book "Diamond in the Rough" (pg. 217). Leitner cites an 1895 sporting guide. In addition the New York *Times* (Jan. 24, 1915), the Boston *Globe* and the New York *Sun* all wrote stories crediting Mac with the development of the glove while playing for Fall River in 1875.

The team dropped back to second place in 1877. The Fall River *Daily Herald* (Oct. 25) said: "Mac is the wonderful general player among the pilecrepi, good everywhere, particularly as pitcher, catcher and right fielder—honest and a hard worker he hates to be swindled, therefore free to express his mind. He is the greatest right fielder we ever saw."

In 1878, McGunnigle moved to the International League's pennant winning Buffalo Bisons as right fielder and change pitcher behind future Hall of Famer Pud Galvin.

The Bisons joined the National League in 1879, and McGunnigle won the New York *Clipper* gold badge as the best right fielder in the league. According to the *Clipper*, McGunnigle "played right field like a shortstop—he could save an imminent home run as a single." That season his right arm cut down many runners at first base on what should have been base hits to right.

As a pitcher in 1879, he won nine and lost five as Buffalo tied for third place. He pitched three games in succession against Cap Anson's Chicago nine, allowing just eleven hits, to insure the third-place tie.

In 1880 Mac served briefly as captain of the Bisons, then came down with a sore arm. He played a game with Worcester, but the arm problem was serious enough to keep him out of baseball for two years. He bounced back in 1883 as field captain for Saginaw, Michigan, in the newly formed Northwestern League. In 1884, he led the Bay City, Michigan, team to the league pennant, sometimes catching future Hall of Famer John Clarkson.

After Bay City folded McGunnigle returned to Brockton where he established a team in the newly proposed Eastern New England League. The best known member of the team, outside of Mac, was Jim Cudworth, who was said never to have had a superior as a judge of difficult fly balls hit into the glare of the sun.

The Brockton *Times*, years later recalling the baseball of the 1880s, described McGunnigle in this manner: "As a player McGunnigle was picturesque, and as captain probably never had a superior. He be-came famous throughout the country for his aggressiveness. Who of the followers of New England baseball did not remember that favorite move of Mac's running in from right field to home plate to lay down the law? Jim Cudworth was his right hand man, and they made a remarkable duo. McGunnigle then wore side-whiskers. He was a strict manager, yet a kind one, and brought out many men who figured as stars of the diamond."

He is undoubtedly the best captain in the league. When he tells a player what to do it is plain he means it.
—Biddeford (Maine) *Journal* 1885

Although he earned a reputation as a "kicker," McGunnigle's judgment was respected by all the other clubs. In 1886, the team took a tumble. Dissatisfied with its performance the directors asked Mac to impose a fine. He refused. The directors then fined the entire team (including Tommy McCarthy, a future Hall of Famer). McGunnigle responded by asking for his release and joining John Irwin's Haverhill team. Haverhill finished second. Brockton ended in fourth place and disbanded.

In 1887, McGunnigle took over a Lowell team that was called a "bunch of bummers who liked their drink." Hooted and derided at the opening of the season, Lowell, which included future Hall of Famer Hugh Duffy and future major league catcher Morgan Murphy, tied Portland, Maine, for first place, then clinched the pennant in a playoff, winning two out of three with Mac pitching one of the winning games.

"McGunnigle's a king" was the cry as the team received appropriate honors from the city of Lowell. Brockton and the Boston *Globe* also presented gold medals to the players.

"The brainiest man the game ever knew."
—Owen F. Canary

He was apparently brainy in more ways than one. On March 10, 1888, the Brockton *Daily Enterprise* wrote in part: "Manager McGunnigle of the Brooklyns has invented a little device which is creditable to his ingenuity and ought to have money in it. McGunnigle's device—which he has patented and in which Mr. Samuel Kingston of East Bridgewater, the machinist, has a half-interest—allows the spikes plate being detached from the shoe after using, and is readily readjusted. The umpires in the American Association will be provided with these spikes."

Signed by Brooklyn of the American Association in 1888, Mac completely reorganized the "Bridegrooms," so-called after six of its members got married. The team started poorly but put it all together and finished in second place just behind the St. Louis Browns. In 1889, McGunnigle's team nosed out the Browns, and the "rag" flew over Brooklyn. The next year, McGunnigle led the same squad to the National League pennant, well ahead of Cap Anson's second place Chicagos. This gave Mac the unlikely distinction of being the only manager to win consecutive pennants in two different leagues with the same team.

The Brooklyn *Citizen* wrote: "There isn't a Brooklyn player who works harder, physically, to win a game than McGunnigle. Always with a bat in hand, sliding from one end of the bench to the other, he uses it to telegraph his plays. He understands the game and knows just what to do at every stage."

In October, 1890, *Sporting Life* published the following article:

A great deal has been said at odd times of various players and managers who have been connected in their time with many champion teams, but one man, with a more remarkable record than any of the many mentioned, has been entirely overlooked, simply because he is altogether too modest for pushing baseball world and never blows his own horn. That man is Manager McGunnigle, of the Brooklyn Club. Here is his unequaled record, which speaks for itself:

With Brockton, Massachusetts League
First   1874
With Fall River, New England League
Second   1875
With Fall River, New England League
First   1876
With Fall River, New England League
Second   1877
With Buffalo, International League
First   1878
With Buffalo, National League
Third   1879
With Saginaw, Northwestern League
First   1883
With Bay City, Northwestern League
First   1884
With Brockton, New England League
First   1885
With Brockton, New England League

Fourth   1886
With Lowell, New England League
First   1887
With Brooklyn, American Association
Second   1888
With Brooklyn, American Association
First   1889
With Brooklyn, National League   First
1890

If there is any man with a better record as a winning team leader we have yet to hear of him. Even Anson doesn't approach McGunnigle's record of handling winning teams by a long shot. Nine firsts and three seconds in 14 years is simply phenomenal.

Despite his success, the politics of baseball's consolidation after the "Brotherhood War" of 1890 gave the managership of the single Brooklyn team that emerged to John Montgomery Ward. Many years later, sportswriter Frank Graham observed that McGunnigle probably coined the phrase: "There is no sentiment in baseball."

In 1891, McGunnigle organized the new Providence Grays of the Eastern League, and agreed to manage the team without a contract. That left him free to accept in July, when he was called back to the National League by J. Palmer O'Neill, president of the last place Pittsburgh Pirates.

Mac's arrival in the big city landed him in the middle of what the local media variously called "monkey and parrot time" and "snarl of the century." A group of dissident directors, in defiance of O'Neill, refused to replace manager Ned Hanlon. The Pittsburgh *Chronicle* wrote: "O'Neill has made a bold play, but he stood these directors on their heads more than once"—and did it again. McGunnigle was in.

Although the team did not move up in the standings, the turnabout in their play drew raves from sportswriters. The New York *Press* wrote:

Since Manager McGunnigle has taken charge of the Pittsburgh team there has been a complete transformation in their style of play...this is in such a contrast to their slouchy, listless playing in their games at the Polo Grounds on their first trip, that it is especially noticeable, and Manager McGunnigle and his players are to be congratulated. Tail end honors are not for such a team as played against the Giants yesterday, and if they can keep up their good works they will surely get much further from the last hole than they are now.

He also set the style on how a manager should dress. The *Chronicle* wrote: "One of the most interesting sights of the game was Billy McGunnigle. Arrayed in a beautiful pair of lavender trousers and weighed down with a solid gold watch and guard of huge proportions, he capered about near the bench."

A Boston paper, in a special to the Pittsburgh *Post*, called him "the tin whistle manager, with an extremely novel method of infusing life into the tailenders while they are sent tooting to last place." But Louis Bierbauer had this to say about his new manager:

How do the players and McGunnigle hit it off? Why, tip top. Mr. McGunnigle is a hustler and is no way to blame for the poor work of the club since he took hold. Those stories sent out from Boston about 'his tin whistle,' and 'blue yachting caps' were greatly exaggerated. Those caps were bought by the players themselves; we purchased a job lot of them and McGunnigle had nothing to do with it. We gave him a white one and he wore it. The whistle story does him a great injustice, and grew out of the fact that while on the bench one day he requested Berger to whistle for one of the players, as Mac was unable to attract his attention in any other way. If the directors let McGunnigle alone he will have no trouble with his players.

However, the directors did not leave McGunnigle alone. The dissidents got the upper hand, O'Neill resigned, and Mac was out.

In May, 1892, McGunnigle returned to Brockton, taking the reins of the local club which had been struggling under manager Tommy Cotter. The team went on a roll, winning eight in a row before playing to a twelve-inning tie with Pawtucket. Mac himself returned to the lineup after a five-year hiatus, banging out thirty-eight hits in his first thirty games. However, the talent was not there and the team finished fourth, a few chips shy of the top.

The next year McGunnigle returned to Lowell, moved the team to Manchester, New Hampshire, then finally to Boston as the Boston Reds. It was a tough year for the financially strapped New England League.

Mac returned to the "ring" in July, 1896, replacing John McCloskey as manager of the last place Louisville Colonels. Another party seeking terms was John Montgomery Ward—shades of Brooklyn and Pittsburgh! Mac agreed to a two-year verbal agreement—a big mistake.

As in Pittsburgh in 1891, Mac gained the respect of the league while finishing in the cellar. He had only two players, Tom McCreery and Fred Clarke, who could be called stars. The team lost thirty-two games by one run.

At the annual baseball meeting in Chicago the Philadelphia men were impressed enough with Mac that they offered him the management of their club, but Dr. T. Hunt Stucky of Louisville would not listen to any proposition, even the offer of a good player to sweeten the deal.

No man in baseball is better able to teach a lot of young players in the science of the game than William McGunnigle, the Louisville manager. This is a strong statement with men like Hanlon, Tebeau, Ewing and Joyce in view ....
—Boston *Globe*, December, 1896

Despite the fine press, rumors persisted that Mac would not be back in 1897. It was Pittsburgh all over again, only worse. Tim Murnane of the *Globe* wrote:

The Louisville Club is honor bound to keep their verbal agreement with Manager McGunnigle, just as the Boston club is bound to treat Manager Selee fair and honest. During the last meeting at Chicago, McGunnigle was offered $1,000 more salary by the Philadelphia club, if he could get away from Louisville. McGunnigle replied that he had given his word that he would remain in Louisville next season and his word was good as a contract.

Mac went to Louisville people and asked to be released, as Vice President Dehler had blocked him in every deal he attempted to make, but the Louisville people would not listen to their manager when he asked to be allowed to go. Now, after the Philadelphia club has secured a new manager, a lot of directors talk of letting McGunnigle go.

The axe fell in January, 1897—Mac was out. Ironically, the Louisville club, which had been $5,000 in the red when Mac took the reins, had finished $13,000 ahead of the previous year.

Mac declined to take the club to court and, instead, chose to go before the annual meeting of the National League. Murnane of the *Globe* wrote:

Billy McGunnigle promises to take his case to Baltimore and lay it before the National Board. If he does I am willing to go on record as a prophet, and here is the prophecy: Mac will tell all he knows and the board will show him that he has no case, and advise him to call it off. Who ever heard of a board of this kind giving themselves the worst of it.

If the manager has a good case, and first-class lawyers have said he has, why then the proper place is in a court of law, unless the Louisville club can fix up the wrong they have done the Brockton boy without going into the law business. McGunnigle has faith in Mssrs. [Arthur H.] Soden and [Charles H.] Byrne doing him justice. Unfortunately for the game Louisville has given the national sport more unwholesome notoriety than any other city that ever held a league franchise.

On May 24, 1897, Murnane wrote:

The McGunnigle case promises to become nearly as famous as the [pitcher Amos] Rusie case before it is settled. [Rusie, the "Hoosier Thunderbolt" was baseball's first fireballer in the modern style, and National Laegue's biggest drawing card. He had refused to pay fines leveled by Giant owner Andrew Freedman, sat out, and threatened to attack the reserve clause.] The ex-Louisville manager is now at his home in Brockton reflecting on the beautiful hand-painted dinky dink he received from that prince of smooth and oily magnates known as the "Louisville Doctor." Mr. McGunnigle was warned by friends to keep away from the league meeting at Baltimore, but he went there and got just what every man, woman and child has received since the league was organized, the small end of fair play.

The case seems never to have been settled. It appears that Murnane was, indeed, a prophet. Although removed from the game Mac was not forgotten. On July 1, 1897, the *Globe* wrote: "The Phillies made a mistake in not securing Billy McGunnigle for a manager. Men like Arthur Irwin, Bill McGunnigle and Tom Burns of Springfield, know more baseball than Stallings can be expected to learn for years to come in the big league." (George Stallings, of course, went on to a fine managerial career that included leading the "Miracle Braves" to their 1914 World Series sweep of the great Philadelphia A's.)

On the evening of July 22, 1897, Mac and three friends were riding in a carryall in Salisbury Square when the electric car from Whitman, bowling along, struck the wagon, throwing the four men to the ground. Mac sustained severe injury to a hip.

His whole left side became affected by paralysis and his general health declined. On March 9, 1899, "Billy Mac" died, leaving a widow and seven children. A strange coincidence: Mac, his son William E., and his daughter Agnes, were all born on New Year's Day and all died on March 9.

Perhaps the best summation of Mac's career as a manager was made by the Brockton *Enterprise*: "He was a great schemer as a captain and manager. With ordinarily sharp men in any team that he controlled he was able to conceive and have carried out points of play that had seldom or never been tried before. Any crew of players in McGunnigle's control was a team to be feared."

"I was associated with Billy McGunnigle for many years on and off the diamond," Murnane told the Brockton Knights of Columbus. "He was a real old-timer with a warm personality and when he died I lost a close friend. I predict that some day there will be an institution to honor the pioneer heroes of the diamond and also the modern stars. When that day arrives, Billy McGunnigle, because of outstanding playing ability, sagacious leadership and aggressiveness, should be one of the first enshrined therein ..."

Well, at least you now know who Billy McGunnigle is, and why Murnane made his as yet unfulfilled prediction.

Bibliography:

North Bridgewater *Gazette*, 1874-79; 1884-92

Brockton *Daily Enterprise*, 1884-1902

Brockton *Times*, 1895-1902; 1915

Boston *Globe*, 1896-97; 1959

Louisville *Courier Journal*, 1896

Pittsburgh *Chronicle*, 1891

The Portable Batting Cage

Ninety years old and still going strong

Ken Tillman

Connie Mack had an enviable career in baseball, but even he couldn't match the longevity record of a piece of baseball equipment that is taken for granted by baseball teams spanning the competitive level from Little League teams to each of the major league teams. It was on April 9, 1907, that a patent was issued to Wellington Stockton Titus for a Portable Batting Cage. There were batting cages before that date and, in fact, Amos Alonzo Stagg, the famous football coach, is credited with developing an indoor batting cage. But prior to the invention by Mr. Titus, batting cages were stationary and references to them indicated that they were constructed as an inside facility. His invention is the prototype of the present day batting cages that are used in every major league baseball stadium and by most teams at most levels.

Titus was born on April 21, 1872, and died on October 5, 1942, after arriving at a hospital to have a broken hip set. He broke his hip when he fell from a ladder in Yardley, Pennsylvania, where he was dismantling an airport hangar.

It is fitting that his death resulted from an activity of this type as he was known throughout his community as a person who could fix anything and who would never ask anyone to do something he wouldn't do himself. He was a multitalented, self-taught, individualistic person who typified the small town handyman who led the way in the technological development of the United States of America during the late nineteenth and early twentieth centuries.

The idea—Titus lived near Hopewell, New Jersey, about fifteen miles north of Trenton. On the patent he received for the Portable Batting Cage his address is listed as Glenmore. Glenmore once included a post office where Mr. Titus served as postmaster, and a railroad stop near the current site of the Hopewell Valley Golf Club, where the portable batting cage was first used.

In addition to being a postmaster, Titus was a house builder, house mover, civil engineer, and farm foreman. It was while he was foreman of the farm of his uncle, E. S. Wells, that he developed the idea of a portable backstop. His uncle was a wealthy man who moved to Hopewell from Jersey City after acquiring large land holdings in the area. He had a race track on his farm, which is now the location of the Hopewell Golf Club. Wells, a pharmacist by training, became a millionaire in the 1860s by developing a formula for rat poison which was called "Rough on Rats." He sold his product worldwide by mail order in 10¢, 15¢, and 25¢ packages, and also had salesmen on the road, using horse and buggy.

There are conflicting reasons given for the factors that motivated Titus to design a portable backstop. His daughter, Susie T. Snook, wrote that her father "probably got the idea for a backstop after chasing balls he had missed when two people were engaged in

Ken Tillman *is a retired professor/coach/administrator from The College of New Jersey. His publications include two books on teaching and coaching wrestling.*

batting practice." This could have been the case, since Titus was a third baseman for the Hopewell town team.

His son, Livingston Titus, feels the major impetus came from an experience his father had as foreman of his uncle's farm. Wells had a son, George Titus Wells, who was an extremely talented second baseman. In fact, he became captain of the 1908 Princeton University team and signed with the New York Giants. Unfortunately for him, the New York Giants had a pretty fair second baseman named Larry Doyle at the time, so he never made it to the majors. To prepare his son, Wells had his farm hands throw batting practice to him and field balls he hit. Titus grew frustrated with the time lost chasing missed balls, so he rigged up a rough batting cage with pipes and chicken wire. This led to his designing the more sophisticated backstop. Joe Pierson, a longtime Hopewell resident who knew Titus, also gave this as the origin of the backstop.

The patent application submitted by Titus, states that this portable device "may be moved to any desired point in a baseball field." It then gives a more technical explanation of why his invention is needed:

This photo of Wellington Titus with his backstop was taken on the Wells farm where the backstop was developed.

> As is well known, it is customary during the fielding practice of the team to utilize two batsmen, one of whom bats to the infield and the other to the outfield, and as the infield batsman usually stands in front of the stationary backstop, balls thrown or pitched to the outfield batsman, who is stationed some distance from the infield batsman, pass him and are lost where the field is unenclosed.
>
> It is the chief object of the invention, therefore, to provide a portable back-stop which may be moved with great readiness to any position on the field to suit a batsman, so that he may stand in position to bat with greater certainty to any particular fielder or portion of the field

without the danger of any ball pitched or fielded to him being stolen by any onlookers.

A further object of the invention consists in the provision of a portable backstop which may be utilized in the practice of bunting to take the place of a catcher and which may be further utilized in connection with batting practice while the remaining members of the team are engaged in fielding or batting practice and during the game.

The patent application included seven illustrations (Figures 1, 2, and 3). It also contained three pages that describe in detail how and of what it should be built. For example, the "screens" on the cage should be of "heavy twine or other similar material, so as not to cut or otherwise injure a ball that passed the batsman or when struck foul by him."

Business—On February 26, 1907, even before he received his patent, Wellington Stockton Titus signed a Memorandum of Agreement to have A.G. Spalding and Bros. "manufacture a device known as a Portable Batting Cage which he had perfected." Manufacture was contingent on receipt of the patent, for which application had been submitted on December 20, 1906. Titus was to receive "$5.00 upon each and every Portable Batting Cage so manufactured and sold, and upon the further basis of a royalty of ten per cent upon the selling price of extra nets appurtenant to the said device and in the nature of repairs and replacement." This royalty was to be received "for the full end and term for which Letters Patent may be received."

Legend has it that the Philadelphia A's baseball team was the first professional team to use portable batting cages. One of their scouts came to Hopewell to scout George Wells. He was so impressed with the batting cage that he bought one for the A's. Prior to that time, the professional teams employed ball chasers—young boys from the neighborhood who would run after the balls that eluded fielders.

Titus made one further foray into the world of sports. He manufactured a baseball bat called the "Black Diamond" with this term burned into it. The bats were produced on lathes and many had orange and black stripes to give them a tigerish appearance—no doubt due to the influence of George's college, Princeton. Titus called his bats "positive groove bats" because they had longitudinal grooves spaced evenly around the handles. The bat business folded quickly. The company hired to store and season them put them over a boiler to speed the drying process. Some bats became brittle and broke when the first ball was hit. Black Diamond's reputation was ruined and Titus stopped manufacturing them.

Legacy—Wellington Stockton Titus had little formal education, but he was considered to be a "natural born civil engineer" by those in his community. He was known throughout the United States and Canada and frequently traveled to construction sites to find solutions. According to local accounts, he provided information that allowed construction of New York's George Washington Bridge to resume after work was halted due to engineering difficulties. His son, Livingston, recalled that his father was called to replace trolleys that ran off their tracks. His analytical mind enabled him to solve technical problems that occurred in his community.

Titus's fertile mind was always at work. For instance, he designed a horse and buggy swing set, made a rolling hammock, worked on an automatic record changer for the Edison record player, and even built a machine that he operated as an automobile in his community.

However, Titus was best-known as a house mover. He could move brick houses without putting a crack in them. He moved churches, lodges and, on one occasion, a courthouse with prisoners inside. He developed a device whereby a horse would walk

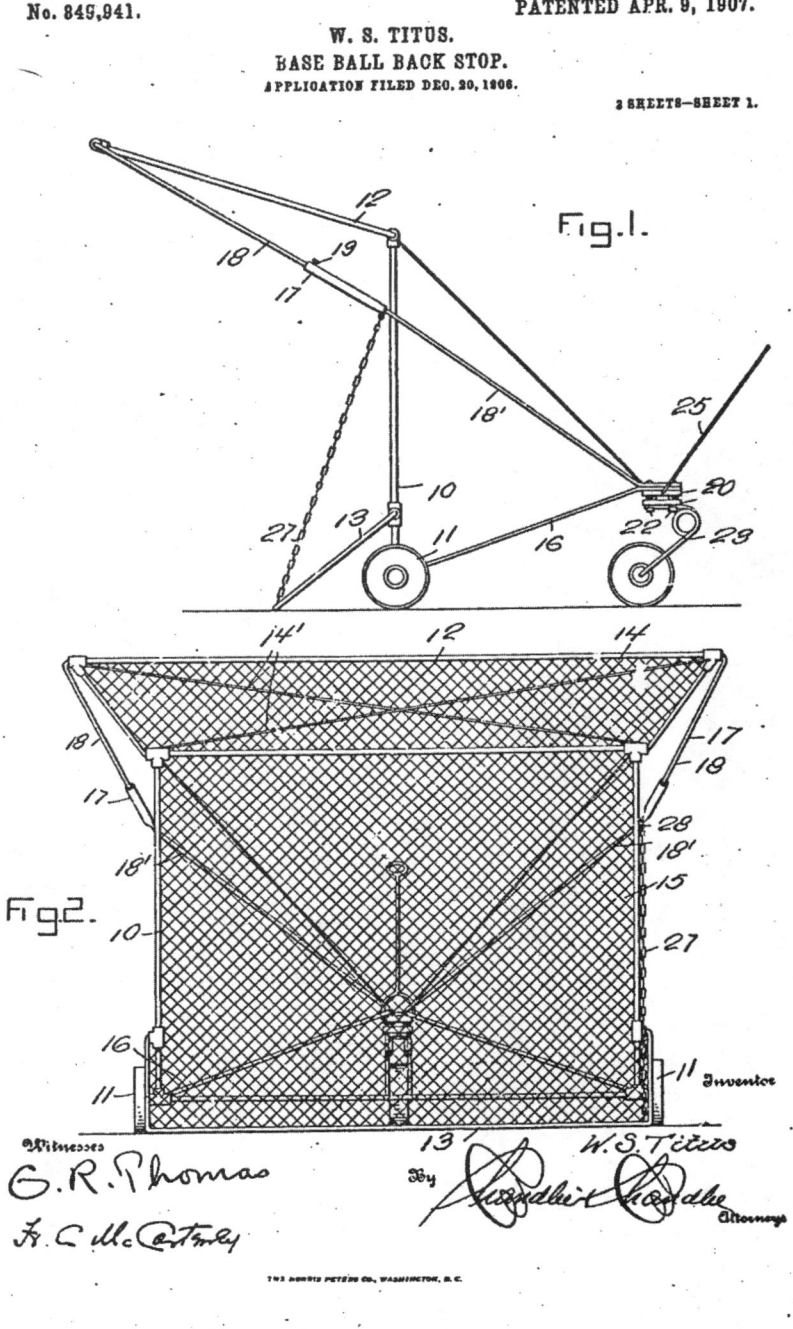

ILLUSTRATION 1

around a house and slide the house on wood beams. He used as many as 2,000 beams, which were greased with soap or crankcase oil. He is also credited with being the first to use the technique of cutting a house in half to move it. Engineering classes came from Princeton to watch him move buildings, because of his advanced techniques.

Many of Titus's innovations continued to have an influence on engineers and scientists for many years. However, his legacy is most visible in baseball—every

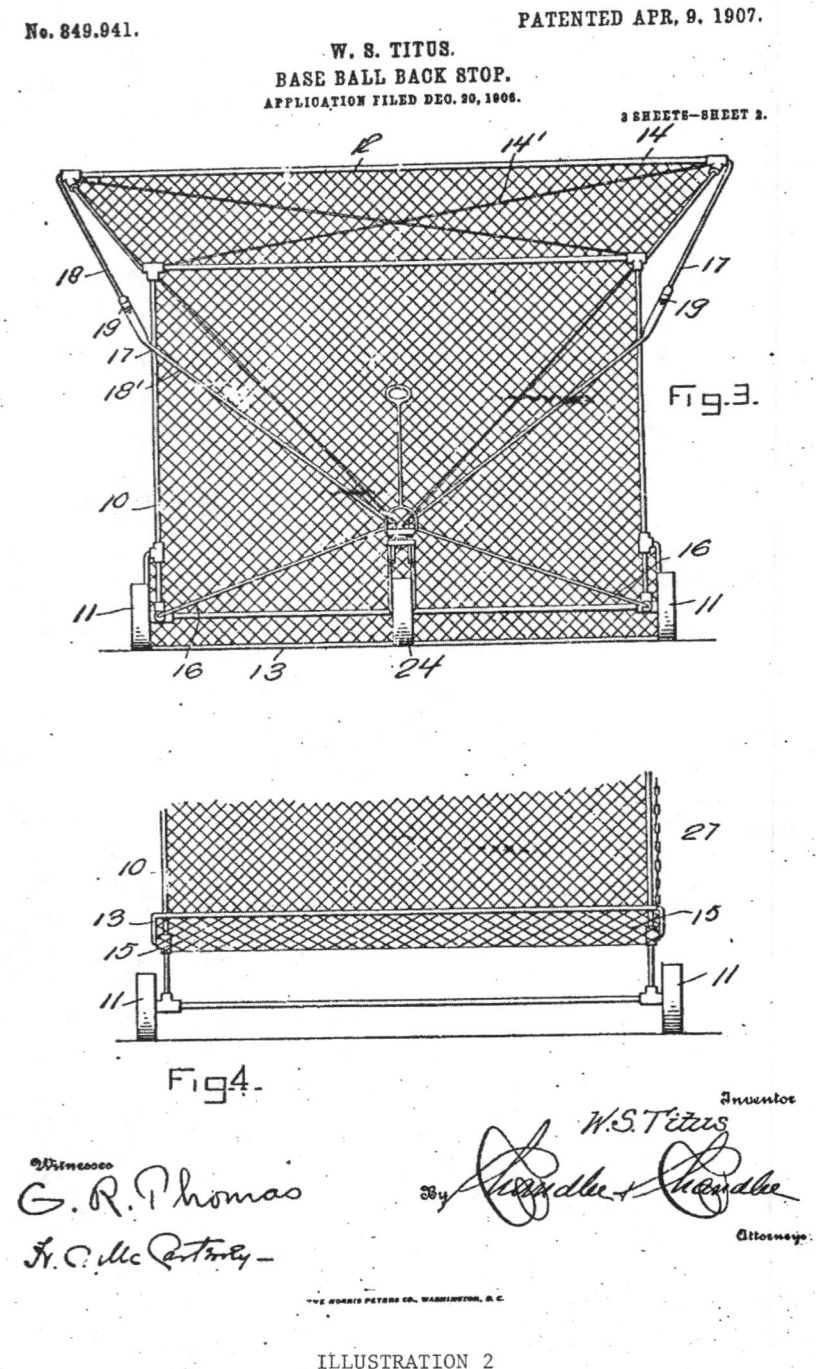

No. 849.941.
PATENTED APR. 9, 1907.
W. S. TITUS.
BASE BALL BACK STOP.
APPLICATION FILED DEC. 20, 1906.
3 SHEETS—SHEET 2.
Fig.3.
Fig4.
Inventor
W.S. Titus
Witnesses
G. R. Thomas
By
Attorneys

ILLUSTRATION 2

The wheels (11) on the early models were solid steel. They were later changed to cast iron with spokes and wider rims so they would not cut into the ground.

time the batting cage is rolled out on the field for batting practice.

References:

Bennett, J. & Pravitz, J. (1982). *The Miracle of Sports Psychology*. Englewood Cliffs: Prentice Hall, Inc., 132.

Litsky, F. (1975). *Superstars*. Secaucus, N.J.: Derbibooks, Inc., 312-313.

Memorandum of Agreement. W. S. Titus and A. G. Spalding & Bros. February 24, 1907.

Stagg, A. as told to Trout, W. (1927). *Touchdown*. New York: Longmans, Green & Company, 102-103.

Titus, W. (1907). *Base ball back-stop*. United States Patent Office.

Titus, W. (1908). *New and useful improvement in boot jacks*. Dominion of Canada Patent Office.

Zoda, F. & Monteleone, J. (No date given). *Hopewell Valley Golf Club—A History*. Hopewell, New Jersey: Hopewell Valley Golf Club. 1.

The Chicago Baseball Wars

Competition in a hotbed of the game

Barrie Ribet

Chicago is the best baseball city in the country because of the loyalty displayed by Chicago fans, who support their teams enthusiastically, in bad years as well as in good ones.

—Charles A. Comiskey

From the beginning of the century until the collapse of the Federal League in 1915, two Chicago baseball teams fought to survive in one city. The struggle was especially fierce in Chicago largely because each team was instrumental in the creation of its league. The National League was the creation of Chicagoan William Hulbert in 1876, and his team, led by Adrian "Cap" Anson, was one of the game's early dynasties. The American League's claim of major league status in 1901, and the immediate strength of Charles Comiskey's White Sox, turned Chicago into a two-team baseball town. As direct competition intensified, each team sought the love of the city's fans and domination of the Chicago baseball scene.

With the challenge of the upstart Federal League in 1914, each team had a new and common enemy, and the nature of the competition between them changed from franchise survival to success on the baseball diamond. Once the Federal League was eliminated the competition between the Cubs and the White Sox never returned to pre-1914 levels. Each team was able

Barrie Ribet *is a senior at Homewood-Flossmoor Community High School in Flossmoor, Illinois. As a result of her keen interest in baseball history, she wrote this paper for the Chicago Metro History Fair, where it advanced to the State Finals.*

to benefit from the rivalry, yet never again did both teams simultaneously reach the high level of play they exhibited between 1900 and 1915.

Baseball and the city—As early as 1909, Americans understood the importance of baseball to their image of themselves. "An American City does not deem itself metropolitan without a baseball team," according to Hugh Weir, who wrote on the subject in that year. "An American state does not consider itself progressive unless it numbers at least one baseball league."

For most of this century, baseball has been our national pastime. At one point or another almost every American has played it, and they all feel they have enough personal experience to be experts. The game has also appealed to people from all social classes. In the early 1900s, almost anyone could afford tickets ranging from 25 cents to $1.50. In 1908, over thirty million people paid more than $10 million to watch professional baseball games.

In the early years of the twentieth century, baseball was a growing and profitable business to both owners and players, a new and exciting American industry. Baseball also provided jobs for people who manufactured, marketed, and sold balls, bats, uniforms, shoes, masks, gloves, and other equipment.

The owners who ran the National League had long tried to protect its dominant position and maximize management's income. By 1900, it had put out of business three competing major leagues and had won battles with the players over salary structure and the practices that determined it. The Reserve Clause was firmly in place, eliminating what we now call free agency, and holding salaries down by binding players to teams in perpetuity.

The American League, and eventually the Federal League, would take advantage of the resulting low wages by raiding the National League and offering quality players more money.

American League founder Byron Bancroft "Ban" Johnson, the league's visionary president, wanted teams in large-market cities, so that the teams would have an established fan base. The Chicago *Tribune* noted, "The establishment of an American League club in Chicago…undoubtedly would add a great deal of interest to baseball. The big Western cities look to Chicago as their metropolis. They are interested in Chicago's enterprise and progress. Their business interests link them with Chicago." Johnson's theory turned out to be correct. Competition between Comiskey's White Sox and the team soon to become the Cubs sparked fan interest. James Hart, Chicago's National League owner, was less certain that two teams in the same city would increase fan interest for both, but he said that he was "willing to accept the situation and make the best of it. Where there are two clubs in a city it cannot be helped now, and I think the best way is to let the public in time to decide whether it can support them both. If not, let the same public decide which team must seek other territory."

The two leagues battled it out in the courts as well as on the field. Eventually, the National League had seen enough, and on January 10, 1903, a formal treaty between the two leagues was signed at the St. Nicholas Hotel in Cincinnati. Johnson promised to refrain from further raids on National League players, and the National League formally recognized the American League. A three-man national commission was formed to oversee the leagues jointly. Later in the year, the first World Series between the champions of the two leagues took place, an anual event that was formalized in 1905. It was this "peace" in 1903 that enabled the competition between the Cubs and the White Sox to intensify and draw the people of Chicago into the fray.

Charles Comiskey

Strong fans, strong teams—Charles Albert Comiskey, the prominent owner of the White Sox, was the son of the illustrious Chicago Alderman John Comiskey, and a great and famous ballplayer in his own right. On February 24, 1900, he announced his intentions to move his St. Paul, Minnesota, team to Chicago as an entry in Johnson's new and not yet major American League. Comiskey's "magical misfits" did not have one big star to lead the way. Nevertheless, the White Sox won their first pennant and the hearts of many of the Chicago fans.

Their first location was an old resodded weed patch that had once served as the home of the Wanderers cricket team, located at 39th and Wentworth. In 1910, they moved a few blocks to the "Baseball Palace of the World," variously known as Comiskey Park and White Sox Park, at 35th and Shields.

Southsiders responded enthusiastically to their "hometown" team. Comiskey concentrated on making his team and fans into a community. He charged 25-cent admissions instead of the normal 50 cents. Comiskey was always on hand to meet and greet his fans, buying them drinks at local pubs as he listened to their suggestions. The White Sox also had a special fan club called the Rooters. They went to all home games, and often traveled with the team.

An intense rivalry grew up between the White Sox and the Cubs, who in those days played at the West Side Grounds. As the Sox, with their South Side lo-

Ban Johnson

cation and Irish-dominated lineup appealed to their ethnic, blue-collar home community, the Cubs appealed to the people of the northern and western suburbs, many of them businessmen. Thus, the geographical location of the teams was one of the contributing factors to the development of their distinct fan bases.

Another reason that the fan base for the two teams became so broad in the first twenty years of the century was that the Cubs and White Sox of this era were among the best that either club ever had. Collectively they made ten World Series appearances between 1900 and 1918, with the Cubs winning the National League pennant in 1906, 1907, 1908, 1910 and 1918, and the White Sox capturing the American League flag in 1900, 1901, 1906, 1917, and 1919. In the *Baseball Register* of 1946, Fred Lieb ranked the outstanding team of each major league club. He chose the 1907 Chicago Cubs and the 1917 Chicago White Sox. There were also a number of Chicago players from this era who were eventually inducted into the Baseball Hall of Fame, including the famous Cub infield of Joe Tinker, Johnny Evers, and Frank Chance, who were immortalized by Giants fan Franklin P. Adams:

These are the saddest of possible words:
Tinker to Evers to Chance
Trio of bear Cubs and fleeter than birds,
Tinker to Evers to Chance
Ruthlessly pricking our gonfalon bubble
Making a Giant hit into a double-
Words that are weighty with nothing but trouble:
Tinker to Evers to Chance.

City Series—Fan interest in the Cubs and White Sox in Chicago was also sparked by the annual City Series played between the two local rivals. The first City Series were played in 1903, as fans in New York, Boston, Philadelphia, St. Louis, and Chicago were given the opportunity to see their National and American League teams play each other for a city title.

In Chicago, the series was originally to be won by eight of fifteen games, but since weather required the first series to be called a draw, four games out of seven became the standard format. In Chicago, a pattern emerged, as mediocre White Sox teams would defeat the strong, powerful Cubs. Ring Lardner, when he was a Chicago *Tribune* sportswriter, wrote:

Will someone obligingly slip me the reason,
They don't play like that in the regular season?

The pattern continued to play out in 1906, the only time that the Cubs and White Sox won pennants in the same year. The Cubs were an all-powerful team that won a record 116 games in a 154-game schedule, while the White Sox, whose team batting average was .228, were dubbed the "Hitless Wonders." The Cubs were three-to-one favorites to win the World Series.

The city was in a state of bedlam. The *Tribune* reported, WEST SIDE TEAM'S SUPPORTER, SINGLE HANDED, ATTACKS CROWD OF WHITE SOX ROOTERS AND IS LOCKED UP. On the day of the first game City Hall closed so the payrollers would be able to attend. The game was scheduled for October 9, exactly thirty-five years to the day after the great Chicago fire swept through the city. A *Tribune* reporter called on history to write that, "Today a fire is raging through the city that has been smoldering for weeks past and will burst into its full fury at 2:30 o'clock this afternoon, when Chicago's two teams of champions face each other on the green battlefield which is bounded by Polk, Wood, and Lincoln streets on the West Side."

The White Sox upset the Cubs in six games. After the final game, jubilant Sox fans rushed onto the field in celebration of their upset victory. Frank Chance, the player-manager of the Cubs displayed his shock at losing the Series: "It was the greatest series ever played and we have got to give it to Comiskey's champions. The Sox played grand, game baseball, and outclassed us in this series just ended. But there is one thing I never will believe, and that is that the White Sox are a better ball club than the Cubs. We did not play our game and that's all there is to it." The Cubs regrouped to win the World Series against Ty Cobb and Detroit the following year.

The rivalry remained strong after 1906, but it became a little less frantic. Both teams made a number of World Series appearances over the next decade and more, but never again in the same year. Many Chicago fans "crossed over" and rooted for the other hometown team rather than supporting a team from another city. Finally, the creation of the Federal League challenged the territory of both teams, and united them in a common purpose.

The Federal League challenge—The Federal League was founded in 1913, but it didn't become a threat until it was taken over by James Gilmore, a thirty-seven-year-old Chicago businessman determined create a major league. Gilmore relinquished his interest in the ChiFeds to two local businessmen, William Walter, a wholesale fish distributor, and Charles Henry Weeghman, a successful restaurant owner who had made several unsuccessful attempts to buy the Chicago Cubs. The Federal League did not observe the Reserve Clause, and began raiding American and National League teams, offering established stars big money.

The Chi-Feds shocked the baseball world and the city of Chicago by immediately signing Cubs shortstop Joe Tinker to a three-year contract as player-manager. This move gave the Federal League real credibility, especially in Chicago.

Weeghman built his team a new ballpark. During construction, the Chicago *Daily News* reported, "Many north side residents stepped over the police line...to shake hands with the young man who had the nerve to buck organized baseball and give the north siders a baseball park which, he says, will outshine any in either the National or American Leagues, with the exception of the Polo Grounds in New York."

With attendance lagging in 1915, Weeghman tried to increase attendance by signing two high-profile players: Cub favorite Mordecai "Three Finger" Brown, and baseball's best pitcher, Walter Johnson. The war among the leagues was still bitter, and Johnson was persuaded to return to the American League Washington Senators after White Sox owner Comiskey agreed to pay three-quarters of Johnson's salary to keep him out of the hands of his Federal League rival.

On January 20, 1915 the fledgling Federal League filed a suit in federal court, charging organized baseball with monopoly and criminal conspiracy. The presiding judge was Kenesaw Mountain Landis, a loyal Cubs fan and the future commissioner of baseball. Unwilling to upset the order of the game he had followed since boyhood, he told the attorneys that he would reserve judgement for a year, then made a public statement indicating his unwillingness to disrupt the two-league system. It looked like time for the leagues to settle.

In negotiations, the Feds insisted on admission of four of their teams to the established leagues, and the right to purchase two established teams. In the end, Weeghman was allowed to buy the Cubs, Phil Ball purchased the St. Louis Browns, and other Federal League owners were given financial settlements. Organized baseball assumed control of Federal League

stadiums, and players were auctioned off to the highest bidders. The Federal League was dead. It had a lasting effect in Chicago, though. Weeghman Park eventually became Wrigley Field, the famous "friendly confines" of the Chicago Cubs.

The Black Sox scandal of 1919 had a terrible effect on Chicago baseball. The Sox didn't return to respectability until the '50s. The Cubs, though they made Series appearances in the '20s, '30s, and '40s, never returned to the greatness of the century's first decade. Fervor moderated, but never disappeared.

The competition that had been so characteristic of the early 1900s helped shape the teams and their identities. The rivalry between the two clubs gave each a distinct identity comprising not only uniforms, owners, and players, but fans and neighborhoods, too.

Had the competition between the two not been so intense the history of the Cubs and the White Sox would not be so rich. Their rivalry is just a part of the history of the sport that has conquered the hearts of the American people in general and specifically so many of the citizens of Chicago.

Sources:

Baseball in Old Chicago. Federal Writers' Project (Chicago: A.C. McClurg &Co, 1939).

Weir, Hugh C., "Baseball: The Men and the Dollars Behind It," (*The World Today*, 1909).

Evers, Johnnie and Fullerton, Hugh S., *Baseball in the Big Leagues* (Chicago: Reilly and Britton, 1910).

Lindberg, Richard C., *Stealing First in a Two-Team Town: The White Sox from Comiskey to Reinsdorf* (Champaign , IL: Sagamore Publishing, 1994).

Ahrens, Arthur R., "Chicago's City Series: Cubs versus White Sox," *Chicago History* (Winter 1976-1976), 248.

Catton, Bruce, "The Great American Game," *American Heritage* (April, 1994).

Leonard, Will., "Tinker to Evers to Chance," *Chicago History* (Fal,l 1970) 69.

Lieb, Fredrick G., "Each Major League Club's Outstanding All-Time Team," *The Baseball Register* (1946).

Lindberg, Richard C., "The Chicago Whales and the Federal League of American Baseball, 1914-1915," *Chicago History* (Spring, 1981) 7.

Chicago Daily Tribune. "Bound to Place Club in Chicago," Feb. 25, 1900: p. 17.
　　"New York the Vital Question," Dec. 18, 1901: p. 6.
　　"Fans Fight; One Arrested," Oct. 14, 1906: p. 2.
　　"Great Ball Games Begin Today," Oct. 9, 1906: p. 1.
　　"'Fairly Won,' Says Chance," Oct. 15, 1906: p. 2.

Cubs Trades

Oh, dear

Eddie Gold

Imagine a ballclub trading away more than 1,000 home runs for fewer than 50. The Cubs have disposed of a shower of power in five futile deals.

The departed quintet went on to slugging stardom with other teams. Their names are Cy Williams, Dolph Camilli, Andre Thornton, Joe Carter, and Rafael Palmeiro.

In return, they might as well have received Moe, Larry, and Curly. At least they would have provided some slapstick in deference to slap hitters.

The Guys That Got Away

Cy Williams: The Cubs gift-wrapped slugger Cy Williams to Philadelphia the day after Christmas in 1917 for Dode Paskert. When the switch of outfielders was consummated, many fans sang an ode to Dode, but they later sighed for Cy.

Paskert, an acrobatic center fielder, helped the Cubs win the 1918 pennant, batting .286, but Dode was more of a dud. He lasted only three seasons in Cubs flannels and hit only nine homers.

Williams, a long-legged bean pole, played thirteen seasons with the Phillies and wound up with 251 homers. In 1923, he matched Babe Ruth in homers, each leading his league with forty-one. Unfortunately for him, Cy couldn't match the Babe's paycheck.

Dolf Camilli: Two decades later, the Cubs again dealt a promising prospect for a fading veteran. On June 11, 1934, Cubs manager Charlie Grimm reported to

Eddie Gold *is a semiretired sportswriter and a long-suffering Cubs fan.*

Cy Williams

Wrigley Field. He looked about for Dolf Camilli, who was to be his replacement at first base. Grimm was told Camilli had been dispatched to Philadelphia for aging first sacker Don Hurst.

Hurst, who hit as many as thirty-one homers and had driven in 143 runs in separate seasons with the Phillies, was fading fast. In fact, Hurst was more like a hearse in a Cubs uniform. He hit three homers and drove in twelve runs, batted .196, and dropped out of sight at the conclusion of the season.

Camilli, meanwhile, went on to torment the Cubs for the next decade. He led the Brooklyn Dodgers to the 1941 pennant by hitting a league high thirty-four homers and 120 runs batted in and won the Most Valuable Player Award. He finished his career with 239 homers, but only hit six with the Cubs.

Andre Thornton: It was another era and another first baseman. The Atlanta Braves took the troubled Joe Pepitone off the Cubs' hands on May 19, 1973. In return, they threw in Andre Thornton, an unheralded rookie.

Thornton, a fine-fielding first baseman, showed a penchant for power during his brief Cubs stay. Getting his first shot as a regular in 1975, Thornton responded with eighteen homers, sixty RBIs, and a respectable .293 batting average.

The Cubs had a shortage of home run power, but a bigger shortage of brain power. They dangled Thornton on the market. The Montreal Expos grabbed Andre and sent journeymen Larry Biittner and pitcher Steve Renko to the Cubs on May 17, 1976.

What did the Cubs miss? Thornton played briefly with the Expos, but became a fixture with the Cleveland Indians, blasting 234 homers in their cleanup spot through the 1980s.

Joe Carter: Here's one trade you can't fault the Cubs for. General manager Dallas Green felt his club needed a big pitcher to put them on top. He risked the future by sending slugging rookie outfielder Joe Carter to the Cleveland Indians in a six-player swap on June 13, 1984.

The deal paid immediate dividends as newly ac-

Dolf Camilli

Transcendental Graphics

quired pitcher Rick Sutcliffe rolled down the stretch with a 16-1 record to lead the Cubs to the NL East title and garner a Cy Young Award.

But in the long run the Cubs missed the long ball provided by Carter, who went on to blast 396 homers, mainly with the Indians and Toronto Blue Jays.

In addition, Carter was the hero of the 1993 World Series, hitting a three-run homer off ex-Cub "Wild Thing" Mitch Williams in the ninth inning for an 8-6 victory over the Philadelphia Phillies.

Rafael Palmeiro: The Cubs brought up first baseman Rafael Palmeiro near the end of the 1986 season, and he looked like the best pure hitter on the team.

But the following spring, they moved Rafael to left field. It seemed that the braintrust of the Cubs, GM Jim Frey and manager Don Zimmer, preferred veteran outfielder Jerry Mumphrey and sent Palmeiro back to the bushes. Jerry Mumphrey?

Palmeiro finally got his chance as a regular in 1988 and banged out forty-one doubles to go with his .307 batting average. And he showed promise as a power hitter with twenty-two homers in his short stint.

Raffy looked like a solid .300 hitter for the next decade. The Cubs brass, however, claimed Palmeiro wasn't a "clutch hitter."

It was the Cubs who choked. On December 5, 1988, they shipped the young prospect to the Texas Rangers in a six-player trade that landed them the enigmatic Mitch Williams. (The Wild Thing keeps popping up.)

The result? Palmeiro kept pumping homers, totaling 361 by the end of 1999, and was usually above .300, with the Rangers, the Baltimore Orioles, and back with the Rangers.

Baseball in the Virgin Islands

Our eastern outpost

Rory Costello

When the year 2000 arrives, the first place the sun will hit American soil is the U.S. Virgin Islands. St. Croix and St. Thomas are only eighty-four and thirty-two square miles apiece, yet these low-key Caribbean isles have made a contribution to baseball that belies their size. Consider that the territory's population is about 110,000 now, and in 1960 it was a mere 32,000. As a pocket of talent and passionate support for the game—especially during the '50s and '60s, but still today—the USVI have forged a distinctive tradition.

There have been ten true Virgin Islanders in the major leagues, plus two special Puerto Rican cases. In addition, there was one Negro League player and even a nineteenth-century black baseball manager (see table). Since 1957, there has been at least one V.I. ballplayer active in the majors in every season but 1985. In particular, Crucians and St. Thomians have made their mark in the Puerto Rican Winter League, including four Rookies of the Year and a Triple Crown winner.

No one has yet been able to pin down the exact date when baseball was first played on St. Thomas or St. Croix. The most likely theory is that it spread from elsewhere in the Caribbean. There was a longstanding pattern of migration between the Virgin Islands and Cuba, the Dominican Republic, Puerto Rico, and Panama.

A driving force was the search for work as sugar-cane cutters throughout the region, which also ties in with the presence of cricket. As Rob Ruck portrays vividly in his book *The Tropic of Baseball*, cane cutters were playing cricket on the British Virgin Island of Tortola as far back as the 1890s. Tortolans brought cricket to the Dominican Republic, breaking the ground for baseball, and they most likely did the same in St. Croix.

It is possible, though, that the States exported baseball directly. Confederate blockade runners and Union warships both dropped anchor in St. Thomas harbor during the Civil War. As early as 1865, the U.S. sought to buy the Virgin Islands from Denmark, but it took more than fifty years of stop-start negotiations before the sale finally took place in 1917. One intriguing conjecture is that early black baseball organizer S.K. Govern—a native of St. Croix—may have returned to his birthplace during the 1880s or 1890s, talking about the game or even organizing a match.

The key to getting baseball entrenched as a popular sport in the Virgin Islands was the U.S. armed forces. After the Spanish-American War of 1898, and especially under Teddy Roosevelt, military teams played throughout the Caribbean basin. Fear of German sea threats during World War I pushed the Wilson administration into clinching the deal with the Danish. The Navy governed the Virgin Islands until 1930, and sailors often went ashore and played against the locals. According to oral history, though, baseball was being played before the Navy arrived.

Rory Costello *is a Mets fan who made his one World Series game count—it was Bill Buckner's boot in 1986. He is preparing a full-length history of Virgin Islands baseball.*

Virgin Islands players have ranged throughout the hemisphere

	Position(s)	MLB	Negro Leagues	Puerto Rico	Other
Alfonso Gerard	OF		1945-49	1944-58	Mexico, Canada, D.R.
Valmy Thomas	C	1957-61		1949-63	Canada, D.R.
Joe Christopher	OF	1959-66		1954-69*	Mexico, D.R., Venezuela
Al McBean	P	1961-70		1958-71*	
Elmo Plaskett	C-IF-OF	1962-63		1957-71*	D.R.
Horace Clarke	2B	1965-74		1959-68	MLB scout
Elrod Hendricks	C	1968-79		1960-78*	Mexico, MLB coach
José Morales	C-1B-DH	1973-84		1963-84	MLB coach
Jerry Browne	2B-IF-OF	1986-95		1986-87, 97-98	
Midre Cummings	OF	1993-			
Calvin Pickering	1B	1998-		1998-99	
Also:					
S.K. Govern	Mgr.		1880s-90s		
Julio Navarro**	P	1962-66, 70		1955-77	
Henry Cruz**	OF	1975-78		1972-86	Mexico, MLB scout

*Did not play in one or more seasons.
** Self-described Puerto Ricans who lived on St. Croix in their youth.

Following are sketches of the most prominent members of the Virgin Islands baseball fraternity, in chronological order. (Quite a few others played in Puerto Rico and the minor leagues.)

Alfonso "Piggy" Gerard, the pioneer pro, shaped the course of this story. The lone V.I. ballplayer in the history of the Negro Leagues, Gerard spent most of his career (fourteen winters) in Puerto Rico with the Santurce Cangrejeros. The very young Roberto Clemente broke in behind him in right field. The sporting hero of Horace Clarke and Elmo Plaskett was also on Branch Rickey's list of candidates to break the color line.

After starring in Puerto Rican amateur ball, the Crucian was co-winner of the Rookie of the Year award in 1944-45, batting .348 and leading the league in steals. This won Virgin Islanders a special exemption from the roster limits on non-Puerto Ricans and also impressed George Scales, who was skipper of the Ponce Leones. Scales brought Gerard up to play with his New York Black Yankees in 1945.

In 1946, Gerard became one of the many players from the majors and the Negro Leagues to join Jorge

Pasquel's would-be major league in Mexico. In the early '50s, he was part of a wave of black ballplayers who played in racially tolerant Canada. He also spent a couple of summers in the Dominican Republic, before the league switched to winter play in 1955.

Alfonso played on three champion clubs with the Crabbers (1950-51, 1952-53, and 1954-55), which also won the Caribbean Series. The 1954-55 squad is widely regarded as the best winter league club ever assembled. Gerard's lifetime batting average of .303 (with just six homers) stands eighth on the all-time list in Puerto Rico. He was described as "a pesky hitter who could hurt you."

Piggy ended his playing career in 1957-58 and returned home to St. Croix, where he managed local teams and worked with the government's baseball development program. He also kept an eye on local talent as a bird dog. Gerard retired in 1984 and lives today, age eighty-three, outside of Christiansted.

Valmy Thomas, the first big leaguer from the Virgin Islands, was born in Santurce, Puerto Rico, where his mother had gone for better medical care, and was brought home to St. Croix. Valmy remembers the main sports of his youth as cricket and soccer, but his generation embraced baseball.

Valmy spent the years 1943 through 1949 with the Navy in Puerto Rico, playing ball with local teams and traveling to international competitions. He joined Gerard on the great Santurce Cangrejeros teams of the early '50s, winning Rookie of the Year honors in 1950-51. During his thirteen seasons in Santurce, the team won five championships.

In 1951, Thomas became another of the black players who went to Canada's Provincial League, but he spent the next three summers playing in Santo Domingo for better money. Valmy got his shot at the majors because New York Giants owner Horace Stoneham and Santurce honcho Pédrín Zorrilla had a friendly working relationship. To get drafted, he had to return to Canada and play for St. Jean in 1955.

Valmy's first major-league season, 1957, was also his best. He was a semiregular with New York. He played in sixty-three for the first San Francisco Giants and sixty-six for the '59 Phillies, but spent most of '60 and '61 in the minors. He wrapped up his Puerto Rican career in 1962-63. Although he felt he could have played another year, he wanted to come back to St. Croix and get more involved in local business and sporting affairs. Valmy has owned a sporting-goods store for forty-one years, ran for the Virgin Islands Senate a few years ago, and still has a radio show. He remains full of ideas and has a droll sense of humor.

Joe Christopher played for a champion in the U.S., several in Puerto Rico, and another in the Dominican Republic—yet U.S. fans mainly remember him today as one of the original Amazin' Mets.

As a teenager, the Frederiksted native played shortstop for a local team called the Athletics, plus three years of varsity ball at St. Patrick's High School. When he was eighteen in 1954, the Christiansted Commandos journeyed more than 3,000 miles to Wichita, Kansas, to play in the National Baseball Congress (NBC) tournament. Joe impressed the late Pirates superscout Howie Haak, whom Branch Rickey had commissioned to hunt for talent throughout Latin America. After signing Christopher, Haak visited the Virgin Islands for many years to come in search of prospects.

In 1957, Joe, who was switched to the outfield when he turned pro, led the Mexican League in steals, though he played in just sixty-four games. In 1958-59, he became Puerto Rico's stolen-base king for the first of four times. A consistent .300 hitter in the high minors, Joe was obviously ready for The Show. He was a

backup outfielder with the Pirates from 1959 through 1961, making his debut in Harvey Haddix's masterpiece. With the 1960 champs, he pinch-ran in three World Series games and scored two runs.

Christopher got his chance to start with Casey Stengel's comical crew from 1962 through 1965. In 1964, he recorded what is still the finest season by any V.I. batter in the majors, hitting .300 with sixteen homers and seventy-six RBIs. However, the Mets traded the outspoken Crucian to Boston in 1966, where he played only briefly. Joe remained active in the minors through 1968 and in Puerto Rico through the winter of 1968-69. He won two more championships in his last two Puerto Rican seasons, also developing his knack for counseling younger players.

Joe Christopher lives in the Baltimore area today. As ever, he is an individual thinker with a fondness for debate. He loves to talk about hitting and would make a fine instructor, but he doesn't want to be part of the old boys' club. Since retiring, art has been his great passion, along with spiritual knowledge and delving into the workings of the universe.

Al McBean, the only big league pitcher from the Virgin Islands, was a showman with a live arm. He performed at a high level in the majors more consistently than any other V.I. player, and his flamboyance made him memorable. He loved playing for the crowd.

Born in Charlotte Amalie, McBean became the first St. Thomian to make the majors. Haak discovered him in 1957 at a tryout camp. Al, a press photographer for one of the local papers, had been assigned to cover the event. His friend Lealdo Victoria (manager of a local club, the Texaco Stars) suggested that he had nothing to lose by giving it a whirl. McBean's limber arm and natural hard-running sinker caught Haak's eye, and an invitation to spring training with the Pirates came a couple of months later.

In Puerto Rico, Al won Rookie of the Year honors with the Ponce Leones in 1958-59. One of his teammates was Elmo Plaskett, whose best man he would become. Pittsburgh called him up first in July, 1961. The next year, McBean posted career highs in starts (twenty-nine) and wins (fifteen). From 1963 through 1965, though, he was as effective as any reliever in the game. He complemented Elroy Face at first, but when Face suffered one of his few poor years in '64, Alvin won Fireman of the Year with an 8-3 record, 1.91 ERA, and twenty-two saves.

McBean showed his flexibility by returning to the

Pirates rotation in 1968, but he was exposed to the expansion draft and selected by the Padres in 1969. San Diego traded him to the Dodgers after just one start, and the Pirates reacquired him in 1970. His major league career then wound down, though he did his best to revive it with an effective return to Puerto Rico and some good work for the Phillies Triple-A club in Eugene, Oregon, in 1971.

Al then joined the Housing, Parks, and Recreation department on St. Thomas, rising to deputy commissioner. He supervises crews in charge of maintenance, construction, and beautification projects. The Al McBean Center near his home in the hills has a baseball diamond. At age sixty-one, he is still brimming with restless energy and vociferous opinions, especially about baseball in the '90s. Yet despite this combative streak (which served him well as a player), what still distinguishes Al McBean is his enjoyment of friendly company, family and fans alike.

Elmo Plaskett, one of just four men to win the Triple Crown in Puerto Rico, passed away in November 1998 at the age of sixty. Despite his talent as a hitter, Plaskett enjoyed only two brief stints in the majors. Yet he remained devoted to baseball throughout his life, always striving on behalf of local youth. The unanimous memory of this big-hearted man is his luminous smile.

From the time he was a small boy, the Frederiksted native lived to play his favorite game. At St. Patrick's School, he followed a few years behind Joe Christopher, whom he credited with teaching him. The sixteen-year-old Elmo was also on the Virgin Islands team that went to the 1954 NBC tournament. Three years later, Howie Haak signed him for the Pirates. Haak may or may not have remembered him from the tournament; Christopher recommended his friend.

Elmo came up as a pitcher and played all positions during his minor league career. He earned his call-up with a marvelous season for the Asheville Tourists of the Sally League (Class A) in 1962. Plaskett edged future three-time AL batting champ Tony Oliva, .34979 to .34978, and was named Player of the Year. His lone major league home run came in the thick of the pennant race, dropping the Giants (who beat the Dodgers in a playoff) four games back with thirteen to play.

But Plaskett's greatest feats came in Ponce. In 1960-61, though Luis Arroyo beat him out for MVP, he became the second of four players to win the Triple Crown. (Willard "*Ese Hombre*" Brown, who did it twice, Wally Joyner, and Héctor Villanueva are the others.) At age twenty in 1958-59, Elmo led the league in hits and triples and became the third of ten players to hit three homers in a game. He also led the league in RBI in 1962-63.

However, the Pirates of the time were well stocked at Plaskett's various positions. They decided to convert him to catcher. Perhaps most damaging to his career, though, was a badly broken ankle suffered in Ponce early in the 1964-65 season. After the injury, Elmo put on weight and was really never the same. He continued to play in the minors through 1969 (nurturing the young Vida

Mickey Mantle was one of Al McBean's favorite players growing up listening to Armed Forces radio. Yet before meeting him in spring training, Al had no idea what he looked like. At right is Elmo Plaskett.

Rory Costello

Blue in the A's chain) and had one last at-bat for the Arecibo Lobos in the winter of 1970-71. After retiring, Elmo became a baseball specialist for the Department of Housing, Parks, and Recreation. His partner was Horace Clarke.

Horace Clarke played more games in the majors than any other Virgin Islander. For seven seasons from 1967 through 1973, he was a durable fixture at second base for the New York Yankees, averaging 151 games. A pesky hitter with speed and a good glove, Clarke admits that he was bothered by criticism while he was playing. Looking back on it now, though, his mind is at rest.

Horace's introduction to baseball came via softball, because there were no Little Leagues on St. Croix when he was young. At age thirteen or so, he remembers seeing Navy teams playing hardball against the locals. From then until age seventeen, when he signed his first pro contract, he played in the St. Croix Baseball League. Horace also competed in interisland high school meets against St. Thomas.

Yankees scout José "Pepe" Seda discovered Horace and also arranged for him to play in Puerto Rico starting in 1959-60. Clarke believes that playing winter ball definitely sharpened his skills on the way to the majors, and it was also an important source of earnings. During the 1962-63 season, at Elmo Plaskett's urging, Ponce traded for Horace. He was an All-Star for the Leones in 1965-66, leading the league in triples and runs scored.

Horace progressed steadily in the minors, hitting for good average and showing his speed. He broke in as a utility infielder with the Yankees in May, 1965, and Ralph Houk gave him a chance to play every day late in '66. Horace's career on-base percentage of .310 was less than ideal in the leadoff spot, but his lifetime success rate on stolen bases was 72 percent. In retrospect, he regards himself as underrated defensively. Overall, his career may not have been stellar, but it was certainly decent.

Gabe Paul dealt Clarke to San Diego in 1974 as part of his housecleaning for George Steinbrenner. After that season, Horace returned to St. Croix, teaming with Elmo Plaskett in the local baseball programs. For several years in the early 1980s, he was an associate scout with the Kansas City Royals. Horace's two sons, Jeff and J.D. (also middle infielders), have each played minor league ball. J.D., who played with the Class A Daytona Cubs in 1999, is hoping to play for Ponce. Horace took early retirement in 1997 and enjoys the quiet life in Frederiksted. Among other things, he plays vibes in a local jazz combo.

Elrod Hendricks, the embodiment of Baltimore Orioles tradition, has made a greater lifetime contribution to baseball than perhaps any other Virgin Islander. He has worn the Orioles uniform for far more games than anybody else—his major league career spanned twelve seasons, and he is now in his twenty-second year as the O's bullpen coach. He also played seventeen seasons in Puerto Rico and became known as the "Babe Ruth of Mexico" during four summers there.

The Charlotte Amalie native did not come to baseball until age thirteen because of a childhood accident that broke his feet. However, he then started playing with the Texaco Stars in the local men's league thanks to his uncle and Lealdo Victoria. Four years later, Ellie signed to play pro ball with the Milwaukee Braves organization—largely owing to Hank Aaron, who came to St. Thomas on a hitting exhibition after the 1958 World Series.

The Braves released Hendricks in December, 1960, but he was able to hook on with Santurce. Ellie backed up Valmy Thomas and then shared catching duties with him during the next two seasons. He salutes Valmy, as well as many other Puerto Rican veterans, for helping him learn the craft of baseball. Around that time, Ellie also roomed for a couple of years with Horace Clarke at the San Juan YMCA. He jokes about the St. Thomas–St. Croix rivalry with both Valmy and Horace.

The Puerto Rican connection also helped keep Hendricks' career alive after the Cardinals chain cut him. His closest friend with the Cangrejeros, pitcher William de Jesús, found him a chance to play every day with Jalisco in the Mexican League. His slugging for the Charros caught the eye of future Orioles manager Earl Weaver, who was then Santurce's skipper. Hendricks became a regular in Puerto Rico too, and Weaver insisted that the Orioles draft him in 1966. Ellie then became a cog in the superb Baltimore machine of 1969-71. He peaked in Puerto Rico in 1968-69, winning the MVP award. In recognition, Santurce played a game at Lionel Roberts Stadium on St. Thomas the next winter—a unique honor.

The winter of 1977-78 was Ellie's last with the Cangrejeros. He still ranks third lifetime in Puerto Rico with 105 homers, and he played on five league champs. In November, 1977, Earl gave Hendricks the Orioles bullpen spot, and ever since (including cameos as a player-coach in 1978 and 1979) he has been Baltimore's most loyal lieutenant. Ellie served as interim manager for two periods during 1988, and though he admits that in the past he had the desire to get the job full-time, he says that he put it on the back burner some years ago. He loves coming to the ballpark every day, and he is so popular and friendly to fans that it is hard to imagine him ever leaving.

José Morales, a line drive master, made his reputation in the U.S. with twenty-five pinch hits in 1976. That record stood until John Vander Wal stroked twenty-nine in 1995. José's mental approach to the demands of pinch hitting helped him to a total of 123, which still ranks fourth on the career list. It has also led to a productive career as a batting coach in the majors.

Morales was born in the Frederiksted area and recalls playing in a diamond cut out of the middle of a big cattle pasture. He remembers that there were several more naturally gifted players among his friends on St. Croix, but he credits his determination for making the difference. The Giants signed "Shady" in 1963 after "Piggy" Gerard recommended him to Pedrin Zorrilla.

At that time, José went to play in Puerto Rico. He spent twenty-one seasons there, ranking third on the league's all-time RBI list with 467. One of his achievements was batting .402 in the winter of 1968-69, though his 112 at bats were not enough to qualify for the title. He also starred in the 1978 Caribbean Series, hitting .421 and leading Mayagüez to the title. The Indios were just 29-31 in the regular season but went on a late roll.

It took Morales ten years to make it to the majors with Oakland in 1973. The main problem was his fielding. Broadcasters referred to him often as "a catcher by trade," though he played first most often in the majors. During his major league career, he appeared in the field in only 104 of his 733 total games, and he never had more than 242 at-bats in a season. José set his pinch-hit record with Montreal, was a very effective part-time DH with Minnesota, and finished up as a specialist with Baltimore and Los Angeles. He had his eye on Manny Mota's career pinch-hit mark of 150, but L.A. released him partway through the 1984 season at age thirty-nine.

Morales returned to the Orioles as a minor league instructor in 1985, inventing a special short, heavy exercise bat in order to help prospects hit more line drives. He then spent three years as batting coach in San Francisco, four in Cleveland (where Kenny Lofton swore by him), and one and a half with the Florida Marlins. Shady was active most recently when Carlos Baerga, another of his devoted former pupils,

enlisted his help in the winter after the 1998 season. He was in spring training with the Cardinals, who gave Baerga a brief look, but did not join St. Louis in any official capacity. Morales lives in the Orlando area and occasionally visits family and friends in St. Croix.

Jerry Browne, "the Governor," picked up the baton for the Virgin Islands—nearly two seasons went by without a V.I. player in the majors after the Dodgers released Morales. The Texas Rangers called up the twenty-year-old Crucian in September, 1986. Jerry stuck around for nine years, and were it not for a personal decision he could still be active today.

Growing up, Browne played Little League, Babe Ruth League, and American Legion ball. He was also in the Horace Clarke/Elmo Plaskett youth program. The Rangers signed him as an undrafted free agent in 1983, thanks to scout Orlando Gómez, who had played and managed in Puerto Rico alongside Clarke, Morales, and Christopher, among others.

In the winter of 1986-87, Jerry became the fourth Virgin Islander to win Rookie of the Year in Puerto Rico, batting .316 and scoring a league-leading thirty-six runs for Santurce. He was also the Rangers' top rookie in 1987, hitting .271 and stealing twenty-seven bases as their regular second baseman. Texas third base coach Dave Oliver, a Californian, nicknamed him that year after the Golden State's quirky politician.

After the 1988 season, Browne was sent to the Indians in the four-player swap that brought future batting champ Julio Franco to Texas. Jerry hit a career-high .299 for Cleveland in 1989 and remained the regular at second in 1990. The Tribe released him in spring training '92, but he caught on with Oakland, where Tony LaRussa made excellent use of him in a utility role. In 1994, Browne signed as a free agent with Florida, joining fellow Crucian Morales. The Marlins chose not to re-sign Browne after a decent year in 1995. The next spring, he went to camp with the Mets and appeared to have won a job, but when Dallas Green decided to carry eleven pitchers, Jerry was optioned to Norfolk.

He refused the assignment, irritating his old boss, then-Tides manager Bobby Valentine. Following a year's layoff, the Rangers invited him to their minor league camp in 1997, but his comeback fell short. Still, Jerry wasn't quite ready to hang it up. After ten seasons away from Puerto Rico, he played for Arecibo in the winter of 1997-98. Since then, though, he has remained with his family in Arlington, Texas.

Midre Cummings, a talented enigma, may be as close to a five-tool player as the Virgin Islands have ever produced. However, he has displayed only tantalizing glimpses of production in the majors. Though generous and likable, Cummings is an unusual personality who polarizes opinion. He has attracted many supporters and also caused much frustration. It was once said of Midre, perhaps unjustly, "Being from a laid-back culture, he may be a little too laid-back."

In 1987, the fifteen-year-old Crucian played on a team coached by Elmo Plaskett that upset perennial power Taiwan in the Senior Little League World Series. The father of one of his teammates urged several of the boys to move to Miami to find more competition. At Edison High, Midre starred for the baseball team and also set state records running track. The Minnesota Twins drafted him with a supplemental first-round pick in 1990, which they got when the Red Sox signed Jeff Reardon.

The Pittsburgh Pirates slashed their payroll in 1992, starting when they traded John Smiley to the Twins for Denny Neagle and Cummings. At the time the Bucs regarded Midre—labeled by *USA Today* as a possible 30/30 player—as the key to the deal, not Neagle. Cummings hit strongly at all levels in the minors, and got his first callup in September 1993. At Triple-A Buffalo in 1994, though, the press was scathing in its criticism of his work habits and attitude. The next year, Midre won the starting right field job with the big club, but he was sent down after seven games with a lecture about nonchalance from Jim Leyland.

Over the next couple of seasons, Cummings was called up on various occasions, but he never put it together. Pittsburgh finally waived him in July, 1997, but after Phillies GM Lee Thomas gave him a chance, Midre responded with a .303 average in sixty-three games as the starting center fielder. Still, the Phillies released him during spring training in 1998, as hard-nosed batting coach Hal McRae voiced the same old concerns about motivation. The Reds tried him out briefly, and then Thomas, who had joined the Red Sox front office, rescued him again.

As a reserve for Boston, Cummings was the AL's leading pinch hitter. But a "sprained wrist" actually turned out to be a torn ligament. Midre needed surgery much earlier than he got it, and he wound up as odd man out during spring training in 1999. In May, however, he accepted a minor league deal with the Twins, and he won his way back to the majors in September. At age twenty-eight, Midre is certainly young enough to re-establish his big-league career.

Calvin Pickering, the latest heir to the V.I. baseball tradition, could turn out to be a legitimate slugging star. Although he started off as a thirty-fifth round draft pick, "Picko" has established himself as a top prospect for the Baltimore Orioles. The twenty-three-year-old has enormous size—6-foot-5, 283 pounds—and power to match. As a result, he has drawn comparisons to Mo Vaughn, among other hulking first basemen.

Pickering is only the third St. Thomian to make the majors. He competed in youth leagues from the age of ten, and like Elrod Hendricks before him, played as a teenager in the local men's recreational league. His high school did not have a team. Fortunately, Calvin also had his aunt's husband, Addie Joseph, who devoted much of his time to coaching the local boys. Calvin's own training wrinkle was thirty-yard ocean sprints in water ranging from waist- to chest-deep.

A crucial step for Calvin came when he moved to Tampa for his senior year in 1995. Hurricanes Hugo (1989) and Marilyn (1995) had driven two of his aunts from St. Thomas. Aunt Lois went back for a vacation, saw her nephew play, and knew that she would bring him back to find his dream. At King High, Calvin made the all-state second team in left field and caught the eye of Orioles area scout Harry Shelton. Shelton believes that he might have been the only scout interested—he thinks the young man's body structure may have scared off the others.

In the minors, however, Pickering has clearly made many baseball people snap to attention. In 1996, he became the first Oriole to be named the club's minor league player of the year from the Rookie League level. His fine 1997 season at low-A enabled him to skip to Double-A in 1998, where he was Eastern League Player of the Year. During his September call-up, Calvin excited all of the Virgin Islands when he hit his first big league homers against two premier pitchers, David Cone and Pedro Martínez.

A tired Pickering did not produce in fifteen Puerto Rican games in the winter of 1998-99. In spring training 1999, Gold Glover Will Clark generously tutored Calvin on his weak point, fielding. When the veteran's thumb was broken, Pickering was called up briefly, also starting in the first exhibition game against Cuba on May 3. He was recalled again in September. Overall, 1999 has been his least successful year, but Hendricks, who first saw Calvin as "a fat kid" of seventeen at a St. Thomas baseball clinic, thinks he'll be all right. Pickering has monitored his weight, and he is an agile big man with a selective eye at the plate. If necessary, the DH role is available as a failsafe. And if he goes on to greater success, one of the benefits could be heightened interest in baseball back in the islands.

Special Cases:

Julio Navarro was born on the Puerto Rican island of Vieques, but his family moved to St. Croix when he was four years old. His father was a cane cutter. Known as "Juju" growing up, he was another member of the team that went to Wichita for the NBC tournament. In February, 1955, not long after he graduated from St. Patrick's school, Navarro impressed "Piggy" Gerard while playing in a series between Puerto Rican winter leaguers and a combined Virgin Islands team. For many years this was an annual affair after the Puerto Rican season ended. Gerard helped arrange a tryout for Juju in Puerto Rico, where he worked out for Pedrin Zorrilla with Orlando Cepeda and José Pagán. All three then signed with the Giants. *El Látigo* (or "Whiplash," for his sidearm fastball) pitched for parts of six seasons in the major leagues but played during twenty-two winters in Puerto Rico, tied for third in league history. In another distinctive link, José Morales is godfather to Julio's son Jaime, a major-league pitcher since 1989.

Henry Cruz was born in Christiansted in 1952. Although older Cruz brothers played for local teams in St. Croix, Henry's family moved to Puerto Rico's easternmost city, Fajardo, when he was young. Cruz was a backup outfielder for parts of four seasons with the Dodgers and White Sox. He continued at the Triple-A level until 1981, and he played in the Mexican League from 1982 through 1985. However, he spent thirteen seasons in Puerto Rico, all but one with Arecibo, finishing up in 1985-86. Henry joined the Indians as a part-time scout covering Puerto Rico in 1997 and was made a full-time scout later that year.

S.K. Govern (c. 1854–1924) was a Renaissance man. A labor organizer, journalist, and Shakespearean actor, Govern also managed the first professional black team, the Cuban Giants. This "smart fellow and shrewd baseball man" not only established the business model for the Negro Leagues but also deserves credit as the father of Latin American winter ball. The Cuban Giants went to Havana during their 1885-86 winter tour, and though it has not been confirmed, Govern may have taken another club, the Washington Manhattans, to Cuba as early as 1881 or 1882. His Caribbean background could have led him to spot baseball's role in the nexus of commerce and culture throughout the region.

The Outlook for V.I. Baseball—Baseball's heyday in the Virgin Islands was the '50s and '60s—even into the early '70s, says Horace Clarke. You could have assembled a pretty fair little franchise then with the homegrown talent. In fact, Valmy Thomas says he had a well-developed plan for a V.I. sports complex and entry in the Puerto Rican league. Owing to some interisland intrigue with St. Thomas, though, it never got off the ground.

Lack of athletic talent is certainly not one of the reasons for the erosion of the game's hold on V.I. youngsters. The main culprits—all intertwined—are changing population patterns, a small and oddly distorted economy, notoriously messy politics, the punishing hurricanes, the popularity of basketball (led by Crucian superstar Tim Duncan), and television.

Nevertheless, baseball still enjoys considerable grassroots support in the Virgin Islands, as evidenced by healthy rec-league activity. The Little Leagues are named for Al McBean and Elrod Hendricks on St. Thomas, and for Elmo Plaskett on St. Croix. Adult hardball leagues also remain popular. Horace Clarke believes the key to producing major league prospects is what happens to players once they hit their teens, and he thinks there will always be a select few from the islands who are willing to work and do what it takes.

Despite the changes in society and misfiring cylinders, Virgin Islands baseball still continues to turn out viable prospects. A few dozen players have been drafted in the '80s and '90s, though most were low selections. However, the 1999 draft produced two upper-level picks in pitcher **Terry Byron** (taken in the second round by the Florida Marlins) and shortstop **Mackeel Rodgers** (a fourth-rounder for the Kansas City Royals).

The major leagues continue to look farther and farther afield in search of talent. The recent success of Curaçao and Aruba shows that small Caribbean islands can develop bonafide prospects, including solid starters like Sidney Ponson and even stars like Andruw Jones. With some more of the right kind of nurturing, St. Croix and St. Thomas could resume their rightful role as producers.

The author wishes to acknowledge the research of SABR members José Crescioni, Tom Van Hyning, and Jerry Malloy.

Joe Gordon

A Reliable view of Flash

Tom Henrich
with Richard Nickas

From the first time that I set foot upon the outfield grass at Yankee Stadium early in the 1937 season to my last at bat thirteen years later, I was privileged to play with and alongside some of the greatest names in baseball: Gehrig, Gomez, Crosetti, DiMaggio, Keller, Lazzeri, Mantle, McCarthy, Mize, Rizzuto, Reynolds, Raschi, Rolfe, Ruffing, Berra, and Stengel.

Many of these names are rightfully enshrined in that most hallowed place of baseball tradition, the Baseball Hall of Fame. One of my former teammates, however, deserves to be and is not. That man is Joe "Flash" Gordon. It was natural that we would call him "Flash." Even big leaguers marveled at his athleticism and grace around second.

Joe Gordon was my kind of ballplayer. He was a tough competitor on the diamond and a quick wit off of it. In the decades that have passed since we last played, I have always wondered why Joe has been overlooked for enshrinement in Cooperstown. See if you don't agree.

An acrobat at second base—He started out as a shortstop at the University of Oregon. When he wasn't on the diamond you could find Joe in the gymnasium. Today you would call Gordon a gymnast, back then we called him an acrobat. At Oregon he would tumble every afternoon, developing the moves that he would later import to Yankee Stadium.

A scout for the Yankees signed Joe out of college sending him to play for the Oakland Oaks of the Pacific Coast League. During the year that he spent by the Bay he developed the power that would mark his days in New York. Lefty O'Doul once said of Joe, "Not only can that kid hit, he plays the field as if he had wings." The next year Gordon brought his wings to Newark where he played with the Bears on the greatest minor league team of all time.

When he joined the Yankees in the Spring of 1938 he faced the expectations that came with replacing an aging legend named Tony Lazzeri at second base. Throughout camp we saw Joe McCarthy watch with awe as Joe leapt into the air around the bag. McCarthy never smiled much, but I can still see him grin watching his rookie find.

Reading *Baseball in '41* by Robert Creamer a few years ago, I saw that Joe was described as a "nonpareil." I had an idea what the word meant but looked it up anyway. The dictionary defined the term as "without equal" or "peerless." McCarthy stamped our club with a sense of professionalism that never left those of us on the team. Lazzeri had been a star who began his career when the Babe still held my spot in

---

Tom Henrich *played right field and first base for the New York Yankees from 1937 to 1942 and 1946 to 1950. With Joe DiMaggio and Charlie Keller he was part of one of the greatest outfields of all time. "Old Reliable," who has always preferred "Tom" to "Tommy," soldiers on in Prescott, Arizona with his wife Eileen. He wrote about DiMaggio for* The National Pastime *earlier this year, and hit a long home run as keynote speaker at SABR's national convention in Phoenix. Richard Nikas is an admiralty lawyer practicing in Long Beach, California. He is a SABR member and a pitcher for the Greek National Baseball Team, which will compete in the 2004 Olympic Games in Athens, Greece.*

Flash works out at first. "Gordon can play anything, including the violin."

could play anywhere. When Phil Rizzuto and Gerry Priddy came up in 1941 as the next pair of highly touted rookies from the Yankee farm, McCarthy moved Joe—an All Star at second base the two previous seasons—to first. He even talked about moving him to third if Red Rolfe retired. When asked about such a move, McCarthy replied, "Gordon can play anything, including the violin. He'd be as good at third as he is at second, or anywhere else for that matter." Evetually, though, he realized that at second base Gordon had no equal and moved him back.

McCarthy once overheard a reporter criticize Joe for failing to hit for average. McCarthy replied curtly, "We play to win. Gordon hits homers, drives in runs, and plays to kick your teeth in. It's enough." When I heard what he had said, I had to agree.

Comparisons—The rivalry between Gordon and Bobby Doerr existed only in the minds of the reporters. Off the field Joe and Bobby were good friends and felt their rivalry was overplayed. For what it's worth, Ted Williams, when asked whom he would choose to play second base for him, replied diplomatically, "Joe had more power and sparkled in the field, but Bobby was just as good." I have my own opinion, having played alongside Joe all those years. Bill James ranks Joe Gordon as "the top second baseman of his time," and I agree with him.

Even the voters who chose the MVP agreed that Joe was tops. I can't remember a year when he wasn't among the league leaders in voting for the MVP. Of course, Joe won the American League MVP Award in 1942 with one heck of a season. He was named to *The Sporting News* All Star team back when only one team was named for both leagues. He was selected to represent the American League in the All Star Game nine times. When I thought about that, I realized that the only times that he was left off the roster were during his first and last seasons.

right field, yet when Gordon arrived we all knew that the second base job would be his. There wasn't a lot of sentiment over Lazzeri's loss, Gordon was just better. It was that simple. I can think of a couple of second basemen who played at the same time as Joe who were good, but few came close to him as a player, and even fewer came close to his ability to win. You name any player at second who might be comparable and I guarantee that if you matched nine Joe Gordons against a starting nine of anybody else, the team of Gordons would win hands down.

Gordon was so good that McCarthy thought he

Two fellows named Eugene and Roger McCaffrey

Transcendental Graphics

did a survey of more than six hundred former ballplayers. When the players were asked to name the best second baseman of all time, Joe finished among the top five of those who ever played the game. Rated on glove work and defense, Joe was ranked among the top three. He was also named with Rizzuto and Lou Boudreau as the second baseman for two of the top five double-play combinations to ever play the game.

When the survey asked players to name the top second baseman among those who played from 1921 to 1945, Joe placed behind only Rogers Hornsby and Charlie Gehringer—pretty good company, and last time I checked both were in the Hall of Fame. Perhaps most importantly, however, when asked to name the all-time greats for each franchise, Joe was named twice! His fellow ballplayers named him as the greatest second baseman to have ever played for the New York Yankees *and* for the Cleveland Indians. Those were both great teams, and I will tell you straight up that Joe made every man that played with him a better player. It's no coincidence that the two managers he played for, Joe McCarthy and Lou Boudreau, loved him for both his ability and attitude.

Toughness and teamwork—Although the story has been told countless times, it is my favorite for what it says about Joe as a player and a man. Once a sportswriter hanging around before a game asked Joe McCarthy why he liked Joe Gordon so much. McCarthy turned to the infield and hollered, "Joe! C'mere!"

Joe trotted over and when he reached the pair, McCarthy asked him, "Joe, what's your batting average?"

Gordon replied, "I don't know."

McCarthy stared back at him and asked Joe, "Well then, what's your fielding average?"

"I don't know that either," answered Joe.

McCarthy turned to the writer with a big grin on his face, and honest to God, said, "That's what I like. All he cares about is beating you."

McCarthy demanded that we played for the team first instead of ourselves. Our individual statistics were not always overpowering. Our record, though, almost always was. Gordon typified the Yankee emphasis on toughness and teamwork. If Joe had been more selfish, I wouldn't feel that I wanted to write this article today. He did all the unselfish things that team players do: hitting the ball to the right side with a man on second base and nobody out, hitting the outside pitch to the opposite field to start a rally in the late innings, taking the extra base every chance he got instead of running the bases ninety feet at a time, and taking charge of anything hit near him in the field.

I once wrote that if Lou Gehrig's life story was entitled "Pride of the Yankees," then mine would have to be "Pride in the Yankees." Well, I am mighty proud to have had Joe as one of those Yankees.

When I put on that Yankee uniform I knew that I was with a bunch of pros. Joe was as professional as any of the guys that I ever played with. He just wanted to go and beat you by playing as hard as he could. Over his career Joe hit 253 home runs. No American League second baseman has ever hit more. He helped us win the World Series in 1938, 1939, 1941, and 1943. To top that off he helped the Cleveland Indians win it all in 1948. Oh boy, could he play!

God only knows how his statistics were slaughtered by playing all those years in Yankee Stadium, and then later at Municipal Stadium in Cleveland. As with the great DiMaggio, the house that helped Ruth never let Joe pad his numbers with that right handed swing of his. Bobby Doerr once told me that he thought that Yankee Stadium was the hardest ball park to hit in for a righthanded hitter. "Tom," he said, "You know how those shadows started to creep in about the fourth or fifth inning. You couldn't see a darn thing. Most of the time you'd have a white background from the white shirts of the fans sitting in the center field stands. How Gordon and DiMaggio hit there amazed me."

Like so many fine players, Gordon lost three full seasons to the second World War. He never complained, and even after he left us Yankees we still knew that he was the best second baseman that we would ever play with or against. After Gordon was traded to the Indians for Allie Reynolds we ended up playing the Tribe in Cleveland early in the season. Somebody on the Indians hit a single into right field and tried to get to second. Rizzuto fielded the ball and was promptly slid into, clean but very hard. The next inning DiMaggio singles and stretches it into a double. Gordon, his old teammate and friend, was covering. DiMaggio slid and hit Gordon so hard you could hear the contact all over the park. Nobody said anything or had to. Both Gordon and DiMaggio expected nothing else. That's what I loved about both of them. Flash is no longer with us, but I'd like to see him get the recognition he deserves.

The Greater Glory of Doubles and Triples

Excitement leaders

Guy Waterman

Why do home runs please the fans so much more than doubles and triples? Yes, anyone can thrill to that explosive moment when the bat connects solidly and the ball arches skyward, soaring far beyond the earthly confines of the park. But what happens then? The batter trots sluggishly around the bases, head down. Fielders stand around dejected. Two or three teammates wait to high-five the hero when his uneventful tour of the bases is concluded. Dullsville.

Contrast this ho-hum scene with what transpires with a ball shot into the alleys or down one of the lines. Will the runner on first go all the way home? Will the batter settle for two or go for three? Which outfielder can get to the bounding ball quickest? What kind of rebound will it take off the fence? How strong is that throw-in? Hit the cutoff? Is there a play either at the plate or at one of the bases—or both? A lot of action unfolds, full of drama, uncertain outcome, several players involved in key moves, perfect execution demanded on what may prove a close call.

A home run inside the park, of course, may even exceed doubles or triples in electrification. The point is: if the ball is still in play, tension mounts as the action hurtles toward its climax. Hit out of the park, it's all downhill with a home run.

Yet the record is clear: it's homers hit out of the park that put fans in the seats. That's what they come to see. *Baseball Weekly*'s Paul White put it this way:

"It's why Thomas-Griffey-Williams means 'oooooh' and Gwynn-Boggs- Molitor means 'uh-huh.'" (July 19-25, 1995, p. 2.)

The Boston *Globe*'s Peter Gammons claims that homers are "our most American act" and argues "there is nothing comparable in sport to the home run." (*Baseball Digest*, July 1999, pp. 30-31.) It must be conceded his is the majority view.

Ask any owner, with his eye on the gate receipts. Ask any agent negotiating next year's multimillion-dollar contract for the thirty-homer behemoth. Fifteen triples, you say? Forty-five doubles? Have a seat in the outer office, please, and we'll get to you in a minute. But thirty homers? Step right this way, sir. Let's see what we can get you.

I don't understand this. I recall seeing a video in the Hall of Fame on World Series highlights of the last thirty years or so. It consisted of shot after shot of game-winning or Series-winning homer. What we saw was a batter taking a swipe, an outfielder or two taking a few desultory steps toward the fence, then the slow trot around the bases, maybe a bunch of fans cheering. Sure, at the time these epic clouts, in the context of a game or an entire Series on the line, must have been exciting. But the drama of the play itself dies with the echo of the crack of the bat.

By contrast, that same day in Cooperstown, I saw a video of Slaughter's dash for home in the 1946 Series. In the primitive state of the art of catching baseball on film in 1946, there was but a single camera angle on the play, apparently behind first base. Black and

Guy Waterman, *a retired writer and infrequent singles hitter from Vermont, is a contributor to* Baseball Digest, The National Pastime, *and* Nine.

white, of course. When Slaughter came into third, the cameraman (like everyone else in the park) obviously expected him to stop there. You can tell because all the way to the plate Slaughter almost runs off the left edge of the screen, the cameraman desperately trying to catch up to his headlong dash. Watching even more than half a century later, any fan feels a mounting excitement as this brazen charge gambles with fate, dares the Red Sox' excellent defense. Gripping drama all the way.

But ask any budding buff to name the fifteen 500-homer hitters and he'll (she'll) rattle 'em off. Ask him (her) for the top fifteen career triples leaders? Bid McPhee? Fred Clarke? Roger Connor? Who they?

After 1998's home run orgy, everyone seems hopelessly addicted to this dull event. It was not always thus. For example, recall the protracted excitement of the 1946 pennant race, when from midseason on, never much more than two games separated the Cardinals and the Dodgers.

That year the Cards' biggest home run hitter was Enos Slaughter with eighteen. Pistol Pete Reiser led the Dodgers with eleven (three of them inside the park). In their final ten head-to-head encounters, plus the two playoff games to settle their regular season tie, the two teams clobbered fifty-six extra base hits: thirty-seven doubles, fifteen triples, and only four homers. Half the games were decided by margins of one or two runs, usually featuring a triple by Reese or a double by Slaughter, or one of the six doubles and two triples rapped out by Musial.

In one contest, the Brooks scored first when Stanky doubled and scored on Reiser's single. Pistol Pete took

second on the throw-in, seized third when the Cardinal catcher bobbled the throw, and scored when Dixie Walker's double ricocheted off the crazy Ebbets Field scoreboard. But the Cards roared back the very next inning on Schoendienst's triple, Dusak's double, Kurowski's triple, and Slaughter's sacrifice fly.

Can it be possible that the modern fan would regard all this as dullsville compared with watching McGwire and Sosa hit those long shots and trot around the bases?

What follows is intended as a small contribution to righting the balance, for the greater glory of doubles and triples, and the men who hit them—and run them out at top speed, challenging a hurried throw, hurtling toward the distant base.

First, who are the career leaders in doubles and triples? Check the box at lower left. Scan those names. What a tremendous number of thrilling at-bats these players gave the fans. Four men are on both top ten: Cobb, Speaker, Wagner, and Waner. The first three are found in practically every offensive pantheon (except slugging stats), but Waner is often overlooked when all-time greats are honored. Big Poison sprayed a lot of baseballs through the alleys and down the lines—a lot of exciting moments for the Forbes Field faithful.

Cobb and Speaker lead the combined total. What tremors those two must have provided for the lucky fans of their day. But we've had our share of kicks in the latter half of this century, too. Four of these top ten played for our eyes. Stan the Man once told a sportswriter that he'd rather hit a triple than a home run because he liked to run (*Baseball Digest*, February 1986, p. 73). Pete Rose, whatever his morality, sure brought fans to their feet by hustling to second and third. So did George Brett. And Hank Aaron.

Career leaders often reward simple longevity (combined with top-flight ability, of course). Hence, Aaron's homers surpass Ruth's, and Rose amasses more hits than Cobb. So let's look at whose names repeatedly show up among the league leaders in doubles and triples. In this case we'll sort them out by time periods, because otherwise we'll get too many Dead Ball stars.

Don't those lists conjure up treasured memories and legends of electrifying batters and baserunners? Lou Brock, Vada Pinson, Rod Carew, Brett Butler, Heinie Manush, Minnie Minoso, Willie Wilson. Also some big home run hitters who treated the crowd to some extra-base melodrama too: Dimag, Greenberg, Aaron,

Career leaders

Doubles			Triples			Combined	
1. Tris Speaker	792		1. Sam Crawford	309		1. Ty Cobb	1019
2. Pete Rose	746		2. Ty Cobb	295		2. Tris Speaker	1014
3. Stan Musial	725		3. Honus Wagner	252		3. Stan Musial	902
4. Ty Cobb	724		4. Jake Beckley	243		4. Honus Wagner	892
5. George Brett	665		5. Roger Connor	233		5. Pete Rose	881
6. Nap Lajoie	657		6. Tris Speaker	222		6. Nap Lajoie	820
7. Carl Yastrzemski	646		7. Fred Clarke	220		7. George Brett	802
8. Honus Wagner	640		8. Dan Brouthers	205		8. Paul Waner	796
9. Hank Aaron	624		9. Joe Kelley	194		9. Sam Crawford	767
10. Paul Waner	605		10. Paul Waner	191		10. Henry Aaron	722
Paul Molitor	605		**Players Active in 1999:**				
Players Active in 1999:			1. Lance Johnson	117			
1. Wade Boggs	578		2. Tim Raines	112			
2. Cal Ripken	571		3. Willie McGee	94			
3. Tony Gwynn	522						

Snider. You didn't think Medwick or Mize could run? They each got up enough gas to place high in triples three different seasons. Don't you have to wonder what kind of an exciting player Sherry Magee must have been? Almost totally unsung today.

triples, and tied Mize for the doubles lead with thirty-nine.

In 1965, Zoilo Versalles tied for the lead in both categories: matching Yaz at forty-five doubles and Bert Campaneris at a league-leading twelve triples.

Seasons among top three in doubles and triples

Dead Ball Era	D	T	Big Swingers Era	D	T	Post WW II, mostly pre-expansion	D	T	Recent Years	D	T
1. Honus Wagner*	8	7	1. Paul Waner	4	7	1. Stan Musial	12	7	1. Pete Rose	10	2
2. Ty Cobb	8	7	2. Rogers Hornsby	6	4	2. Lou Brock	4	6	2. George Brett	5	4
3. Sam Crawford	5	9	3. Joe Medwick	7	3	3. Vada Pinson	5	5	3. Brett Butler	0	8
4. Tris Speaker	12	2	4. Charlie Gehringer	5	3	4. Willie Mays	3	5	4. Al Oliver	7	1
5. Sherry Magee	7	5	5. Edd Roush	2	5	5. Enos Slaughter	1	6	5. Lance Johnson	0	7
6. Joe Jackson	5	6	George Sisler	2	5	6. Mickey Vernon	4	3	Willie Wilson	0	7
7. Nap Lajoie*	7	0	7. Heinie Manush	3	4	7. Hank Aaron	6	1	7. Rod Carew	2	5
8. Bobby Veach	4	3	8. Lou Gehrig	2	4	Tony Oliva	6	1	8. Robin Yount	4	3
9. Frank Baker	3	2	9. John Mize	3	3	Carl Yastrzemski	6	1	9. Wade Boggs	7	0
10. Ed Konetchy	1	3	10. Hank Greenberg	5	1	10. Roberto Clemente	1	5	10. Juan Samuel	1	5
Cy Seymour	2	2				Joe DiMaggio	1	5	Dave Parker	3	3
Zack Wheat	4	0				Minnie Minoso	3	3	Hal McRae	6	0

*Lajoie and Wagner were also among the leaders in some years before 1900; only post-1900 seasons included here.

A select few even led the league in both doubles and triples in the same year (below). Think of the sparkling moments they provided in those years of hard hitting and fast running. Cobb and Musial jump out of this list. Three times each! And only four others in the history of the game! Musial just about made it four: in 1949 he led the league in doubles and tied teammate Slaughter in triples.

Some others came very close to making this elite list. In fact, four more names would be there had we not insisted that these championships be undisputed, not muddied by a tie:

In 1921, Rogers Hornsby led with forty-four doubles, and tied for the lead in triples at eighteen.

In 1929, Charlie Gehringer led with nineteen triples, and tied Manush and Roy Johnson with forty-five doubles.

In 1941, Pete Reiser led the league with seventeen

When was the last time anyone recalled how much sheer excitement Versalles generated at bat and on the basepaths (and in the field) during the Minnesota Twins first pennant run? And Pete Reiser—oh, my gosh, what a ballplayer! When I was young, the oldtime fans used to talk about Gehringer and Hornsby, and you knew they prized the memories of many intoxicating moments as those two bid for the extra base on many a close play. Joe Vosmik? He must have been something in 1935.

Enough of the overall stats though. Before we leave this subject, let's linger a moment over a few of the greatest doubles and triples in baseball history.

October 13, 1906: The Hitless Wonders erupt.

Start back in 1906, the Chicago Series between the 116-victory Cubs of Tinker-to- Evers-to-Chance and the "Hitless Wonders" White Sox. In Game 5, with the Series tied at two wins apiece, the Hitless Wonders lashed eight doubles, the Cubs three more.

In the fourth inning, the score tied, 3-3, the Sox put two men on with a walk and a single. Frank Isbell then belted the third of his four doubles that day, a long fly dropping in the alley between right and cen-

2B & 3B leaders, single year

1905 Cy Seymour	1911 Ty Cobb	1935 Joe Vosmik	1948 Stan Musial
1908 Honus Wagner	1917 Ty Cobb	1943 Stan Musial	1968 Lou Brock
1908 Ty Cobb	1919 Bobby Veach	1946 Stan Musial	

ter, scoring the tie-breaking run. The next batter, George Davis, placed another double to left for two more runs. Jiggs Donohue followed with another two-bagger to left to score Davis.

These four runs were the winning margin—but not before the Cubs threatened in the sixth, Wildfire Schulte blasting one into the alley to score two scampering teammates. The White Sox victory that day, fueled by all those doubles, set them on the road to the world championship.

October 10, 1923: Stengel's dash to glory.

Move now to the 1923 Series, opening game, described in the first words of the conservative New York *Times*' front-page story thus: "In the greatest game of baseball ever played between championship teams …"

What evoked this modest claim was one thrilling moment in the top of the ninth, the score tied, 4-4. This wasn't a double or a triple technically, but the spirit is the same. Here is how the *Times* recounted it:

"…There were two out when Casey Stengel stepped to the bat. It was 'Casey at the Bat' all over again, but this time the great Casey did not strike out. He waited [Joe] Bush out patiently, worked the count to three balls and two strikes and then hit the next pitch on a sharp line to left centre.

"The ball struck between [Whitey] Witt and Bob Meusel and rolled to the fence. Witt was going like the wind after that pellet, but not much faster than old Casey Stengel was going around the bases. With one leg injured and the other not as young and spry as it used to be, Casey ran the race of his life. Out at the fence Witt was gathering the ball in. He turned and flung it to Meusel, and Meusel turned and threw it toward the plate.

"By now Stengel was rounding third, badly winded but still going strong. It was a race between man and ball, but the man won easily for Casey slid into the plate and up onto one knee in a single motion. Then he waved a hand in a comical gesture that seemed to say, 'Well, there you are,' and the game was as good as over."

October 15, 1925: Traynor's gallant failure—and Cuyler's shot.

Two years later came another sequence of extra-base excitement: the seventh game of the 1925 Series between Pittsburgh and Washington. At the seventh inning stretch, in miserable weather, cold and rainy, the Senators held a 6-4 lead.

But in the home seventh, with Eddie Moore aboard after a Senator error, Max Carey rocked a two-bagger to left, Moore racing all the way home. With two outs, Pie Traynor came up. Here's the *Times* account:

"It was right here that Pie Traynor cut loose and showed what was in him. Pittsburgh has been waiting throughout the Series for the big third baseman to show some of the baseball he is capable of. Pie delivered. He socked one of [Walter] Johnson's fast balls into the gathering fog in right centre field. The ball jarred off his bat so fast that no one saw it.

"Sam Rice and Joe Harris disappeared into the darkness as Carey hurried over the plate with the tying run and Traynor tore over the muddy base paths like one possessed. The expectant crowd was on its feet cheering every stride Pie took in his mad circuit. The mud splashed from his spiked shoes as he rounded second and tore down to third.

"Joe Harris and Rice by this time had dug the ball out of the mud in deep right centre. Traynor wheeled around the sticky ground at third and rushed toward home. Joe Harris hurled the ball to his namesake, Stanley, and the Washington manager sent it into Ruel. Muddy stood at the plate, tagged Pie with the ball and robbed him of a home run. It may not have been a home run, but don't overlook the fact, neighbors, that it was a man-sized three-bagger."

Washington came back to regain the lead in the eighth on a homer (out of the park) by [Roger] Peckinpaugh. That merely set the stage for more Pirate fireworks of extra-base hits. Two two-baggers brought the home crowd to its feet again and tied the score. Then, with the bases loaded by a walk and an error, Kiki Cuyler lashed a screaming liner just fair by first base. One foot to the right, it's a foul; one foot to the left, it's caught by the Senators' fine-fielding Joe Judge.

With a frenzy of base running, all three Pirates scored, and even Cuyler dashed home when the throw-in went amiss. However, the ball had gone into the crowd on its way to right field's further reaches, so it was declared a two-base hit and only two of the runs were allowed. That proved enough for the winning margin, 9-7, the game, the Series, and a world championship for Pittsburgh.

October 8, 1940: Did Bartell hold the ball? (Foreshadowings of Pesky in '46!).

In 1940, the Cincinnati Reds and Detroit Tigers locked horns in a thrilling seven-game Series. In the crucial finale, the Tigers lucked out with an unearned run early. Until the seventh, that 1-0 lead held. But after the seventh inning stretch, the Cincinnati home crowd never sat down.

Popular Frank McCormick led off with a double to left. Jimmy Ripple lofted a fly deep to right, and that's when the excitement mounted. McCormick held at second, hoping to advance after the catch. When Ripple's belt caromed off the railing on the fence— inches higher and it would have been a homer—McCormick took off. Even then he might not have made it, but Dick Bartell, the Tigers' shortstop, took the throw-in, held it long enough to see was happening, and the tardy runner reached home in time to tie the score.

After a sacrifice moved Ripple over to third, with still but one out, the stage was set. Here's how the New York *Times* reported it:

"Then came the game's most dramatic moment.

"Out of the Cincinnati dugout emerged [Ernie] Lombardi to bat for [Eddie] Joost and the crowd beseeched their favorite Schnozzolo to give the ball a ride. But Newsom took no chances with the long-clouting Lombardi, who, even on one leg, can smash a ball a country mile if he can connect with it. Bobo intentionally passed Ernie and [Lonnie] Frey trotted out to do the running.

"Only Ripple was doing any of the running that counted. Myers landed viciously on the ball and drove it on a line for center field. For a moment it looked as if the drive would smack the wall, but it lacked just enough carry, and [Barnie] McCosky, his back to the barrier, hauled it down. Ripple, however, dashed home the moment the ball landed in Barney's glove, and that tally eventually was to decide the conflict."

October 5, 1941: Keller batting, DiMag on the tear.

The next year came Mickey Owens' infamous passed ball and the first of many Yankee humiliations of Brooklyn's ever-striving Bums.

Tommy Henrich's dash to first and Joe DiMaggio's subsequent single are etched in memory. But the big play was yet another two-bagger. There were still just runners on first and second, two out, the Dodgers ahead 4-3. Hugh Casey got two quick strikes on Charlie Keller. One pitch away…

But on the third pitch—no cute curve in the dirt this time—King Kong belted it high off the diabolical right field wall in Ebbets Field. Careering like a runaway stallion, DiMag tore all the way from first to follow Henrich across the plate with the winning run before the beloved Dixie Walker could fire the ball in.

After a walk, Joe Gordon laced another two-run double, but that was just icing. The key blow was

Keller's, the key baserunning Joe D's.

October 15, 1946: Slaughter's dash.

We've already described Slaughter's celebrated scamper in 1946, one of World Series history's most prized moments. Well-meaning efforts to exalt Slaughter's achievement have tended to distort some pedestrian facts of the case. It was not a single on which he ran, but scored unmistakably as a double at the time. Nor did he run through his third base coach's stop sign, at least according to his own testimony in the clubhouse as reported the next day. Even so, it was indeed an epic moment.

October 13, 1947: Bevens' lost no-hitter.

Yet another hugely famous Series moment from the 1940s: the Yanks' Bill Bevens mowed 'em all down at Ebbets Field, without a hit for 8-2/3 innings. In the ninth two walks put the potential winning run on first and brought "the swarthy-complexioned" Cookie Lavagetto up to pinch-hit for Eddie Stanky. One out away from the first Series no-hitter in history!

On the first pitch, Lavagetto swung wildly and missed. Two strikes away! The *Times*:

" …Then he swung again and connected, the ball sailing toward the right field wall.

"Over raced Tommy Henrich. The previous inning the brilliant Yankee gardener had made a glittering leaping catch of a similar fly ball to rob Gene Hermanski of a blow and keep the no-hitter alive.

"There was nothing Tommy could do about this one, though. It soared over his head and struck the wall. Desperately he tried to clutch the ball as it caromed off the boards in order to get it home as quickly as possible, but that sloping wall is a tricky barrier and as the ball bounced to the ground more precious moments were lost.

"Finally Henrich hurried the ball on its way. [George] McQuinn caught it and relayed it to the plate, but all too late. [Al] Gionfriddo and [Eddie] Miksis already were over the plate while in the center of the diamond Dodger players and fans were all but mobbing Lavagetto in their elation."

October 16, 1962: Mays' double—and Maris' fielding gem.

In 1962, the Yankees and Giants went to the last of the ninth of the seventh game, the ultimate all-or-nothing finish. The Yanks led, 1-0, behind Ralph Terry. Little Matty Alou led off with a pinch-hit infield scratch hit, but had to remain standing at first while the next two Giants were retired.

Next came Willie Mays, swinging from the heels. Played as a pull hitter, he surprised the Yanks' defense by lining a smash to the extreme right field corner. The speedy Alou was running full speed from first, the incomparable Mays rocketing after him.

Here came one of the greatest fielding plays of Series history, seldom given the credit it deserves. Roger Maris, so often put down as the sullen loner of 1961, played Mays' hit perfectly, getting to the ball much faster than anyone could have thought possible. In an instant he wheeled and let loose a powerful throw right on target to the plate. Alou was forced to hold at third, Mays at second. It saved the Series: on the next play, Bobby Richardson made his famous catch of Willie McCovey's liner to end the game and the Series.

Maris' play was a truly perfect defensive gem, a splendid illustration of the excitement that doubles and triples generate at crucial moments.

October 10, 1968: Northrup's big blow.

Another seven-game Series occurred in 1968 between the Cards and Tigers, the last World Series undiluted by prior "League Championship Series."

The seemingly invincible Bob Gibson, with five straight complete-game Series wins (and an ERA of 0.80) in this one and 1967's, retired twenty of the first twenty-one Detroit batters he faced. He had two out in the seventh—but the Tigers' Mickey Lolich was pitching almost as well, and the score was 0-0.

Then Gibson's tidy world came apart: Norm Cash and Willie Horton singled. Jim Northrup knocked the next pitch to deep center field. Curt Flood misjudged the fly, then slipped and stumbled, and the ball dropped fatally in front of the fence. Cash and Horton ran madly all the way home and Northrup was on third before the ball got back to the infield.

A third run scored when Lou Brock couldn't make a clean grab of Bill Freehan's sinking liner to left center, giving the Tiger catcher an RBI double.

That triple and double gave Detroit the Series, as the final score was 4-1.

October 20, 1982: Lonnie Smith, hero.

In 1982, the Series went to the seventh game for the twenty-eighth time (more than one in every three Series). Tension further mounted when it was all tied, 1-1, after five innings, between the Milwaukee Brewers and St. Louis Cardinals. Both teams scored in the sixth, and doubles played key roles.

The Brewers made the first move when Jim Gantner led off with a double to left center. Paul Molitor's bunt single, another infield hit by Robin Yount, and a sacrifice fly netted two big runs.

But in the bottom of the inning, Ozzie Smith got a one-out single. Lonnie Smith sliced a double down the left field line, the Brewers' defense playing flawlessly to hold those two speedy runners to second and third. A walk filled the bases. Keith Hernandez singled to right center for two, the inspired Smith tearing in from second with the tying run. George Hendrick then delivered the game-winning RBI with an opposite field poke to right.

Smith doubled again in the eighth to spark a further two-run rally, which with Bruce Sutter's masterful relief pitching, nailed down the Series for the Cards.

October 27, 1991: Lonnie Smith, goat.

The World Series of 1991 is one of a half dozen or so regarded, at the time and ever after, as among the greatest Series ever staged. Four of the first six games were decided by one run, two in extra innings, as two Cinderella last-to-first clubs went to the wire: Atlanta's Braves and Minnesota's Twins.

The tension mounted through nine scoreless innings. But in Atlanta's ninth, the hero of 1982, Lonnie Smith, poked a leadoff single. When Terry Pendleton doubled into the left-center gap, the stage seemed set for the speedy Smith to electrify the crowd again with a dash all the way home for the winning run and the championship. But for reasons he refused to discuss afterwards—and to the great relief of the Minnesota fans—Smith held up for fatal seconds at second, apparently unsure where the ball was coming down. So he only reached third, where he and Atlanta's chances expired.

In the Twins' tenth, it was Dan Gladden who led off with another double, moved to third on a sacrifice, and scored on a single by Gene Larkin.

Thus far, our epic moments in doubles and triples have been drawn from the October Classic. But other exciting extra-base action sparkles almost daily during the regular season. A few such moments have been writ especially large in the baseball record book. Here are some.

August 7, 1915: Cravath connects.

On a late summer day in Cincinnati, Philadelphia's visiting Gavvy Cravath, the premier NL home run hitter of the Dead Ball Era, helped himself to a feast of doubles. The Phillies were in a pennant race, the first they won in the twentieth century, so it was an important team contribution.

Cravath contributed a double to a three-run Phillie first, then found himself coming up with the bases loaded in the second. He doubled again, sweeping the bases in a whirlwind of grey uniforms to give the team a 7-0 lead. When the Reds closed the gap to 7-2, Cravath doubled again in a four-run fourth. Finding the bases loaded again when he came up in the eighth, Cravath smashed a fourth double, again sending all three runners pell-mell for the plate.

For his day's work, Cravath had eight RBIs. It remains the only time in the twentieth century that one man has hit two three-run doubles in the same game.

Four doubles is a record, too, but much tied, most recently (as of the 1995 official Record Book) by Kirby Puckett of the Twins in the AL and Billy Hatcher of the NL Reds.

September 8, 1958: Clemente's three straight triples.

Reggie Jackson's three consecutive home runs in the 1977 World Series are justly celebrated in baseball lore. Almost completely forgotten is Roberto Clemente's three consecutive triples (tying a record that still stands) in the heart of a pennant race in 1958.

Though the young Pirates didn't win a pennant until 1960, it wasn't for lack of stirring effort by Clemente. On that September day, he became the only player since 1940 to blast three straight triples.

In his second at-bat he tripled, but was left stranded. The next time up he found a teammate on base and tripled him home, climaxing a three-run rally to break a scoreless tie. In the eighth he belted yet another triple, and this time he trotted in on Dick Stuart's single, locking up a 4-1 victory and closing the gap a bit on the idle, pennant-bound Braves.

August 2, 1959: Bruton's two base-clearing triples

Another epic triples achievement involved the next year's pennant race. Going into the games of August 2, the three front-runners of that summer were packed tighter than sardines: the first-place Giants, and, half a game back, both the Dodgers and defending champion Milwaukee.

That day the Giants and Dodgers both won, while the Braves lost the first game of a doubleheader with the Cards. A lot was riding on the outcome of the second game.

In the first inning, Billy Bruton, batting seventh, came up with Henry Aaron, Joe Adcock and Andy Pafko on base. His towering triple sent all three scurrying home to get the team off to a 4-0 start.

In the sixth, with the score 7-3, the Braves loaded the bases again, and again Bruton wiped them clean with a mighty clout. Bruton remains the only twentieth century National Leaguer to clear the bases twice with triples in one game.

July 30, 1959: National League, meet Mr. McCovey

Three days earlier, the San Francisco Giants had been in a four-game losing streak, so manager Bill Rigney took a gamble, reaching down to the Pacific Coast League to bring up a twenty-one-year-old giant who was leading the PCL in average (.377), home runs (twenty-eight), and RBI (ninety-one—in July!). Willie McCovey had never played an inning in the majors. Rigney benched third baseman Jim Davenport and moved the great Orlando Cepeda to third to make room for the newcomer, whom he audaciously placed third in the batting order between Willie Mays and Cepeda.

How did Rigney know? The raw rookie sizzled four hits in four trips to the plate, and two of them were gigantic triples. He scored three of the team's seven runs that day, and drove in two more, as the Giants broke their losing streak, 7-2, beating Robin Roberts and the Phils. On one day, a National League record for most triples in a first game was set and a Hall of Fame career was launched.

May 13, 1989: Puckett's four doubles

Kirby Puckett became the thirty-fifth man in major league history to power four doubles in one game—and the last in the AL, as of the 1995 record book. His feat fueled a hectic 10-8 slugfest, with no fewer than eleven doubles, a record-tying seven by the Twins and four more by the losing Blue Jays.

Both teams scored in the first, the Twins getting theirs on Puckett's first double of the day. A six-run fourth sent the Twins ahead, with one of Puckett's doubles knocking in one of the runs. In the sixth Greg Gagne opened with a double, scored on a single by John Moses, who in turn scored on Puckett's third two-bagger of the day. His fourth came in a scoreless eighth inning.

Eleven doubles provided a lot of base-running excitement that day, and a special chance for Minnesota fans to cheer their favorite player.

The Manager Of The Year

An evaluation

Lawrence Hadley and John Ruggiero

Manager of the Year" is one of major league baseball's annual awards. Since 1983, the award has been voted by the Baseball Writers Association of America (BBWAA) to the best manager in each league. On the surface, the purpose of the award is obvious: league recognition of the season's best manager. However, a careful probing of the concept of "best manager" uncovers some ambiguities. These ambiguities result from the multidimensional nature of a manager's work. A manager is the team's field leader, who is responsible not only for training, motivating, and disciplining players, but also for game tactics and the team's strategy over the entire season. The Manager of the Year award should identify the one manager who best integrates these many responsibilities. But how can these intangible responsibilities be collapsed into one overall measure of managerial effectiveness?

Despite the complex nature of the job, the manager's basic duty is to produce the maximum winning percent (MAXWP) for his team. He is constrained in this task by the quality of the players on the team roster. Theoretically, there is a MAXWP that any manager can achieve given the quality of his players. The efficiency of a manager can be judged on the basis of his team's actual winning percent compared to the theoretical MAXWP. The most efficient

(and perhaps best) manager is the one who comes the closest to his maximum winning percent.

Our methodology for measuring managerial efficiency is regression analysis, which generates an equation that predicts a team's winning percent based on the performance of the team's players. The team whose actual winning percent exceeds its predicted winning percent by the largest percentage is defined as having achieved the MAXWP. This team is the benchmark for the computation of our efficiency indexes, and is assigned an index of 1. Once MAXWP is determined for this most efficient team, a MAXWP can be determined for all the other teams based upon the regression equation.

After MAXWP is established for all teams, an efficiency index can be computed for all the teams. It is equal to the team's actual winning percent divided by the team's MAXWP. Teams that have a winning percent equal to their estimated MAXWP achieve an efficiency index of 1. Teams that do not win as many games as possible will achieve an index value of less than 1. Managers who achieve a high efficiency index (close to one) have used their available players in a strategic manner that generates an actual winning percentage close to the team's MAXWP.

It is important to note that each team's MAXWP is based upon the quality of the team's pitching, hitting, and fielding by the players who are actually on the field. Our efficiency index evaluates each manager on the basis of the performances of his current players. If key players are injured, they are not included in the

Lawrence Hadley *and* **John Ruggiero** *are associate professors of Economics at the University of Dayton.*

estimation of MAXWP, nor in our efficiency index, because they are not on the field. Therefore, a manager's efficiency rating will not be adversely affected by injuries.

If key players experience prolonged slumps, their poor performances are the basis for the manager's efficiency rating. Therefore, a manager's rating will not be adversely affected by players who fail to perform up to expectations. (For a technical discussion of our efficiency index, see John Ruggiero, Lawrence Hadley, and Elizabeth Gustafson (1996), "Technical Efficiency in Major League Baseball" in *Baseball Economics: Current Research*, J. Fizel, E. Gustafson, and L. Hadley, eds., Greenwood Publishers, Westport, CT.)

The relationship between our efficiency index and the MAXWP for any team can be illustrated by the following example. Suppose that a hypothetical team has an efficiency index of 0.85. Further assume that this team's record is 85-77 for a winning percent of 0.525. If this team had been managed at maximum efficiency, it would have won 1/.85 = 1.176 as many games or 17.6 percent more games. This translates into a potential season's record of 100-62 and a MAXWP of 0.617. The additional fifteen wins the team should have won represents fifteen percent inefficiency (fifteen games not won divided by 100 potential games won) due to the manager's inefficient use of the team's inputs.

Efficiency Indices—Does the Manager of the Year award correlate with managerial efficiency? The purpose of this paper is the comparison of Managers of

Table 1

Descriptive Statistics

(n=314)

Variable	Mean	Standard Deviation	Minimum	Maximum
Winning Percent	0.500	0.064	0.335	0.667
Batting Average	0.258	0.010	0.233	0.285
Slugging Percentage	0.389	0.025	0.327	0.455
Stolen Bases	123.8	43.3	30	314
Fielding Percent	0.979	0.003	0.971	0.986
Earned Run Average	3.900	0.439	2.910	5.410

Data consist of team aggregates taken from the seasons 1982 through 1993.

Table 2

Baseball Production Model Results

(OLS Regression Coefficients, n = 314)

Variable	Coefficients	T-statistics
Intercept	2.116	13.24
Slugging Percent	1.175	12.44
Batting Average	0.501	3.50
Stolen Bases	0.054	5.30
Fielding Percent	7.965	6.17
Earned Run Average	-0.823	-22.94
Adjusted R-square	0.76	

The Cobb-Douglas production function is estimated using OLS with team data for years 1982 through 1993. All variables are measured in logs. The dependent variable is the log of team winning percent. T-statistics are reported in parentheses.

the Year with their peers using the efficiency index defined above. In order to make these comparisons, we have estimated efficiency indexes for all major league teams from 1982-1993.

Table 1 presents descriptive statistics for all variables used to measure team inputs in our analysis. These include team batting average, team slugging percent, team stolen bases, team fielding percent, and team ERA. The team's winning percent is the measure of the output.

Table 2 presents the coefficients of the regression equation used to predict each team's winning percent. All of these coefficients have the expected sign and are statistically significant with ninety-nine percent confidence. The coefficient for ERA is negative because lower values correspond with superior pitching, which in turn generates a higher MAXWP. The coefficients for all the other variables are positive because higher values correspond to superior performance, which corresponds to a higher MAXWP for the team.

Tables 3 and 4 present our efficiency indexes for selected American and National League managers, respectively. For each year and each league, the first manager listed (in bold) is that year's Manager of the Year. The tables also present the efficiency index for all managers whose efficiency rating exceeded the efficiency rating of the Manager of the Year. They are listed in ascending order below the Manager of the Year. For those years in which only one manager is listed, the Manager of the Year had the highest efficiency rating in his league.

Table 3

American League Manager Performance

Year	Manager	Team	Efficiency
1982	**Harvey Kuenn**	Milwaukee Brewers	0.796
	Rene Lachemann	Seattle Mariners	0.799
	Don Zimmer*	Texas Rangers	0.803
	Gene Mauch	California Angels	0.805
	Dick Howser	Kansas City Royals	0.806
	Tony LaRussa	Chicago White Sox	0.813
	Bobby Cox	Toronto Blue Jays	0.819
	Gene Michael*	New York Yankees	0.827
	Dave Garcia	Cleveland Indians	0.847
	Billy Martin	Oakland Athletics	0.885
	Earl Weaver	Baltimore Orioles	0.888
	Ralph Houk	Boston Red Sox	0.893
1983	**Tony LaRussa**	Chicago White Sox	0.859
	Ralph Houk	Boston Red Sox	0.862
1984	**Sparky Anderson**	Detroit Tigers	0.840
	Jackie Moore*	Oakland Athletics	0.859
	Billy Gardner	Minnesota Twins	0.860
	Joe Altobelli	Baltimore Orioles	0.864
	John McNamara	California Angels	0.885
1985	**Bobby Cox**	Toronto Blue Jays	0.769
	Sparky Anderson	Detroit Tigers	0.799
	Dick Howser	Kansas City Royals	0.817
	Chuck Cottier	Seattle Mariners	0.829
	Billy Martin*	New York Yankees	0.830
	Ray Miller	Minnesota Twins	0.843
	Jackie Moore	Oakland Athletics	0.843
	Earl Weaver*	Baltimore Orioles	0.851
	George Bamberger	Milwaukee Brewers	0.859
	Tony LaRussa	Chicago White Sox	0.882

Year	Manager	Team	Efficiency
	Gene Mauch	California Angels	0.925
1986	**John McNamara**	Boston Red Sox	0.940
1987	**Sparky Anderson**	Detroit Tigers	0.837
	Tom Kelly	Minnesota Twins	0.851
	Lou Piniella	New York Yankees	0.884
	Tom Trebelhorn	Milwaukee Brewers	0.926
1988	**Tony LaRussa**	Oakland Athletics	0.886
	Sparky Anderson	Detroit Tigers	0.898
	Lou Piniella*	New York Yankees	0.910
1989	**Frank Robinson**	Baltimore Orioles	0.894
1990	**Jeff Torborg**	Chicago White Sox	0.912
1991	**Tom Kelly**	Minnesota Twins	0.777
	Cito Gaston*	Toronto Blue Jays	0.807
	Doug Rader*	California Angels	0.809
	Hal McRae*	Kansas City Royals	0.811
	Stump Merrill	New York Yankees	0.814
	Jim Lefebvre	Seattle Mariners	0.829
	Jeff Torborg	Chicago White Sox	0.829
	Tom Trebelhorn	Milwaukee Brewers	0.841
	Joe Morgan	Boston Red Sox	0.847
	Bobby Valentine	Texas Rangers	0.865
	Sparky Anderson	Detroit Tigers	0.888
	Tony LaRussa	Oakland Athletics	0.961
1992	**Tony LaRussa**	Oakland Athletics	0.944
1993	**Gene Lamont**	Chicago White Sox	0.834
	Johny Oates	Baltimore Orioles	0.851
	Buck Showalter	New York Yankees	0.851
	Sparky Anderson	Detroit Tigers	0.861

Baseball Conclusions—It is our view that the most efficient manager is the best manager. In an ideal world, he should be named the Manager of the Year. The results in Tables 3 and 4 indicate that the voting by the BBWAA often does not select the most efficient manager. The leagues's most efficient manager was named Manager of the Year in only six of the twenty-four cases between 1982 and 1993. These include Frank Robinson and Joe Torre (Giants and Braves respectively, 1982 co-winners in the National League), John McNamara (Red Sox in 1986), Tommy Lasorda (Dodgers, 1988), Frank Robinson again (Orioles, 1989), Jeff Torborg (White Sox in 1990), and Tony LaRussa (A's in 1992).

The BBWAA tends to recognize two types of managers in selecting the Manager of the Year: those who finish first in their division and/or those who manage a team that performs far above expectations. When a team performs far above expectations and also wins its division, the manager is almost certain to receive the award. Some notable examples include Jim Frey (1984 Cubs), John McNamara (1986 Red Sox), Don Zimmer (1989 Cubs), Jim Leyland (1990 Pirates), Tom Kelly (1991 Twins), and Bobby Cox (1991 Braves). In his first year as manager, Dusty Baker (1992 Giants) came within one game of tying the Atlanta Braves for first place in the NL West. In 1993, he was selected as the Manager of the Year.

There are twelve cases (50 percent) in which the Manager of the Year has an efficiency rating that is inferior to three or more other managers in the same year and league (see Tables 3 and 4). In four of these cases, the efficiency rating of the Manager of the Year is below the mean efficiency rating of all 314 team

Table 4

National League Manager Performance

Year	Manager	Team	Efficiency		Year	Manager	Team	Efficiency
1982	Frank Robinson	San Francisco Giants	0.921			Whitey Herzog	St. Louis Cardinals	0.932
	Joe Torre	Atlanta Braves	0.900		1988	Tommy Lasorda	Los Angeles Dodgers	0.886
1983	Tommy Lasorda	Los Angeles Dodgers	0.823		1989	Don Zimmer	Chicago Cubs	0.840
	Frank Robinson	San Francisco Giants	0.858			Jack McKeon	San Diego Padres	0.885
	Russ Nixon	Cincinnati Reds	0.859			Art Howe	Houston Astros	1.000
	Dick Williams	San Diego Padres	0.871		1990	Jim Leyland	Pittsburgh Pirates	0.817
	Pat Corrales*	Philadelphia Phillies	0.877			Don Zimmer	Chicago Cubs	0.824
1984	Jim Frey	Chicago Cubs	0.900			Art Howe	Houston Astros	0.842
	Davey Johnson	New York Mets	0.906			Tommy Lasorda	Los Angeles Dodgers	0.848
1985	Whitey Herzog	St. Louis Cardinals	0.797			Roger Craig	San Francisco Giants	0.851
	Tommy Lasorda	Los Angeles Dodgers	0.810			Nick Leyva	Philadelphia Phillies	0.877
	Jim Frey	Chicago Cubs	0.818		1991	Bobby Cox	Atlanta Braves	0.856
	Davey Johnson	New York Mets	0.822			Joe Torre	St. Louis Cardinals	0.865
	Buck Rodgers	Montreal Expos	0.822			Greg Riddoch	San Diego Padres	0.878
	Bob Lillis	Houston Astros	0.830			Jim Fregosi*	Philadelphia Phillies	0.897
	Eddie Haas	Atlanta Braves	0.835		1992	Jim Leyland	Pittsburgh Pirates	0.859
	Dick Williams	San Diego Padres	0.837			Art Howe	Houston Astro	0.873
	Pete Rose	Cincinnati Reds	0.896		1993	Dusty Baker	San Francisco Giants	0.820
1986	Hal Lanier	Houston Astros	0.832			Don Baylor	Colorado Rockies	0.822
	John Felske	Philadelphia Phillies	0.849			Jim Leyland	Pittsburgh Pirates	0.861
	Whitey Herzog	St. Louis Cardinals	0.870			Felipe Alou	Montreal Expos	0.894
	Pete Rose	Cincinnati Reds	0.880			Jim Fregosi	Philadelphia Phillies	0.900
	Davey Johnson	New York Mets	0.881			Joe Torre	St. Louis Cardinals	0.900
1987	Buck Rodgers	Montreal Expos	0.894					

managers that can be rated in our sample period of 1982-93 (mean efficiency rating for these 314 cases is equal to 0.816). These below-average managers include Harvey Kuenn (1982), Bobby Cox (1985), Whitey Herzog (1985), and Tom Kelly (1991).

A listing of managers with four or more years of managerial service during 1982-1993 is presented in Table 5 in ascending order by each manager's mean efficiency rating.

Table 5

Manager Performance

Manager	Number of Seasons	Mean Efficiency		Manager	Number of Seasons	Mean Efficiency
Chuck Tanner	5	0.761		Sparky Anderson	11	0.828
Doug Rader	4	0.773		Bobby Valentine	6	0.829
Lou Piniella	5	0.797		Davey Johnson	6	0.831
Tom Kelly	6	0.799		Whitey Herzog	8	0.838
Jim Lefebvre	4	0.799		John McNamara	6	0.838
Bobby Cox	6	0.803		Dick Williams	5	0.840
Buck Rodgers	6	0.804		Tom Trebelhorn	5	0.844
Roger Craig	7	0.804		Gene Mauch	4	0.851
Tom Lasorda	11	0.810		Tony LaRussa	10	0.861
Jim Leyland	6	0.816		Frank Robinson	4	0.879
Dick Howser	4	0.822		Art Howe	4	0.885
Pat Corrales	4	0.823				
Joe Torre	5	0.827				

Sorted from least to most efficient. Managers with fewer than four full seasons were excluded. Efficiency ratings for all managers are available upon request.

Art Howe is the top rated manager with a mean efficiency rating of .885 for the four years he managed between 1982 and 1993. However, he was never named Manager of the Year. Of the top five managers listed in Table 5, only two were ever named Manager of the Year (Frank Robinson and Tony LaRussa). Of all the Managers of the Year listed in Table 5, six appear in the top twelve and five appear in the bottom twelve. All of this leads us to the conclusion that there is little relationship between managerial effi-ciency and the BBWAA Manager of the Year award. It is true that the writers do not have access to efficiency ratings when they vote the award. But these writers are baseball experts who should be able to recognize a manager who gets the most wins from his available talent. To look at the same issue from the reverse angle, would the BBWAA writers pay any attention to efficiency ratings if they had this information available when they voted the award? We doubt it.

Can You Recognize 'Em?

The busiest fan—Dooin
Always pleasant—Cross
A mild swearer—Shaw
The greatest sport—Lush
Sticks to the end—Leach
The most devout—Nealon
A pipe—Cobb
The smartest ever—Brain
The oldest pitcher—Young
The most paternal—Storke
Roosevelt admirer—Parent
Runs like a duck—Waddell
The most savage—Killian
Often hits the wall—Stone
The most acrobatic—Turner
Proud of his ancestry—Lord
The most electrical—Sparks
The most appetizing—Rickey
The most military—Marshall
The warmest baby—Bernhardt
Always in demand—Needham
The most combustible—Byrne
Only popular in Detroit—Payne
The fastest ballplayer—Chase
Can mend your watch—Tinker
The only contortionist—Bender
The coolest proposition—Glade
Necessary to every game—Bell
Has the best eyesight—Seymour
The original steeplejack—Clymer
The small change man—Nichols
A regular William Tell—Archer
The labor union's favorite—Overall
Gets rid of salary quickly—Owen
—Dayton Herald, August 13, 1907

André Rodgers

The first major leaguer from the Bahamas

Lyle K. Wilson, Esq.

On April 16, 1957, the New York Giants took the field for their opener against the Pittsburgh Pirates. The Giants' starting shortstop had been picked by *The Sporting News* as the likely Rookie of the Year for the coming season. In '55, this hot rookie had been voted the MVP of the Northern League, where he had hit .387 with twenty-eight home runs. In '56, he was named to the Texas League All Stars and was described as "graceful, deceptively fast and possessing the strongest infield arm in the circuit…"

In an interview years later, this player would recall "the butterflies in my stomach and how I couldn't get my legs to keep still…" as he stepped into the batter's box for the first time in the majors. He would go on to play eleven years in the big leagues and one last year in Japan, posting a .249 lifetime average. The amazing thing about him was that he had played baseball only once or twice before reporting to Melbourne, Florida, for a 1954 tryout with the Giants. This is the incredible story of André Rodgers, the cricket star turned baseball player—the first major leaguer from the Bahamas.

The letter—In June 1953, John Schwarz, secretary of the New York Giants' farm system, received a letter from Harry Joynes, a Canadian educator living in Nassau. Joynes had seen André Rodgers play cricket and softball, and recommended that the Giants give him a tryout. Schwarz replied that the Giants did not have a scout in the Bahamas. Rodgers could attend the Giants' camp in Melbourne, Florida, for a tryout, but he would have to pay for his own travel and expenses. In a follow-up letter to Rodgers in January, 1954, Schwarz sweetened the pot just a little, inviting him to Melbourne and offering to reimburse him for his expenses if he was signed. Joynes had also recommended another Bahamian, Texas Lunn, for a trial. Schwarz advised André to have Lunn come along.

Your passport please—Under U.S. immigration laws, any player imported by a major league team had to have a contract. Since André was coming on a "make good" basis, he was told to inform the Customs people that he was coming for a visit. As he left the Bahamas, he told an official that he was coming to try out for a baseball team. In Miami, he told the immigration officer that he was just visiting. The discrepancy raised concerns, and he was deported within an hour.

Lunn, who had accompanied André, was allowed in and proceeded to Melbourne. He had an unsuccessful tryout, but insisted that the Giants give André a chance. Schwarz conferred with Alex Pompez, owner of the Negro Leagues' New York Cubans and a Giants scout. Pompez recommended that they bring André in as a contract player and processed the papers through the New York Customs office. André finally arrived at the Giants' camp in Melbourne early in the spring of '54.

The ballplayer—When André stepped off the crowded bus in Melbourne, a Giant official greeted

Lyle K. Wilson *is the author of* Sunday Afternoons at Garfield Park, *a history of African-American baseball teams in the greater Seattle area.*

him by name. Somewhat surprised, André asked, "How did you know it was me?" The official replied, "You just look like a ballplayer."

Indeed he did. At nineteen, he stood 6 foot 3 and weighed 190 pounds. Back home, he had been a star college cricket player and a star in softball and soccer. His father had been one of the all-time greats in Bahamian cricket.

Pitching great Carl Hubbell directed the minor league camp in Melbourne. When Rodgers informed him that he was a cricket player and had almost no experience with baseball, Hubbell thought that someone was pulling his leg. But experience or not, André immediately began to draw attention. He was quick for his size and a quick learner. He stayed at the camp for a month, working three extra hours a day to learn the basics. Since he had played shortstop in softball, that is where the Giants started him. Scouts and managers, recognizing his potential and knowing that he would have no chance to improve if he went back to Nassau, volunteered to work with André. By the end of the month, three of the Giants' Class D managers wanted him. His initial assignment was to Olean, New York, where he hit .286 in 125 games.

MVP—André's next stop was St. Cloud, Minnesota, in the Class C Northern League. In only his second year of baseball, he won the league's 1955 batting crown with a .387 average, was voted to the All Star team, and was selected as the League MVP.

From the St. Regis Hotel in Winnipeg, André wrote to Joynes early during the '55 season, telling him he had collected fifteen hits in his first twenty-nine times at bat and closing:

"In the dinners they gave us in St. Cloud, they introduced the ballplayers to the folks on the committee, and gave them a little of their background. Charlie Fox told them that he shouldn't be saying this, but I am going to take Dark's place in three years' time. He told me if I have a good year with him, I may go to AA or AAA next season, and I only pray I do. I am just as sure of you and the Mrs. pulling for me, as I am sure of myself. Mr. Joynes, the only trouble I can find with myself, and that is I always get down on myself, and when I do, in comes the slump, but I am going to try even harder this season. In that banquet they also mentioned your name, and Fox said that was one of the most wonderful things to happen to the Giants, in many a year, thanks to you, and I will do my best not to let you down."

Rodgers' next season was with the Dallas Eagles in the Texas League (AA). There he hit twenty-two

home runs, collected ninety RBIs, and hit .266. Gary Schumacher, assistant to Giants' president Horace Stoneham, touted Rodgers as perhaps "the best shortstop in baseball some day..."

The Big Show—By the spring of '57, André was locked in a battle with Daryl Spencer for the Giants' starting shortstop job. He had an outstanding spring, batting .292 and hitting five home runs. On April 1, the Giants announced that André had made the major league roster and would be their starting shortstop.

"When the Giants launch the National League season April 16 at Pittsburgh, their starting shortstop will be André Rodgers, a long-legged, smooth-swinging, hard-throwing lad of 22. There have been others who were as long of limb and as smooth of stroke and who gunned a baseball across the diamond as Rodgers guns 'em, but none could match Andre's jet-propelled jump to the majors. Until 1952 the [young man] from the Bahamas never had seen a baseball. Until 1953, he never had held a baseball and until 1954 he never had played in an organized baseball game. Yet Rodgers, two weeks hence, will be wearing the traveling gray of the Giants at Forbes Field, entrusted with one of the most important positions on the club." (The New York Times, April 13, 1957.)

Over the next three years, André spent part of each season with the Giants and part in AAA. In '58, he beat out Vada Pinson for the Pacific Coast League batting title, .354 to .343.

André appeared in eighty-one games for the Giants in 1960, then was traded to the Braves for Alvin Dark. At the end of spring training in 1961, he was traded again to the Cubs for Moe Drabowsky and Seth Morehead. His best year in the Majors was 1962, when he hit .278 in 138 games. André was the Cubs' regular shortstop for three years, taking over for Ernie Banks when the slugger was moved to first.

André's last three years in the majors were spent with the Pirates, to whom the Cubs sent him for cash and Roberto Pena. In all, he appeared in 854 major league games. His nemesis was the curve ball. In the minors, he would sometimes take fastballs in order to practice hitting the breaking ball. Occasional flurries of errors also caused him to become discouraged and the inevitable slump would follow.

After a final year in Japan, he returned to the Bahamas where he resides today.

I Want To Be Like André—A generation of Bahamian youth was inspired by André's career. Closest to home, four of his brothers pursued baseball careers, with three of them, Adrian, Randy, and Lionel, ending up in the minors. Lionel may have had the best shot at joining André in the majors. Tragically, just after he returned to Nassau in March, 1961, after hitting .345 to lead the Winter Instructional League he was killed in an auto accident.

André's brothers were not the only Bahamian baseball stars. Four others (Ed Armbrister, Wenty Ford, Tony Curry, and Wil Culmer) played in the majors. Armbrister and Curry had the longest careers, appearing in 224 and 129 games, respectively, and compiling almost identical lifetime batting averages of .245 and .246.

In 1953, there were no scouts in the Bahamas. But, in 1968, the Dodgers and Pirates made the trek to beautiful Nassau to play an exhibition game in front of 4,000 fans. They were followed the next year by the Dodgers and the White Sox.

At one time, there were at least thirty other Bahamians in the minor leagues. The 1961 Indianapolis Clowns had three Bahamians on the roster: Henry McGregor, Earl Innis, and Clifton Wilson. The last of the minor leaguers was Vince Seymour, who was in the Pirates' system as late as 1988.

The Nassau Baseball League today—On July 27, 1998, it was the author's joy to attend the Nassau Baseball League All Star Game. The game pitted the twenty-nine-and-unders against the thirty-and-olders. Armbrister was one of the coaches for the older players, and André's nephew, former Howard University player Terran Rodgers, was one of the coaches for the younger set.

Avenging a '97 loss, the younger players prevailed behind MVP Jamal Johnson. Johnson went 3-5 and played excellent defense at third. He had recently returned from a Dodgers' developmental camp and is expecting to proceed to their camp in the Dominican Republic.

In recent years, many promising Bahamian players have been on the roster of St. Augustine College in Raleigh, North Carolina. The school has had many outstanding athletes from the Bahamas in a variety of sports. Some of the Island's top high-school prospects are going to school in Florida.

Perhaps Jamal Johnson or Dillon Bethel (now at St. Augustine) will make it to the Big Show and become an inspiration to a new generation of youngsters in the Bahamas. But they will never forget who started it all. For the name of the great cricket player who turned to baseball graces the stadium where they will play. Reporting to you live from André Rodgers Field at Nassau in the Bahamas, your roving correspondent, Lyle Wilson.

Sources:

Harry Joynes, who first wrote to the Giants about André, kept the letters from the Giants and clippings of André's career. Shortly before his death, Joynes mailed a box full of materials to André's brother, Randy. The author spent an afternoon with André, Randy, and Randy's son, Terran, in June of '98. Terran had graciously arranged the meeting and made arrangements for me to obtain about eighty pages of copies from "the box." The devotion of a friend preserved this history so that we can now enjoy it. Thank you, Mr. Joynes, and thanks to André, Randy, and Terran.

Gardner's snapper

The 1920 World Series is best remembered for Bill Wambsganss' unassisted triple play, the only one in World Series history. "It should be the thrill of a lifetime," said teammate Larry Gardner, "but it happened so fast that it was over before anyone know what had happened. Elmer Smith's grand-slam homer, the first in World Series history, was much more dramatic. I have a snapper for that one, though. Fifteen years later our entire 1920 team was brought back to Cleveland for an old-timers' game. You wouldn't believe it, but Elmer stepped to bat with the bases full and hit another grand-slammer over the wall."

—Tom Simon, from research collected for *Green Mountain Boys of Summer*, published by Vermont's Larry Gardner Chapter.

Stoolball:
Alive and Well in Sussex

Rediscovering baseball's ancient ancestor

Martin Hoerchner

It amazes me sometimes how life dishes up treats and surprises, how things unexpectedly fall into place, how coincidences solve riddles, and how, as Ray Kinsella quotes Terence Mann, "There comes a time when all the cosmic tumblers have clicked into place, and the universe opens itself up."

So it happened last June when I received a letter from Japan. I don't know anyone in Japan, but it was from a SABR member named Kazuo Sayama, saying he was researching the origins of baseball. He asked if the games of rounders and stoolball were still played in Britain. It struck a special chord with me, because I've always been especially interested in the genealogy of baseball. I sat down to reply to Kazuo that rounders remained common all over this island, but that the more ancient stoolball has long been extinct.

Both sports have a long history in Britain. Rounders is the sport that Robert W. Henderson, baseball's prime genealogist, points to as the direct precedent of baseball, in his 1947 book *Bat, Ball, and Bishop: A History of Ball Games*. Henderson compares *The Boy's Own Book* by William Clarke, published in London in 1829, with *The Book of Sports* by Robin Carver, published in Boston in 1834, where the rules of an English game called "rounders" and an American game called "base ball" are almost exactly the same. I've always questioned Henderson's conclusion that

the similarity meant that baseball was descended from rounders; to me it only proves that rounders and baseball were once different names for the same sport. That's a very big distinction.

Rounders is still a popular game in Britain. In fact, if anything has dampened British enthusiasm for baseball, it's that a similar but lightweight game exists over here. Mention baseball to an Englishman and he's likely to say, "It's just a girl's game," or a "It's just a school game." I presume none of them has ever faced Randy Johnson—or hung in for anybody's curve.

As for stoolball, it's the game that Henderson defines as the common ancestor to both baseball and cricket. The first reference to the game by name is in 1450, but Henderson thinks it could date from as early as 1330. There's a page for "stool-ball" in the *Little Pretty Pocket Book* of 1744, a few pages over from the first illustration of a game named base-ball. In its earliest incarnation, the game was played by two people. One would throw a ball at a stool and the other would use an open palm to keep the stool unhit. The winner was the one who hit the stool the most times. Modifications, like using a piece of wood to hit the ball, running between two stools, and having fielders to retrieve the batted ball, came later. This is the first game recorded as being played in the English colonies in America, in Massachusetts in 1621.

In 1801, Joseph Strutt in his *Games and Pastimes of the People of England*, writes of a variation where runners, after they have hit the ball, race around a course

Martin Hoerchner *is a failed screenwriter who went on to programming computers because he could touch-type. He has been a resident of the Scepter'd Isle for fourteen years and vows to move back when the Giants win a World Series.*

of stools set out in a circle. It is not difficult to see that a two-stool variety could be the progenitor of cricket while a multi-stool variety could be the ancestor of baseball.

Yet as far as I knew stoolball was dead as the dodo. So I had my mouse pointer hovering over the "print" button on my letter to Mr. Sayama. But I had other chores to deal with. I'm the editor the *SABR UK Examiner*, the research journal of the Bobby Thomson Chapter, the UK branch of SABR. I was working on the report of our annual general meeting, which I had videotaped. Going over the tape, I was listening again to our speaker, Allen Synge, a cricket writer and member of the Marylebone Cricket Club (the governing body of cricket), who had presented an excellent piece entitled "Cricket and Baseball—Cross Currents." As an aside to his comments he said, "And then there's stoolball. You should watch it, if only for the comely maidens who play it."

My mouth dropped open when I registered what had obviously gone right past me at the meeting itself. Allen was talking about stoolball in the present tense, without use of a time machine. I was on the phone to him immediately. "Oh yes," he said, "It's still being played. I know of a few matches coming up in Wisborough Green, in Sussex." He said he would check and come back to me with some dates.

I was dumfounded. I asked my wife, who is from Yorkshire, if she ever heard of a game called stoolball. She said she hadn't. I was perplexed.

I learned later that stoolball is very popular not only in Sussex, but also in nearby counties. For instance, Surrey has twenty-five teams in a league and Kent has twelve to fifteen teams. Sussex, however, has a league of sixty teams. In the Eastbourne area alone are ten leagues. Plus there are lots of nonleague teams. In Sussex every village has a team.

Allen got back to me with a few game dates, and we organized a road trip to include SABR UK Chairman Mike Ross. Allen gave me the number of the head of the Wisborough Green Stoolball Club, Mrs. Denman. Helpful and gracious, she told me when the match would start and that we were more than welcome to attend.

Taking in a game—It was a lovely summer's evening as we drove through the Sussex countryside. When we got to Wisborough Green the match had started. It was a classic setting, a huge open town green surrounded by brick houses of varying ages and designs, most with gardens bursting with summer flowers. The obligatory pub was set off on one corner of the green,

and the town church rose up on a hill just beyond. A cricket sight screen was pushed off to the side of the green, and right behind it was a flag pole on which the Union Jack fluttered proudly. Toward the edge of the green was a clubhouse; obviously it was the headquarters of the local cricket club. It had a bar on the ground floor, and above it was a balcony where the score (runs, overs, and wickets) was displayed.

We parked and made our way towards the clubhouse. As we walked, our attention focused on the game. The two teams were all female, although Mrs. Denman told us that mixed teams exist. The basic uniform consisted of a pullover shirt with a few buttons at the top, and a pleated skirt, which was fairly short, over shorts, like lady tennis players. Some team members, more sensitive to the cold, wore a sweatshirt and/or sweat pants. The home team was dressed in yellow and green, like the Oakland A's of the '70s, with a yellow top and green skirt. The away team from Steadham was dressed in dark red or maroon, like that other Philadelphia team of the late '70s and early '80s.

The main action of the game was in the middle of a large circle drawn near the perimeter of a green, which I later learned was ninety feet in diameter. Stoolball has no foul territory. In the middle of the circle were two wickets, sixteen yards apart. Unlike cricket wickets, these were wooden targets, about a foot square, each set on a wooden pole about the height of the players' heads, supported on the ground by four short legs. Each of the two "batsmen" held what looked like outsized ping-pong paddles.

The game was much like cricket, with batsmen running back and forth between the wickets after they hit the ball. The primary difference was that instead of delivering the ball overhand and bouncing it hard off the ground to try to hit a wicket about two feet tall, the stoolball bowler tossed the ball underhand toward a wicket placed on a pole at about the same height as the batsman's head. Indeed, articles I later read called stoolball "cricket in the air."

Mrs. Denman showed us the game equipment. The bat turned out to be a lot more substantial than a ping pong paddle. Made, like cricket bats, of willow, it was hefty, and flat on one side. The handle was wedged in the middle with a soft wood, for extra spring.

Only about 2-1/2 inches in diameter, the ball was white leather with familiar red cross-stitching, not, like a cricket ball, red with its two hemispheres stitched around the equator. This simple connection to baseball delighted us.

Mrs. Denman then explain to us the rules of the

game. There are eleven players on a team. A match is organized into overs, which are six legitimate bowled balls in cricket and eight in stoolball. The number of overs is flexible—usually from fifteen to twenty—and agreed before the match. There are many ways to score. If the batsman hits a ball that isn't fielded immediately, she and her opposite number can run back and forth from wicket to wicket, scoring a run each time they make the traverse. A hit ball that rolls over the boundary on the ground scores four runs, and one hit over it in the air scores six. There are four ways for the batsman to be out: 1) she can be "caught out," if a fielder catches her hit in the air; 2) she can be "run out," if the ball gets to the wicket before she does; 3) she can be "bowled out," if the bowler strikes the wicket with the ball, throwing it past the batsman untouched, or 4) she can be called for "body before wicket (BBW)," similar to cricket's "leg before wicket," if the umpire decides that the batsman would have been bowled out if she had not been standing directly in front of the wicket and deflected the ball. There are no free bases for HBP's in stoolball.

As we watched the game, Mrs. Denman explained how flexible it is. The number of overs can be varied, or the width of the boundary can be changed, depending on the time and space available for a game. We noted how the players came in all ages, all shapes and sizes, and with varying athleticism. There seemed to be something in stoolball for everyone.

Genealogical hints—If you are interested in the genealogy of ball games, you quickly learn that it is easy to find similarities, but hard to prove ancestry. Stoolball, for instance, has a lot of rules in common with cricket, but whether cricket got them from stoolball or stoolball got them from cricket is open to debate. I can't yet prove this, but I think there was a lot of back-influence from cricket to the current game of stoolball.

Cricket probably did spring from stoolball, although this is an opinion not shared by the cricket establishment, which reacts to it as A.G. Spalding reacted to the suggestion that baseball evolved from rounders. R.F. Johnson's article, "Cricket's Village Ancestor" in Country Life, August 25, 1955, reminded readers that "'Cricket' and 'stool' until the seventeenth century, were interchangeable words." This tallies with an edition of the "Little Pretty Pocket Book" which has a drawing of a stool, with the words "A cricket" underneath.

Nonetheless, cricket was codified, while stoolball remained for many years a pastoral pastime with rules that varied from county to county, indeed, village to village. When it was time to set down the official rules of stoolball in 1881, it's likely that gaps or inconsistencies in the stoolball rules were filled in by cricket rules. The version now played probably owes as much to that quintessentially English game as cricket—and baseball—owe to it.

George Davis and Bill Dahlen: Parallel Careers

Year of Birth: 1870 (Davis on August 3; Dahlen on January 5).
Place of Birth: Upstate New York (Davis in Cohoes; Dahlen about forty miles west in Nellisport).
Size: 5'9", 180 lbs.
Major League Career: Davis 1890-1909; Dahlen 1891-1911.
Primary Position: Shortstop.

Games Played: Davis 2,368; Dahlen 2,443. *At Bats: Davis 9,031; Dahlen 9,031.*
Runs Scored: Davis 1,539; Dahlen 1,589. *Hits: Davis 2,660; Dahlen 2,457.*
Doubles: Davis 451; Dahlen 413. *Triples: Davis 163; Dahlen 163.*
Home Runs: Davis 73; Dahlen 84. *RBIs Davis 1,437; Dahlen 1,223.*
Batting Average: Davis .295; Dahlen .272. *Stolen Bases: Davis 616; Dahlen 547.*
Highest Season Average: Davis .355 (1893); Dahlen .357 (1904).
Longest Hitting Streak Davis 33 games (1893); Dahlen 42 games (1894).
League Leader: Davis RBIs (136 in 1897); Dahlen RBIs (80 in 1904).

In addition to their offensive prowess, both Davis and Dahlen were exceptional defensive shortstops. John McGraw secured Dahlen's services for the 1904 season after strenuous legal maneuvers to keep Davis on the Giant roster had failed in 1903. Dahlen went on to shortstop a World Series champion Giants team in 1905 while Davis shortstopped the White Sox champs of 1906. Davis and Dahlen also share a common failing: an inability to manage successfully in the major leagues (Davis 107-139 in parts of three seasons with the Giants; Dahlen 251-355 in four campaigns at the helm in Brooklyn.

—Bill Lamb

Spahn's First "Loss" Wasn't

A forfeit meant a three-year wait

Bob Buege

No lefthanded pitcher in major league history has won as many games as Warren Spahn. The high-kicking, hawk-nosed Hall of Fame hurler of the Boston and Milwaukee Braves won 363 games in his amazing career, punctuated by thirteen 20-win seasons and two no-hitters. Without World War II taking three years out of the start of his career, he would almost certainly have surpassed 400 victories.

The record shows that Spahn also lost 245 games, but the record is only technically correct. His first loss in the big leagues was, as fate would have it, wiped away—ironically, by the same war effort that was to cost him three years and nearly his life from a shrapnel wound in the neck.

Spahn made his major league debut on Patriot's Day, April 19, 1942, at Braves Field in Boston. A gangly youngster four days short of his twenty-first birthday, Spahn came on in relief in the fifth inning of a game with Mel Ott's New York Giants, retired two batters to end the inning, and then was lifted for pinch hitter Sibby Sisti. The Braves went on to lose the ballgame.

The next day, at Ebbets Field, Spahn appeared again in relief, this time working three-plus innings, allowing five hits, four walks, and four runs, but earning no decision in a 9-2 Braves loss to the Dodgers. In this game manager Casey Stengel ordered Spahn to throw at Brooklyn's Pee Wee Reese, but Spahn refused. Stengel assumed his young pitcher had no guts,

and promptly farmed him out to Hartford of the Eastern League.

After winning seventeen games for Hartford, Spahn rejoined the Braves in September, finding Stengel's bumbling Bostons in their customary (fourth straight year) seventh place. On September 13, in the second game of a Sunday doubleheader with the Chicago Cubs, Spahn made his first big league start. He absorbed a ten-hit shellacking in five innings, then yielded to reliever Johnny Sain. The Cubs won, 12-8, despite shortstop Lennie Merullo's record-setting four errors in the second inning, but Spahn did not figure in the decision.

On the next-to-last day of the season, Saturday, September 26, the Braves traveled to the Polo Grounds for a doubleheader with the Giants. The games meant little, with the home club in a distant third place and the visitors out of contention since spring, but fans attending the twinbill witnessed two of the greatest lefthanders of all time, one near the end of a brilliant career, the other just beginning one.

In the opener, Stengel's boys succumbed to screwball artist Carl Hubbell, "the Meal Ticket," the future Hall of Famer who had fanned Ruth, Gehrig, Foxx, Simmons, and Cronin in order in the 1934 All-Star Game. The Braves got homers from Tommy Holmes and Ernie Lombardi, the lead-footed catcher who won the N.L. batting crown in 1942, but the Giants offset those with blasts by Big Jawn Mize and player-manager Ott and won, 6-4. The victory was cheered wildly by a raucous crowd of 14,121, only 2,916 of

---

Bob Buege *is the author of* The Milwaukee Braves: A Baseball Eulogy *and* Eddie Mathews and the National Pastime.

whom had paid for their tickets—the others were youngsters admitted free by the management.

The cause of this generosity by the Giants' ownership was simple: the world was at war. The Russians and Germans were locked in the twenty-ninth day of the Battle of Stalingrad, and U.S. Marines were fighting for their lives at Guadalcanal in the Solomon Islands. Less than ten months after the attack on Pearl Harbor, the United States was in an all-out struggle with the Axis Powers. Major league rosters were already depleted, and the 1943 baseball season was in serious doubt. Along with a manpower shortage, raw materials, notably metal, were desperately needed for the war effort. As part of the nationwide drive to collect materials for the war, several baseball clubs had begun offering free admission to fans bringing donations of ten pounds of scrap metal. On this day, patriotic young Giants fans contributed fifty-six tons of scrap in support of America's fighting men.

Following the Giants' opening triumph, Warren Spahn took the mound in the second game in search of his first major league win, opposing New York's Bob Carpenter. Spahn's supporting cast was woefully weak, having produced fewer runs that season than any team except the pathetic Philadelphia Phillies. The Braves' only real batting threat, Lombardi, had caught Game 1 and was on the bench, replaced behind the plate by the ominously named Clyde Kluttz. The Boston outfield comprised two rookies and Paul Waner, the once-great hitter now nearing forty and batting seventy-five points below his lifetime average. In the infield Boston boasted Max West at first base (batting .254), Skippy Roberge at second (.220 lifetime), Whitey Wietelmann at shortstop (batting .206), and Ducky Detweiler at third (approaching the

end of his thirteen-game big-league career).

From the beginning this was not Spahn's day. The Giants produced two runs on three hits in the first inning, then added a run in the fourth and two more in the seventh to take a 5-1 lead. Spahn himself scored the Braves' run in the third inning, singling and scoring on Paul Waner's double. His teammates got him another run in the top of the eighth, but he faced a 5-2 deficit as he walked to the mound for the bottom of the eighth.

As the Boston players trotted to their positions, though, fate intervened. Suddenly, clusters of screaming youngsters began running onto the playing field. The stadium ushers tried vainly to herd them back to the stands, but hundreds, then thousands of adolescent scrap donors descended onto the ballpark grass and began running riot. The ballplayers fled to the dugout, from whose sanctuary umpire Ziggy Sears ordered a public address announcement warning of forfeit. Amid the clamor no one heard, much less heeded. Under league rules, Boston was declared the winner, 9-0.

Also under league rules, all batting and pitching performances counted, but no pitcher was credited with a win or a loss. Warren Spahn's initial big league base hit counted, but his first pitching defeat disappeared, discarded on the scrap heap of World War II. Spahn's hit was the first of 363 in the major leagues, coincidentally equaling the number of pitching victories he would achieve. After the season Spahn joined the army, serving in Europe with the combat engineers and earning a Purple Heart and a citation for bravery in the bridge collapse at Remagen. His first major league defeat, and victory, had to wait until the summer of 1946.

Bouncers

A fair ball which bounced into the stands was ruled a home run in the American League through 1929 and the National League through 1930. Al Lopez of the Dodgers probably hit the last official bounce homer September 12, 1930. Bounce homers were probably hit ten to twenty times a season, with park architecture the deciding factor. It can be assumed that few were bounced into the leftfield stands at Fenway Park! Weak-hitting pitcher Eddie Summers of the Tigers had two bounce homers in a game on September 17, 1910. On September 4, 1927, brothers Paul and Lloyd Waner of the Pirates each hit a bounce homer in the same inning at Cincinnati's Redland Field. Babe Ruth never bounced any of his 714 home runs. Lou Gehrig hit two—on July 23, 1925, and July 30, 1927.

—L. Robert Davids

Chicago Scores 36 Runs

A stampede by Anson's Colts

Walt Wilson

When the National League operated with twelve clubs from 1892 through 1899, it was dominated largely by two teams: the Baltimore Orioles and the Boston Beaneaters. The other ten franchises, aside from occasional successes, were also-rans.

Such was the case when the Louisville Colonels came to Chicago to meet Cap Anson's Colts late in June, 1897. The Colonels had a 19-32 record and were in tenth place, a half game ahead of the Colts, who were 19-33. Chicago's glory years of the 1880s were past, and their championship years of the first decade of this century, when they came to be known as the Cubs, were undreamed of. As for the Colonels, the league dropped the Louisville franchise after the 1899 season, with most of their best players, including Honus Wagner and Fred Clarke, moving to Pittsburgh to form the nucleus of a strong Pirates dynasty.

The three-game series began on Monday, June 28, at West Side Park, and Louisville won 7-2 behind the seven-hit pitching of LeRoy Evans. The Colonels also won the Wednesday game, but on Tuesday they were demolished as the Chicagoans won by the incredible score of 36-7.

Native-born Chicagoan Chick Fraser, pitching for Louisville, was not treated kindly in his home city, and was excused in the third inning with the score 15-1 against him. An unknown eighteen-year-old

from Kentucky named Jim Jones took over on the mound and pitched the rest of the way, yielding twenty-one runs and nineteen hits. It was his only game with the Colonels. Jones did pop up again in the majors, with the New York Giants in 1901 and 1902, but as an outfielder.

The fans didn't exactly storm the gates to watch the two weak teams. Only 520 folks showed up to see if the Colts could snap out of a prolonged batting slump, and it would be an understatement to say that they did. They whacked thirty hits, including seven doubles, three triples, and two home runs, and were aided by ten walks and ten Louisville errors.

Anson's men elected to bat first, which was allowed under the rules of the time, and they started mildly enough with a three-run first inning.

A charming ceremony took place when future Hall of Famer Clarke led off for the Colonels in the bottom of the first. He was met at the batter's box by a group of gorgeously dressed young ladies who emerged from the stands to present him with a bouquet of flowers and a shower of rice to celebrate the fact that he was to be married in a few weeks. The smiling young charmers were acting on behalf of some of the popular Clarke's Chicago friends. Fred had just started his long career as a manager a couple of weeks earlier, when he replaced Jim Rogers as skipper of the Colonels. Clarke contrived to hand the flowers to teammate Perry Werden, who was probably the homeliest player on the team, a sort of Yogi Berra of the Gay Nineties, and Werden carried the bouquet to

Walt Wilson *is a retired baseball fan who has been doing research for customers for twenty-five years. Wals has been a SABR member since 1985.*

the bench. A blushing Clarke then went to bat and fanned.

The game became one-sided when the Colts scored five runs in the second and seven in the third. That's when the mysterious Jones was called to the mound. He yielded only six runs from the fourth through the seventh inning, but the hit-hungry Colts were merciless in the late innings, scoring seven times in the eighth and eight times in the ninth. It was choosing to bat first that let Chicago run up its record total of runs.

The Colonels were not idle with the bat, coming up with a five-run fifth inning, but Chicago pitcher Jim "Nixey" Callahan was by then too far ahead for the rally to mean much.

There was a weird happening in the Colts' fifth inning. Jimmy Ryan was hit by a pitch, George Decker singled, Jim Connor singled to score Ryan, then Callahan beat out a bunt, scoring Decker. Tim Donahue fouled out and Bill Everitt grounded out as Connor scored from third. That made two outs, but someone on the Louisvilles ran off the field, thinking it was the third out, and all the other Colonels followed him to the bench. Umpire Phil Sheridan couldn't decide quite what to do. So, with the score 18-1, he decided to provide a third out by calling Connor out for cutting third base. "Cutting," in the language of the day, meant rounding a base without touching it before continuing on to the next base. Connor was already on third when the second-out grounder was hit, so that it was not possible for him to have missed that bag, but nobody complained about Sheridan's call.

In addition to the lovely ceremony in the first inning, the second out that became a third out, and all the lusty Chicago hitting, there were other episodes

Jimmy Ryan

Transcendental Graphics

in the game worth noting. Louisville catcher Dick Butler was injured tagging Everitt out at the plate in the second inning, but remained in the game. Colt left fielder Decker was hit in the head by a Jones pitch in the seventh and had to be replaced by outfielder-pitcher Walter Thornton. The blow made Decker dizzy, and that night he got out of bed and fainted. But he was back in the lineup two days later.

More seriously, Louisville second baseman Abbie Johnson (another Chicagoan, by the way) was hit in the eye by a screaming bad-hop grounder off Anson's bat. The game was delayed for about fifteen minutes while Johnson was attended to on the field. A newspaper report says that the eye was dislodged from its socket. He had to leave the game, of course, and was replaced by Tom Delahanty, just returned to the major league from Kansas City of the Western League. Delahanty was one of four brothers of the great Ed Delahanty to play major league ball. It was Tom's last big league game.

Johnson's injury was a severe one. He was never able to make a comeback.

The Colts' big star, Bill Lange, came up with two dazzling catches in the ninth inning. He went to the fence to grab Ollie Pickering's line drive for the first out, then made a splendid diving catch of Butler's pop fly to short center for the out that ended the massacre.

Outfielder Jimmy Ryan blasted a bases-loaded home run over the left-field fence, the ball hitting the wall of a building outside the ballpark. Ryan scored five runs in the game.

Light-hitting infielder Barry McCormick had six hits in eight at-bats for the Colts, including a triple and a home run, and also scored five times.

Anson, forty-two years old and in his twenty-sev

enth and last year as a professional ballplayer, had only one hit but drew four walks and scored four runs.

By the time the ninth inning came around, the players on both sides were weary from so much work under a hot summer sun; Anson mercifully ran intentionally into the third out to end the eight-run top half of the inning. The veteran manager was pretty sure that a twenty-nine-run lead would hold up.

Louisville at Chicago
Tuesday, June 29, 1897

Chicago	AB	R	H	PO	A		Louisville	AB	R	H	PO	A
Bill Everitt, 3b	6	3	2	0	3		Fred Clarke, lf	4	0	3	1	2
Barry McCormick, ss	8	5	6	3	2		Tom McCreery, rf	5	1	0	0	0
Bill Lange, cf	7	4	4	4	0		Ollie Pickering, cf	5	1	2	1	2
Cap Anson, 1b	4	4	1	10	1		Bob Stafford, ss	5	1	0	2	9
Jimmy Ryan, rf	6	5	2	0	0		Perry Werden, 1b	5	1	3	15	1
George Decker, lf	4	2	3	0	0		Charlie Dexter, 3b	5	0	4	1	5
Walter Thornton, lf	2	2	2	1	0		Dick Butler, c	5	0	0	4	1
Jim Connor, 2b	7	4	4	3	2		Abbie Johnson, 2b	0	0	0	0	0
Nixey Callahan, p	7	4	4	1	1		Tom Delahanty, 2b	4	1	1	1	1
Tim Donahue, c	6	3	2	5	2		Chick Fraser, p	0	0	0	1	2
							Jim Jones, p	3	2	1	0	0
	57	36	30	27	11			41	7	14	x26	23

x-Connor called out for illegal base-running.

Chicago	3	5	7	1	2	1	2	7	8	36	30	2
Louisville	0	0	1	0	5	0	1	0	0	7	14	10

Errors - Everitt; Thornton; McCreery; Pickering; Stafford; Werden; Dexter, 2; Butler, 2; Delahanty, 2.
Doubles - Everitt; Lange; Ryan; Decker; Callahan, 2; Donahue; Werden, 2; Dexter; Delahanty; Jones.
Triples - McCormick; Lange; Connor.
Home Runs - McCormick; Ryan.
Stolen Bases - McCormick, 3; Lange, 2; Connor; Donahue.
Sacrifice Hits - Everitt; McCreery.
Left on Bases - Chicago, 5; Louisville, 7.
Bases on Balls - Callahan, 2; Fraser, 5; Jones, 5.
Struck Out - Callahan, 4.
Hits - Fraser, 11 in 2-1/3; Jones, 19 in 6-2/3.
Hit by Pitcher - By Jones, 2 (Ryan; Decker).
Wild Pitch - Jones.
Winning Pitcher - Callahan.
Losing Pitcher - Fraser.
Umpire - Sheridan.
Time - 2:12.
Attendance - 520.

Domination

Carl Mays vs. the Philadelphia Athletics

Ted Farmer

In individual sports, players often assert differing levels of dominance over other players. This occurs much less frequently in team sports, where the proceedings offer fewer opportunities for one player to master or control an entire team of opponents.

In baseball, the pitcher is obviously the player with the greatest chance of mastering another team. There are many examples throughout history of a pitcher achieving great success against certain teams. This success, however, is usually short-lived, as personnel changes, aging, injury, or plain old bad luck tend to level outcomes.

Perhaps the foremost example of a pitcher dominating an opponent involves Carl Mays, the controversial submarine pitcher who spent the bulk of his career with the Boston Red Sox and New York Yankees. Although he was one of the best pitchers in the major leagues during the time he played (1915-1929), Mays will forever be remembered primarily for the fatal beaning of Ray Chapman in 1920.

Mays went to his death arguing that his career warranted Hall of Fame consideration. Maybe so, but if he had been able to pitch against the Philadelphia Athletics every start, he would have been a lock for the shrine. How overwhelming was Mays to the Athletics? Between August 30, 1918, and September 2, 1922, he defeated them an astonishing twenty-three consecutive times. What follows is a brief description of each victory.

1918

August 30—While still a member of the Red Sox, Mays begins his streak by pitching both games of a doubleheader. He hurls a shutout in the first game, a four-hitter in the second, and goes the distance in both. Mays helps his own cause with five hits in the two games.

1919

May 29—Mays allows only four hits as no A's runner reaches base after the third inning.

July 7—Although the A's manage eleven hits, they are outscored, 5-4. Mays' outstanding control (two or fewer walks in twenty-one of the twenty-three victories) iss a key factor in his success against Philadelphia.

August 31—Mays allows seven hits (all singles) and doesn't permit a runner to reach third base in a 6-0 whitewash. The New York *Times* writes, "Carl Mays took his exercise yesterday and scarcely got up a perspiration."

September 26—Mays strikes out seven and goes nine innings in an 8-2 victory. Both A's runs scored on errors in the ninth.

1920

April 24—Mays goes ten innings and edges the A's, 3-2. As was the case in many of the twenty-three victories, the majority of the hits allowed (six) were singles (five).

June 6—Although Mays allows six runs and twelve

Ted Farmer *is historian who lives in Blacksburg, Virginia.*

hits, only three of the runs are earned and ten of them are singles.

July 3—It takes only 1:23 for Mays to dispatch the A's, 5-0.

September 7—Mays twirls a 2-0 shutout at the Polo Grounds, giving up only four hits and one walk.

September 27—Mays pitches another shutout, again allowing only four hits.

1921

April 13—Mays gets the opening day assignment and pitches a gem, facing only thirty batters en route to an 11-3 victory. He gets offensive support from Babe Ruth, who goes 5 for 5.

April 21—The A's achieve thirteen hits, all singles, but cross the plate only once as they lose to their nemesis, 6-1.

May 28—Mays holds the A's to just one run on seven hits and records his fourteenth consecutive victory over Connie Mack's squad.

August 13—In front of the largest crowd to see a baseball game in Philadelphia since 1914 (33,000), Mays mows down the A's, 7-2.

September 10—Although he doesn't have his best stuff, Mays doesn't need it. The Yankees score nineteen runs while the A's muster only three. Carl allows twelve singles, a home run, and hits a batter, but his streak is never in jeopardy.

October 1—Mays' 5-3 victory clinches the Yankees' first-ever pennant. This game is close, but "Sub" and New York prevail, 5-3.

1922

April 24—Mays goes eleven innings (his longest effort during the streak) and the Yankees finally prevail, 6-4.

May 6—In one of the best performances of his career, Carl faces only twenty-nine batters and gives up only two hits (both to Bing Miller). He needs to pitch superbly, for he gets little support in the 2-0 victory.

May 29—In typical five o'clock lightning fashion, the Yankees score seven runs in the seventh inning and provide Carl with a 7-4 victory.

June 4—Babe Ruth hits a tremendous three-run homer over the right-field grandstand and Mays goes

3 for 4 as the Yankees win, 8-3, at the Polo Grounds.

July 3—Bob Meusel hits for the cycle and Mays pitches his twenty-second consecutive complete game victory over the Mackmen. The Yanks cruise to an easy 12-1 win.

September 2—Although he notches his twenty-third consecutive victory against the A's, "a Philadelphia crowd had the rare spectacle of seeing Mays obliged to quit the pitching throne." He is driven from the mound with one out in the sixth, leading, 7-2. The Yanks hang on for an 11-6 victory that concludes Mays' incredible dominance over the Philadelphia Athletics.

Following the 1922 season, Carl Mays fell out of favor with Yankees manager Miller Huggins and was used sparingly. He made his last start against the A's on October 4, 1923. Mays lasted only five innings, giving up ten hits, three walks, and seven runs, while striking out none. The Yanks lost, 7-6, and the streak was over. Mays spent the rest of his career in the National League.

To understand fully how effective Mays was against the Athletics, it is necessary to examine the critical statistics associated with pitching excellence. These include earned run average, WHIP ratio (hits plus walks, divided by innings pitched), opponents batting average, and innings pitched.

Of the twenty-three victories he achieved, all but one were complete games. He logged a total of 206-1/3 innings. He faced 783 batters; 168 hit safely, while twenty-seven walked. May's WHIP ratio adds up to an astonishingly low 0.95, while the opponents batting average was a paltry .215. Of the 168 hits, all but twenty-seven were singles. Surely Mays' ability to prevent extra-base hits, combined with his superb control, were key factors in his success.

There were several other factors as well. During this stretch, the Red Sox won a world's championship and the Yankees were pennant winners twice. Not only did Mays receive excellent run support (6.7 runs per game during the streak), but he also had skillful defense behind him. Not unimportantly, the A's were the worst team in baseball during this period, finishing last in the American League four times and next to last once. Nevertheless, Carl Mays' performance was truly one for the record books.

Eighteen Stalwart Pitchers

A decade that spawned sturdy moundsmen

Richard Holody

Don Sutton's election to the Baseball Hall of Fame provoked predictable controversey about the merits of his worthiness for inclusion in the shrine. "Okay! So he won 324 games! He really wasn't a dominant pitcher of his time!" Though such arguments can and probably will go on forever, his election does provide the opportunity to review a remarkable period of time in baseball history and to devise a method to analyze the comparative dominance of pitchers who competed in the same era.

Between 1962 and 1967, fourteen pitchers who would finish with 200 or more wins began their major league careers. They account for almost fifteen percent of the ninety-six pitchers to achieve this mark. Six of these pitchers won 300 games, twenty percent of the major league total. And with the election of Sutton, nine are now in Cooperstown.

If we extend our historical focus just three more years, we can add four more pitchers to this list, giving us a total of eighteen such sturdy and successful hurlers—just about nineteen percent of the major league total of 200-game winners. Here they are, ranked by winning percentage, along with their career years and lifetime ERAs. Hall of Famers are indicated by an asterisk. (If we had gone back to 1960 we could have added Juan Marichal. But since his effectiveness ended in 1971 and his last pitch was thrown in 1975, he doesn't quite fit into this era.)

Richard Holody *teaches social work at Lehman College/CUNY, Bronx, New York, and co-authored "Throw 'Em Smoke" (Baseball Monologues, Heineman Publishing).*

Pitcher	Years	Wins-Losses	ERA	WP
*Jim Palmer	1965-84	268-152	2.86	.638
*Tom Seaver	1967-86	311-205	2.86	.603
*Steve Carlton	1965-88	329-244	3.22	.574
*Catfish Hunter	1965-79	224-166	3.26	.574
Luis Tiant	1964-82	229-172	3.30	.571
Vida Blue	1969-86	209-161	3.27	.565
*Don Sutton	1966-88	324-256	3.26	.559
*Ferguson Jenkins	1965-83	284-226	3.34	.557
Tommy John	1963-89	288-231	3.34	.555
*Gaylord Perry	1962-83	314-265	3.11	.542
*Phil Niekro	1964-87	318-274	3.35	.537
Jerry Reuss	1969-90	220-191	3.64	.535
Bert Blyleven	1970-92	287-250	3.31	.534
Mickey Lolich	1963-79	217-191	3.44	.532
*Nolan Ryan	1966-93	324-292	3.19	.525
Joe Niekro	1967-88	221-204	3.59	.520
Jerry Koosman	1967-85	222-209	3.36	.515
Charlie Hough	1970-92	202-191	3.67	.514

A quick review of this chart shows that except for the "brief" fourteen-year careers of Hunter and Lolich, these pitchers had very long careers, pitching in at least parts of from eighteen to twenty-three years. Twelve finished with ERAs from 3.11 to 3.36, a range of one-quarter of a run. And by the way, looking only at these cumulative numbers, Sutton's qualifications for the Hall, compared to his contemporaries, are solid: tied for second in total wins, tied for sixth for career ERA, seventh-best winning percentage.

To place the historical coincidence of seeing eighteen 200-game winners beginning their careers in a period of eight years, consider these facts.

• No decade has ever seen the first pitch of so many 200-game winners. The 1910s (with thirteen) and the 1880s (twelve) rank second and third.

• The 1920s, 1930s, and 1940s *combined* included the start of only seventeen pitchers with 200 victories.

• Only eight pitchers who began their careers after 1970 have 200 wins at the end of the 1999 season: Rick Reuschel (began 1972, finished with 214 wins); Frank Tanana (1979, 240); Dennis Martinez (1976, 241); Jack Morris (1977, 254); Bob Welch (1978, 211); Roger Clemens (1984, 247); Greg Maddux (1988, 221), and Orel Hershiser (1983, 203). This list will grow, of course, but not by much. Only eight active pitchers are within fifty wins of the 200 plateau: Kevin Brown, David Cone, Chuck Finley, Tom Glavine, Dwight Gooden, Randy Johnson, Mark Langston, and Bret Saberhagen.

These eighteen 200-game winners are a remarkable bunch who had nearly contemporaneous careers. They worked in the same era and so faced the same changing conditions and, in effect, competed against each other every year for Cy Young awards and for leadership in such pitching categories as most wins and best ERA. Comparisons may be odious, but in the case of these pitchers, they're also fair.

Let's look at their records using an analysis that seeks to discover how dominating each one was year in and year out. It includes a consideration of their statistical accomplishments, their contribution to their team's records, and of how sportswriters of the time viewed their importance. It works like this:

• Give one point for every time a pitcher 1) wins twenty games; 2) has a winning record with at least ten victories; 3) has a winning record when his wins exceed his losses by at least ten games, and 4) leads the league in one of seven categories: Wins, Winning Percentage, Complete Games, Shutouts, Strikeouts, ERA, and Innings Pitched.

• Deduct one point every time a pitcher has a losing record with at least ten losses.

• Award one point every time a pitcher 1) wins a Cy Young award; 2) receives at least one vote in the Cy Young voting; 3) finishes in the top ten MVP voting, and 4) receives at least one MVP vote.

• Divide the total number of points (**Quality Points**) by the number of years the pitcher qualified for the ERA title (**Full Years**) to produce a **Quality Average**.

A few comments about this analytical framework before applying it to our eighteen pitchers. Like it or not, winning twenty games is an accepted, easily understandable standard of excellence. But having any winning record is important, and having at least ten more wins than losses indicates the pitcher was a significant contributor to whatever success his team had.

Similarly, having a losing record may well indicate that the pitcher was unlucky (Ryan led the league in strikeouts and ERA in 1987, yet ended the year 8-16) but an unlucky pitcher is of no help to his team. Crediting a pitcher for a winning record only when he has at least ten wins (or debiting when he has at least ten losses) is a quick way of discounting those years when the pitcher was injured, just learning to pitch in the big leagues, or on his way out. Finishing first in any of the seven pitching categories indicates that the pitcher surpassed his contemporaries that year in that category.

I realize that the judgment of sportswriters can be influenced by many factors not related to an honest assessment of the pitcher's performance. Still, given the long careers of these pitchers, it is not too much to expect that their yearly performances would attract the attention of at least their hometown writers. Even if a pitcher never won a Cy Young award, his consistent presence in the award voting would indicate that he was *a*, if not *the*, dominating pitcher of his era. Finishing in the top ten of MVP voting indicates some consensus of the pitcher's importance that year. Receiving one MVP vote may mean only that the hometown voter tossed a bone to the pitcher, but who am I to question the motives of the writer. (By the way, Ryan finished sixth in the Cy Young voting in 1987 with twelve votes despite that .333 winning percentage.)

Thus, a pitcher with, say, a 20-9 record will receive three points: one each for winning twenty games, having a winning record with at least ten victories, and having at least ten more wins than losses. If a pitcher won a Cy Young award, he gets two points, one for winning and one for receiving at least one vote in the balloting. These "duplicate" points for the same achievement reward the pitcher for his special performance that year.

Finally, we all know ahead of time who the best pitchers of this era were: Carlton, Palmer, and Seaver. They were the class of these two decades and any analysis that shows otherwise is suspect.

Twenty-win seasons:

8: Palmer

7: Jenkins

6: Carlton

5: Hunter, Perry, Seaver

4: Tiant

3: Blue, John, P. Niekro

2: Koosman, Lolich, J. Niekro, Ryan

1: Blyleven, Sutton

0: Hough, Reuss

Number of years with ten more wins than losses:

6: Carlton, Palmer, Seaver

4: Hunter, John

3: Blue, Perry, Sutton

2: Blyleven, Jenkins, P. Niekro

1: Koosman, Lolich, J. Niekro, Reuss, Tiant

0: Hough, Ryan

Number of years, winning record, at least ten wins:

16: Ryan, Seaver

15: Carlton, Sutton

14: P. Niekro

13: Blyleven, Palmer, Perry

12: John, Tiant

10: Jenkins, Koosman, Reuss

8: Blue, Hunter, Lolich, J. Niekro

6: Hough

Number of times leading league in one of seven categories:

20: Carlton

18: Ryan

17: Seaver

13: P. Niekro, Palmer

9: Perry

8: Jenkins

7: Hunter

6: Blyleven

5: Lolich

4: John, Tiant

2: Blue, Hough, J. Niekro, Sutton

1: Reuss

0: Koosman

Number of years, losing record, at least ten losses:

7: John, Koosman

6: Hough, Ryan

5: Blyleven, Carlton, J. Niekro, Perry, Sutton

4: Lolich, P. Niekro

3: Hunter, Jenkins, Reuss, Seaver

2: Blue

1: Palmer, Tiant

Cy Young Awards:

4: Carlton

3: Palmer, Seaver

2: Perry

1: Blue, Hunter, Jenkins

0: Blyleven, Hough, John, Koosman, Lolich, J. and P. Niekro, Reuss, Ryan, Sutton, Tiant

Years receiving at least one Cy Young Award vote:

10: Seaver

8: Palmer, Ryan

6: Carlton, Jenkins

5: Blue, Perry, Sutton, P. Niekro

4: Blyleven, Hunter, John

3: Tiant

2: Koosman, Lolich, J. Niekro

1: Reuss

0: Hough

Finished top ten MVP voting:

5: Carlton, Seaver

3: Palmer

2: Hunter, Jenkins, Lolich, Perry, Tiant

1: Joe Niekro, Phil Niekro. Vida Blue did so when he won the MVP. Give him an extra point.

0: Blyleven, Hough, John, Koosman, Reuss, Ryan, Sutton

Years receiving at least one vote, MVP balloting:

10: Seaver

8: Palmer

7: Ryan

6: Carlton, Perry

5: Hunter, Jenkins, Perry

4: Blue, Tiant

3: Koosman, Lolich, Phil Niekro

2: Blyleven, John, Reuss

1: Joe Niekro, Sutton

0: Hough

Let's see what we've come up with and then discuss some of the findings.

Player	Quality Pts	Full Years	Quality Avg.
*Palmer	61	14	4.3
*Seaver	69	19	3.6
*Carlton	63	18	3.5
*Hunter	33	11	3
Tiant	29	12	2.6
Blue	26	11	2.4
*Ryan	45	20	2.2
*Jenkins	38	18	2.1

*Perry	40	20	2
*P. Niekro	37	20	1.9
Lolich	19	13	1.4
Blyleven	23	18	1.2
John	22	20	1.1
*Sutton	22	22	1
Reuss	12	13	.9
Koosman	11	17	.6
Hough	2	11	.2

Does the 1-2-3 finish of Palmer, Seaver and Carlton validate the Quality Points/Average as an effective tool to compare pitchers?

I think so, but with two caveats. First, the method can only be effective with pitchers who have comparable careers. For example, consider another pitcher who began in the big leagues in 1963, Wally Bunker. He actually finished with seven Quality Points in his brief career, and a Quality Average of 2.3. But to compare him to Ryan is absurd, for Bunker's dominance lasted about 1,000 innings while Ryan maintained his standard of excellence for more than 5,000 innings.

Second, because this Quality Points/Average analysis seeks only to determine the dominance factor, it can only supplement other ways of measuring the success of a pitcher's career—for example, a pitcher's postseason record.

How dominating was Sutton in his era?

About as dominating as Bert Blyleven and Tommy John. But his star never burned as bright as Blue's, Ryan's, or Tiant's.

Let's look a little more closely at Sutton's career. He led the league in a pitching category twice: 1972 (nine shutouts) and 1980 (2.20 ERA). How did the sportswriters gauge these accomplishments? In 1972, Sutton tied for fifth in the Cy Young voting and when he had the league-best ERA he did not receive even one mention in the balloting. In 1976, his only twenty-game winning season, Sutton had his best Cy Young finish (third, behind Randy Jones and Jerry Koosman) and his only MVP mention (twenty-second, with seven votes).

How dominant was Sutton on his own team?

Eight times he led his team in innings pitched, four times in victories. Compare those indicators with those of Blyleven's and John's. Over his twenty-two-year career, Blyleven led whatever team he was pitching for (Minnesota, Pittsburgh, Cleveland, Minnesota again, and California) in IP a total of twelve times and nine times was the top winner on his team.

John was a less dominating presence on his teams. He was the workhorse starting pitcher six times and led the team in wins five times. Incidentally, John never led the Dodgers in either category when he pitched alongside Sutton.

On the other hand, Sutton was very durable (200 or more innings pitched in his first fifteen seasons, twenty years altogether) and remarkably effective keeping men off the base paths (fewer hits than innings pitched in each of his first sixteen years; and only once did he issue more than ninety walks–91 in 1969).

But again, compare those accomplishments with Blyleven's and John's. Blyleven finished with sixteen years with 200+ innings, fewer hits than IP in seventeen years and only two years with more than ninety walks (ninety-two and 101). John was less durable (twelve 200+ IP years), gave up more hits (only ten seasons with fewer hits than innings pitched) but was stingier with free passes (only two years when he issued more than sixty-five walks).

Some have argued that Sutton may not have been a Sandy Koufax, but that he compares to Don Drysdale; that is, that while he wasn't the best pitcher of his era, he was a consistently good and effective pitcher whose accomplishments were overshadowed by those of others. Sutton certainly wasn't Koufax: Forty-six Quality Points in eight full seasons for a staggering 5.8 Quality Average. But Sutton wasn't the Drysdale of his era either. Though Drysdale gets penalized in this analysis (as does Koufax) because for most of his career only one Cy Young was awarded for all of baseball, he still achieved more Quality Points (twenty-three) in fewer full seasons (twelve) than Sutton, resulting in a Quality Average comparable to Niekro's and Perry's.

So Blyleven and John were as good as Sutton?

Well, no. Or at least to argue so would be to ignore Sutton's almost forty more career victories and edge in career ERA. Comparing Blyleven and John to Ferguson Jenkins in this regard is revealing. Jenkins had almost the exact same career record and ERA as did John and, except for the disparity in losses, as did Blyleven. But Jenkins had a substantially higher Quality Average, because he was a big-time twenty-game winner who consistently received more support in Cy Young and MVP balloting than either of the other two pitchers.

How dominating was Ryan?

Very! Deduct from his point total the eleven times

he led the league in strikeouts, Ryan still accumulated thirty-four points–a Quality Point total that approximates Hunter and a Quality Average that places him near Niekro and Perry. That's still pretty good company. By why penalize him for not being a ground ball pitcher? Strikeouts are significant. Barring a third strike wild pitch or passed ball, you can't score on a strikeout.

Were Blue and Tiant really that dominant?

The answer requires a closer look at their careers as well as consideration of a possible distorting effect of the Quality Point/Average analysis.

Examining Blue's Quality Points reveals that ten of his twenty-six points were accumulated in one year: 1971. (Oddly enough, Lolich, too, secured ten of his Quality Points in that same year.) You can't disregard that year, of course. But it is fair to say that his one fabulous season skews his Quality Average closer to Hunter's than to Phil Niekro's and Gaylord Perry's. Those two sustained their dominance for 2,000 more innings than did Blue.

As for Tiant, his Quality Points and Quality Average are not so dramatically skewed by his big 1968 year. Without the six Quality Points he achieved in that year, he still has more than Sutton in half the full years. Tiant's career, in years of service, cumulative numbers, Quality Points, and Quality Average, closely approximates Hunter's. Let's look at their careers a little more closely:

Don Sutton

	Hunter	Tiant
Total innings pitched	3449	3486
Total hits allowed	2958	3075
Total walks allowed	954	1104
Lifetime baserunner/IP ratio	10.3	10.9
Total home runs allowed	374	346
Led own team in wins	4	4
Led own team in IP	7	3

Tiant's greatest year (21-9, 9 shutouts, 1.60) was overshadowed in the AL by Denny McLain's thirty-one wins and in the major leagues by Bob Gibson's

thirteen shutouts and 1.12 ERA. But Tiant helped people forget his 1968. The following year he was 9-20, 3.71 and 129 walks (forty-seven more than in any other year), then suffered two miserable years (a combined 8-11 in a total of 164 innings). Though he bounced back to be wonderfully consistent from 1972 through 1979 (134-82), including three twenty-win seasons, he never finished higher than fifth in the years he received Cy Young votes. Hunter's Cy Young award finishes are fourth, third, first, and second.

If you have to work this hard to distinguish Tiant from an unquestionably great pitcher, the conclusion is obvious: Luis was one tough, dominating pitcher.

It's a commonplace observation to say that we rarely recognize what makes the era we live in historic until after years have passed and we've had time to reflect. In the 1960s, we thought we knew how to characterize the baseball we saw. It was the era of Koufax and Drysdale, of Gibson and Marichal, and of Denny McLain's thirty-one-win season. We also thought we would sit back and enjoy for a long time what for sure would be the long and great careers of Dean Chance, Jim Maloney, Sam McDowell, and, yes, Wally Bunker. Ooops! They were a combined 38-54 after 1970.

What we didn't know, and needed twenty years to realize, was how many pitchers were beginning together what would prove to be prolonged, productive, historic careers. They were eighteen stalwart pitchers.

Transcendental Graphics

Major League Status for the AL

If 1901, why not 1900?

Joseph M. Wayman

The significant events affecting baseball in 1900 were the National League's reduction from twelve teams to eight and the Western League's name change to the American League.

To lever his renamed league into Chicago in 1900, to downplay his major league intentions to satisfy Chicago's NL ownership, and to remain in the National Agreement, which designated the National League as the only major league, Byron Bancroft Johnson had to hide his major-league intentions.[1] Practically, the AL's status in 1900 was also dimmed by its western locale.[2]

But if the American League was major in 1901, why don't we consider it major in 1900? Ban Johnson certainly could have affected this recognition in retrospect, since from about 1908 through at least 1918 he was the de facto czar of baseball. If the scrutiny of numbers had been as important in those years as it has become, you can bet he would have ruled the AL 1900 averages to be part of the American League's official (read major league) records, especially considering that "opinions of 1900 generally rated the new organization fairly high alongside the established National League."[3]

Players in 1900 "were fearful of new salary cuts, and many were afraid that the contraction of the big league would cause a wholesale loss of jobs. But before long the players realized that Johnson's American League offered plenty of new job opportunities and a chance of breaking the salary log-jam."[4]

In 1900, the pruning of the National League freed four teams' worth of players who would be available for American Leage play. With many of these players, along with independents and minor leaguers, AL rosters were akin to those of high quality expansion teams. The American League in 1900 was stronger than the Union Association had been in 1884, and it rivaled the 1914 Federal League. It was, perhaps, slightly better than the post-1961, expansionist era teams. If the play of today's expansion clubs can be accepted by their leagues as major, then why not the AL in 1900?

The history of the distribution of the lifetime years of AL players appearing in its 1900 games:

	#	Pct.
Played in AL, only major league season	30	14.9
Before/or in part of 1900 played in NL, and in AL 1900 only	56	27.9
Before/or in part of 1900 and after, played in NL only	13	6.5
Before/or in part of 1900 played in NL, after 1900 played in AL only	35	17.4
Before/or in part of 1900 played in NL, after 1900 played in AL and NL	22	10.9
After 1900 played in NL only	10	5.0
After 1900 played in AL only	16	8.0
After 1900 played in both AL and NL	19	9.4
Total Players Appearing in AL, 1900	**201**	**100.0**

The 1900 AL players are from the club rosters in the *All-Time Rosters of Major*

Joseph M. Wayman *is the editor of* Grandstand Baseball Annual. *A version of this artical appeared in GBA in 1994.*

League Baseball Clubs (1967) by S. C. Thompson. Player differences with S.C. Thompson are Tom Carey, who was also listed as Jim Garry (and thus was counted double), Joe Corbett, who was actually Ted Corbett, and Harry Clark, who was W. O. Clark. Michael Hickey was Edward Hickey. Edward Hilley and Jay Nelson are two additional discoveries. Nagle's initials are P.G.[5]

You can see that eighty-six (42.8 percent) of the AL players in 1900 ended their careers that season. Also, seventy (34.8 percent) played before and after 1900 in the majors. Forty-five (22.4 percent) players started in 1900 and played in the majors thereafter. Thus, of the total 201 AL 1900 players, 171 (85.1 percent) were major leaguers either before or after 1900. Of the 171 players, 115 appeared in major league box scores after 1900.

Historian Harold Seymour, in noting baseball's unique employer-employee relationship, states, "The employees not only help create the product sold; they are part of it. There is also a shortage of skilled men. Probably the only time this was not true was in the two-year period from 1898 to 1900, when the National League cut back from twelve clubs to eight."[6] Seymour's observation buoys the contention that major league talent populated AL 1900 rosters.

The real test lies in the starting line-ups. Career-ending years of the starters:

Year	1900	1901	1902	1903+	Total
Position	21	6	3	34	64
Pitchers	7	6	1	10	24

Position: 1 player x 8 positions x 8 clubs = 64 position players.

Pitchers: 3 pitchers x 1 position x 8 clubs = 24 starting pitchers.

Of the career-ending 1900 performances, nineteen of the twenty-one position players and six of the seven starting pitchers had had prior major league appearances.

The 1930s depression years saw many pitiful have-not clubs whose major league talent level was questionable. Consider that the Yankees farm clubs at Kansas City and Newark in those days might have been first-division clubs in either major league. The American League in 1900 had a more even spread of talent.

Major league rosters had about forty percent legitimate major leaguers on them in the World War II years from 1943 through 1945.[7] Realistically, they operated at a major-minor level. The AL in 1900 was stronger than that.

In the American League of 1900, there were enough stars winding down their careers and enough new and promising players to earn it a major league

label. In my mind, a rough rating of the AL 1900-1903 years would look like this: 1900, marginal; 1901, worthier; 1902, acceptable; 1903 and beyond, definitely major.

Following is the dope on the sixty-four primary starting position players (eight positions for each of eight clubs) and on the twenty-four top pitchers (three for each of eight clubs). For purposes of this review I am treating the American League's 1900 season as a major league campaign. My sources are *All-Time Rosters of Major League Baseball Clubs* and *Total Baseball*.

American League 1900 Starting Line Ups, Position Players

Player	Club	Pos	Comments
Abbaticchio, EJ	Mnp	2b	Solid MLer, NL 1903-1910.
Anderson, JJ	Mlk	1b	Reliable MLer 1894-1908.
Andrews, JA	Buf	3b	MLer AL 1900 only.
Bierbauer, LW	Buf	2b	Over-the-hill NLer, AL 1900 final ML season,.
Brodie, WS	Chg	of	Qualified as MLer on basis of 1901-1902 seasons.
Burke, JT	Mlk	3b	Solid NL performer 1901-1905.
Carey, GC	Buf	1b	AL 1902-1903.
Carey, T	Mlk	of	Half ML season only, AL 1900.
Casey, JP	Det	3b	Over 100 G each season 1900-1907.
Conroy, WE	Mlk	ss	AL 1901, 1903-1911 ML with over 100 G seasons.
Coughlin, WP	KC	3b	AL 1900-1908, over 100 G each season.
Davis, AD	Mnp	of	ML rating based on 1900-1903, 1907 play.
Dillon, FE	Det	1b	ML status on basis of 1900-1902, 1904 seasons.
Dowd, TJ	Mlk	of	ML status NL 1891-1899, quality AL 1900-1901.
Dungan, SM	KC	1b	AL 1900-1901.
Elberfeld, NA	Det	ss	Solid ML seasons, AL 1900-1911.
Farrell, JS	KC	of	100 G seasons 1900-1904.
Fisher, N	Mnp	c	9G in 1898. AL 1900 briefly.
Flood, TA	Clv	2b	Recognized on basis of NL 1902-1903 seasons.
Frisbee. CA	Clv	of	Only a few ML games, none after 1900.
Fultz, DL	Mlk	2b	ML performer 1898-1905.
Genins, CF	Clv	of	AL 1900 only full season, good.
Gettman, JJ	Buf	of	Released 1900 NL player. No ML after AL 1900.
Gonding, J	KC	c	AL 1900 only ML season.
Halligan, WE	Buf	of	PL 1890, NL 1891-1892. Last call AL 1900.
Hallman, WW	Buf	ss	Solid ML career: 1888-1898, 1900-1903.
Harley, RJ	Det	of	Six 100 G seasons of seven 1897-1903.
Hartman, FO	Chg	3b	1894, 1897-1902.
Hartsel, TF	Ind	of	Chg (N) 1901 and Phd (A) 1902-1911.
Hemphill, CG	KC	of	1899-1911.
Hickey, ME	Ind	3b	1899-1900. ML season AL 1900.
Hogriever, GC	Ind	of	Bench player 3 seasons. AL 1900 only 100 G season.
Holmes, JW	Det	of	1895-1905.
Hoy, WE	Chg	of	ML 1882-1902. 14 100 G seasons.
Isbell, WF	Chg	1b	Chicago AL career, 1900-1909.
Kelley, MJ	Ind	1b	NL 1899, last ML season AL 1900. Struggled.
LaChance, GJ	Clv	1b	ML career, 1893-1905.

Lally, DJ	Mnp	of	1891, 1897. AL 1900 last ML season.
Madison, A	Ind	ss	Utility 1895, 1899. AL 1900 last ML season.
Magoon, GH	Ind	2b	ML years 1898-1903. NL 1901-1903.
McFarland, HW	Chg	of	ML status on basis of AL 1900-1903 performance.
Nance, WG	Mnp	3b	ML status on basis of 1901 season.
Nicol, GE	Det	of	1890, 1891, 1894. AL 1900 last ML season.
O'Brien, JJ	KC	of	ML status on basis of 1901 and 1903 seasons.
Padden, RJ	Chg	2b	ML, 1896-1905.
Powers, MR	Ind	c	ML, 1898-1909.
Ryan, JB	Det	2b	3-League player: AA 1889-1891; NL 1894-1896, 1898-1899, 1901- 1903; AL 1900, 1912-1913.
Schaefer, HA	KC	2b	Best years Det 1905-1909 and Wash 1909-1914.
Schre'gost, OF	Buf	c	1897-1908. Caught Waddell, 1902-1907.
Seybold, RO	Ind	of	Early Athletics star, 1901-1908.
Shaw, A	Det	c	Utility player, 1900-1901, 1907-1909.
Shay, DC	Clv	ss	Average ML seasons 1900-1901, 1904-1905, 1907.
Shearon, JM	Buf	of	Utility, 1891, 1896. AL 1900 last ML season.
Shugart, FH	Chg	ss	End of NL line in 1897. Rescued by AL 1900-1901.
Smith, GJ	Mnp	ss	1884-1898, 13 100 G seasons. AL 1900 last ML.
Smith, HT	Mlk	c	ML, 1900-1910.
Spies, H	Clv	c	Played only in 1895 before AL 1900. 2 ML seasons.
Sugden, J	Chg	c	Shared catching duties, 1893-1905.
Sullivan, SG	Clv	3b	Released NL player, 1898-1899. AL 1900 last ML.
Wagner, A	KC	ss	Honus's brother. Other ML appearance NL 1898.
Waldron, IJ	Mlk	of	AL 1900, G 139, BA .293, 1901, G 141, BA .306.
Werden, PW	Mnp	1b	In-out ML seasons thru 1897. AL 1900 last ML.
Wilmot, WR	Mnp	of	Good NL ending in 1898. AL 1900 last ML.

American League 1900 Starting Pitchers

Pitcher	Club	T	Comments
Amole, MG	Buf	L	NL 1897-1898. AL 1900 (21-18) final ML season.
Bailey, HF	Mnp	L	NL 1899-1900. AL 1900 (14- 12) only season .
Barnes, FE	Ind		AL 1900 only ML season (13-10).
Cronin, JJ	Det	R	Showed ML ability 1900-1904.
Dammann, WF	Ind	L	NL surplus. AL 1900 (10-12) final ML.
Denzer, R	Chg	R	Below average in NL, great AL 1900. 1901 last ML.
Ehret, PS	Mnp	R	ML 1888-1898. AL 1900 (12-23) last.
Fisher, CB	Chg	R	Marginal NL, Great AL 1900 (18-13). NL 1901 last.
Foreman, FI	Buf	L	Worthy ML career. AL 1900-1902 last ML.
Gear, DD	KC	R	NL 1896, AL 1900-1901. AL 1900 (19-12).
Hart, Wm F	Clv	R	Losing 1890s record. AL 1900-1901 last ML.
Hastings, CM	Buf		Prior to AL 1900 last ML year, four 1890s seasons.
Hoffer, WL	Clv	R	Some great 1890s seasons. AL 1900-1901 last ML.
Kellum, WA	Ind	L	ML career AL 1900-1901, NL 1904-1905.
Lee, WA	KC	L	AL 1900 first (23-21), 1901 (16-16). 1904 last.
McKenna, JW	Clv		AL 1900 (8-10) like 1890s NL (3- 10).
Miller, RC	Det	R	ML1900-1904. AL 2.7 and NL 2.3 seasons.
Parker, HP	Mnp	R	AL 1900 (12-15), NL 1890s. Finished 1901.
Patten, CL	KC	L	Solid ML career. AL 1900-1908, over 100 wins.
Patterson, RL	Chg	R	ML career Chicago AL 1900-07. Best 1900-1902.
Reidy, WJ	Mlk	R	ML 1896, 1899-1904. Best AL seasons 1900-1901.
Sparks, TF	Mlk	R	ML 1897, 1899-1910. Phillies star 1903-1910.
Waddell, GE	Mlk	L	Hall of Fame legend
Yeager, JF	Det	R	ML 1898-1903. AL Det 1900-1903.

Notes:

1. *History of American League Baseball Since 1901*, 1980, page 3, by Glenn Dickey.

2. *Commy*, 1919, page 144, by G. W. Axelson.

3. *Baseball Research Journal*, 1978, SABR, "The Chicago White Sox of 1900," page 91, by Arthur R. Ahrens.

4. *American Baseball: From Gentleman's Sport to the Commissioner System*, 1966, page 272, by David Quentin Voigt.

5. Final player revisions courtesy of Lefty Blasco and Bob Hoie.

6. *Baseball: the Early Years*, 1960, page 105, by Harold Seymour.

7. *Historical Baseball Abstract*, 1968, page 182, by Bill James.

Playing for Pride

League leaders on last place teams

Ron Kaplan

It's tough playing in the basement. The games drag on, the weather seems colder at the beginning and end of the season and hotter in the dog days of summer. If the fans come out at all, they're abusive or, perhaps worse, apathetic. Planes are late, hotel rooms aren't ready. When you're winning you never notice the minor inconveniences. But on a last-place team, you feel every little bump along the way.

So where can you take solace? When you're out of pennant contention by the All Star Game, you have to play for pride.

Roger Clemens of managed this when he was with the Toronto Blue Jays and earned the 1997 American League Cy Young Award. Andre Dawson was NL MVP for the Cubs in the strike-shortened 1987 season. And Hall of Famer Steve Carlton was the unanimous choice for the NL Cy Young as a member of the 1972 Phillies.

Other Hall of Famers to suffer at least one season with cellar-dwellers include Christy Mathewson, Sam Crawford, Eddie Collins, Miller Huggins, Max Carey, Chuck Klein, Jimmie Foxx, Ralph Kiner, Harmon Killebrew, Phil Niekro, and Richie Ashburn.

Pitchers on last place clubs most frequently led the league in appearances (twenty-two times), complete games (eighteen), and innings pitched (sixteen). Those who led in complete games and innings

pitched were probably staff aces, left in as long as possible. For appearance leaders it was the flip side of the coin: the starters were so horrible that relievers were called upon time and time again.

It's no surprise, therefore, to see that only four pitchers on basement clubs have led the league in wins: Clemens, Carlton, Phil Niekro, and Rick Sutcliffe. Carlton led the NL in five categories in his magical 1972 season—the pitcher's triple crown of wins, strikeouts, and earned run average, as well as complete games and innings pitched. Clemens, in '97, also led the AL in wins, strikeouts, and ERA, and he tied with teammate Pat Hentgen for most shutouts.

For batters, the most frequent categories are home runs (sixteen times), walks (twelve), and stolen bases (ten). Richie Ashburn topped the NL in five offensive categories in 1958, including hits, triples, walks, batting average, and on-base percentage. On ten occasions players have led their loop in three categories.

What follows on the next two pages is a register of players who led their league in a given category while playing for such woeful clubs. I didn't list "negative" categories, such as most losses or home runs allowed, because we want the boys to have something to be happy about. I omitted the strike year of 1981, which resulted in split seasons, because it produced too many last place teams. I did include all other seasons plagued by work stoppages.

Ron Kaplan *is a freelance writer from Montclair, New Jersey. His articles and reviews have appeared in such publications as* Nine, The Elysian Fields Quarterly, The Mystery Review, *and* BookPage. *He also has two on-line baseball book columns, at www.Purebaseball.com, and warningtrack.net.*

League Leaders for Last-Place Teams

Year	Team (Record)	Player	Categories, totals
1901	Cinc. (52-87)	Noodles Hahn	CG (41), IP (375.1), K (239)
		Sam Crawford*	HR (16)
1902	NY, NL (48-86)	Christy Mathewson*	ShO (8)
	Balt., AL¹ (50-88)	Jimmy Williams	3B (21)
1904	Phila., NL (52-100)	Roy Thomas	BB (102)
	Wash. (38-113)	Case Patten	Sv (3)²
1905	St. L., AL (54-99)	George Stone	H (187), TB (259)
		Jim Buchanan	Sv (2)³
1906	Bost., NL (49-102)	Irv Young	CG (37), IP (358.1)
1907	St. L., NL (52-101)	Stoney McGlynn	CG (33), IP (352.1)
	Wash. (49-102)	"Long Tom" Hughes	Sv (4-T)
1910	Bost. , NL (53-100)	Al Mattern	G (51), ShO (6-T)
1911	Bost. , NL (44-107)	Doc Miller	H (192)
1913	St. L., NL (51-99)	Miller Huggins*	OBP (.432)
	St. L., AL (57-96)	Burt Shotton	BB (99)
1914	Cinc. (60-94)	Red Ames	Sv (6-T)
1915	NY, NL (69-83)	Larry Doyle	H (189), 2B (40), BA (.320)
1916	Cinc. (60-93)	Hal Chase	H (184), BA (.339)
		Heinie Groh	BB (84)
	St. L., NL (60-93)	Red Ames	Sv (8)
		Lee Meadows	G (51)
1917	Pitts. (51-103)	Max Carey*	SB (46)
1918	Phila., AL (52-76)	Tilly Walker	HR (11-T)
		George Burns	H (178), TB (236)
		Scott Perry	CG (30-T), IP (332.1)
1919	Phila., NL (47-90)	Gavvy Cravath	HR (12)⁴
1920	Phila., NL (62-91)	Cy Williams	HR (15)
1923	Phila., NL (50-104)	Cy Williams	HR (41)
1924	Bost., NL (53-100)	Jesse Barnes	ShO (4-T)
	Chi., AL (66-87)	Eddie Collins*⁵	SB (42)
		Sloppy Thurston	CG (28)
1925	Chi., NL (68-86)	Guy Bush	Sv (4-T)
	Bos., aL (47-105)	Howard Ehmke	CG (22-T)
1926	Phila., NL (58-93)	Cy Williams	SA (.568)
1927	Phila., NL (51-103)	Jack Scott	G (48)
1928	Bost., AL (57-96)	Buddy Myer	SB (30)
		Red Ruffing*	CG (25)
1929	Bost., AL (58-96)	Danny MacFayden	ShO (4-T)
1930	Phila., NL (52-102)	Chuck Klein*	R (158), 2B (59), TB (445)
		Hal Elliott	G (48)
1931	Cinc. (58-96)	Red Lucas	CG (24)
1932	Cinc. (60-94)	Babe Herman	3B (19)
		Red Lucas	CG (28)
1933	St. L., AL (55-96)	Bump Hadley	IP (316.2)
1935	Bost., NL (38-115)	Wally Berger	HR (34), RBI (130)
	Phila., AL (58-91)	Jimmie Foxx*	HR (36-T), SA (.636)
1936	Phila., NL (54-100)	Bucky Walters	ShO (4-T)
1937	Cinc. (56-98)	Lee Grissom	ShO (5-T)
	St. L., AL (46-108)	Beau Bell	H (218), 2B (51)
1939	St. L., AL (43-111)	Harlond Clift	BB (111)
1940	Phila., NL (50-103)	Kirby Higbe	K (137)
1943	NY, NL (55-98)	Ace Adams	G (70)
1945	Phila., NL (46-108)	Andy Karl	G (67), Sv (15-T)
	Phila., AL (52-98)	Joe Berry	G (52)
1946	NY, NL (61-93)	Ken Trinkle	G (48)
1947	Pitts. (62-92-T)	Ralph Kiner*	HR (51-T), TB (361), SA (.639)
	St. L., AL (59-95)	Bob Dillinger	SB (34)
1950	Pitts. (57-96)	Ralph Kiner†	HR (47)
1951	St. L., AL (52-102)	Ned Garver†	CG (24)
1952	Pitts. (42-112)	Ralph Kiner	HR (37-T), BB (110)
1955	Pitts. (60-94)	Bob Friend	ERA (2.83)
		Dale Long	3B (13-T)
1956	Chi., NL (60-94)	Sam Jones	K (176)
	K.C., AL (52-102)	Harry Simpson	3B (11-T)
1957	Pitts. (62-92-T)	Bob Friend	IP (277)
	Chi., NL (62-92-T)	Turk Lown	G (67)
	Wash. (55-99)	Roy Sievers†	HR (42), RBI (114), TB (331)
1958	Phila., NL (69-85)	Richie Ashburn*†	H (215), 3B (13), BB (97), BA (.350), OBP (.441)
	Wash. (61-93)	Tex Clevenger	G (55)
1959	Wash. (63-91)	Bobby Allison	3B (9)
		Harmon Killebrew*⁶	HR (42-T)
		Camilo Pascual	CG (17), ShO (6)
1961	Phila., NL (47-107)	Jack Baldschun	G (65)

In 1961, the American League expanded to ten teams with the addition of a new Washington Senators (the original franchise having moved to Minnesota) and the Los Angeles Angels. The NL followed suit the next year, adding the New York Mets and the Houston Colt .45s (later the Astros) to the standings. In those days, before free agency and multimillion dollar offers to draft choices, expansion teams were expected to bring up the rear and the Senators and Mets did not disappoint. Between 1961 and 1969, when each league added two more teams, the Nats filled the last place slot four times. The Mets became media darlings, the benchmark of baseball futility, with five last-place finishes during that span. They had the misfortune, however, of zooming to the top of the charts in 1969, winning 100 games and, astonishingly, beating the heavily favored Braves for the league title and the Baltimore Orioles for the world championship.

Year	Team (Record)	Player	Categories, totals
1964	K.C. (57-105)	Johnny Wyatt	G (81)
1965	K.C. (59-103)	Bert Campaneris	SB (51), 3B (13-T)
1966	Chi., NL (59-103)	Ron Santo	BB (95), OBP (.417)
1967	K.C. (62-99)	Bert Campaneris	SB (55)
1968	Wash. (65-96)	Frank Howard†	HR (44), TB (330), SA (.552)

The major leagues switched into a two-division format in 1969, allowing two teams the dubious honor of finishing in last place, albeit out of six teams instead of ten.

In the American League, the Seattle Pilots finished last in the new Western Division in their only year for a perfect last-place record of 1.000. They moved to Milwaukee in 1970 and switched divisions with the Texas Rangers (nee Washington Senators) to move to the Eastern Division in 1972. The Kansas City Royals were a very good team by comparison, finishing in fourth place in 1969 and never finishing at the bottom of the standings until 1997.

1969	Cleve., ALE (62-99)	Sam McDowell	K (279)
	Sea., ALW (64-98)	Tommy Harper	SB (73)
1970	Wash., ALE (70-92)	Frank Howard[7†]	HR (44), RBI (126), BB (132
	Chi., ALW (56-106)	Wilbur Wood	G (77)
1971	Mil., ALW (69-92)	Ken Sanders	G (83), Sv (31)
1972	Phila., NLE (59-97)	Willie Montanez	2B (39)
		Larry Bowa	3B (13)
		Steve Carlton*[8]	W (27), CG (30), IP (346.1), K (310), ERA (1.97)
	Tex., ALW (54-100)	Paul Lindblad	G (66)
1973	Phila., NLE (71-91)	Steve Carlton	CG (18-T), IP (293.1)
	Cleve., ALE (71-91)	Gaylord Perry*	CG (29)
1974	Cal., ALW (68-94)	Mickey Rivers	3B (11)
		Nolan Ryan	K (367)
1975	Chi., NLE (75-87)	Bill Madlock	BA (.354)
	Cal., ALW (72-89)	Frank Tanana	K (269)
		Mickey Rivers	3B (13-T), SB (70)
1976	Atl., NLW (70-92)	Jim Wynn	BB (127)
1976	Mon., NLE (55-107)	Dale Murray	G (81)

In 1977, the AL expanded again, adding the Toronto Blue Jays to the Eastern Division and the Seattle Mariners to the Western. Both finished last.

1977	Atl., NLW (61-101)	Phil Niekro*	CG (20), IP (330.1), K (262)
1978	NY, NLE (66-96)	Craig Swan	ERA (2.43)
	Atl., NLW (69-93)	Jeff Burroughs	BB (117), OBP (.436)
		Phil Niekro	CG (22), IP (334.1)
1979	Atl., NLW (66-94)	Phil Niekro†	W (21-T), CG (23), IP (342), ShO (5-T)
1980	Chi., NLE (64-98)	Dick Tidrow	G (84)
		Bruce Sutter	Sv (28)
		Bill Buckner	BA (.324)
1982	NY, NLE (65-97)	Dave Kingman	HR (37)
	Tor., ALE (78-84 T	Dave Stieb†	CG (19), IP (288.1), ShO (5)
1983	Cinc., NLW (74-88)	Mario Soto	CG (18)
1984	Pitts., NLE (75-87)	Johnny Ray	2B (38-T)
	Tex., ALW (69-92)	Charlie Hough	CG (17)
1986	Sea., ALW (67-95)	Mark Langston	K (245)
1987	Chi., NLE (76-85)	Andre Dawson[9]	HR (49), RBI (137), TB (353)
		Rick Sutcliffe†	W (18)
	S. D., NLW (65-97)	Tony Gwynn†	H (218), BA (.370)
	Tex., ALW (75-87T)	Charlie Hough	IP (285.1)
1989	Atl., NLW (63-97)	Lonnie Smith	OBP (.420)
1990	St. L., NLE (70-92)	Willie McGee	BA (.335)
		Vince Coleman	SB (77)

1991	Mont., NLE (71-90)	Marquis Grissom	SB (76)
		Barry Jones	G (77)
		Dennis Martinez	CG (9-T), ShO (5), ERA (2.39)
	Cal., ALW (81-81)	Bryan Harvey	Sv (46)
1992	Phila., NLE (70-92)	Darren Daulton	RBI (109)
		Terry Mulholl,and	CG (12)
	Bost., ALE (73-89)	Roger Clemens	ShO (5), ERA (2.41)
	Sea., ALW (64-98)	Edgar Martinez	BA (.343), 2B (46-T)
1993	Mil., ALW (69-93)	Cal Eldred	IP (258)

In 1994, the leagues split into East, Central and West divisions, allowing yet one more team per year the pleasure of claiming the basement for their own.

1994	S. D., NLW (47-70)	Tony Gwynn†	H (165), BA (.394)
	Cal., ALW (47-68)	Chuck Finley	IP (183.1)
1995	Pitts., NLE (58-86)	Denny Neagle	IP (209.2-T)
	S.F., NLW (67-77)	Barry Bonds	BB (120), OBP (.434)
1996	S.F., NLW (68-94)	Barry Bonds†	BB (151)
	Phila., NLE (67-95)	Curt Schilling	CG (8)
	Det., ALC (53-109)	Mike Myers	G (83-T)
1997	Tor., ALE (76-86)	Roger Clemens[10]	W (21), K (292), ERA (2.05), Sho (3-T), CG (9-T), IP (264-T)
		Pat Hentgen	CG (9-T), Sho (3-T), IP (264-T)
	Phila., NLE (68-94)	Curt Schilling	K (319)
	SD, NLW (76-86)	Tony Gwynn	BA (.372), H (220)
1998	Ariz., NLW (65-97)	Dave Dellucci	3B (12)
	Pitts., NLC (69-93)	Tony Womack	SB (58)
	Oak., ALC (65-97)	Rickey Henderson	BB (118), SB (66)
	Det., ALC (65-97)	Sean Runyon	G (88)
1999	Col., NLW (72-90)	Neifi Perez	3B (11-T)
		Larry Walker	BA (.379), SA (.710)
	Minn., ALC (63-97)	Bob Wells	G (76-T)

Key:

BB=base on balls (for batters only); BA=batting average; SA=slugging average; OBP=on-base percentage; R=runs; H=hits; 2B=doubles; 3B=triples; HR=home runs; TB=total bases; RBI=runs batted in; SB=stolen bases; G=pitching appearances; CG=complete games; W=wins; K=strikeouts; ERA=earned run average; Sv=saves

* Member of the Baseball Hall of Fame; † In top ten for MVP and/or Cy Young award; [1] Baltimore became the NY Highlanders (later the Yankees) in 1903; [2] Not recognized as an official statistic until 1969; [3] This was Buchanan's only season in the majors; [4] Cravath accomplished this feat as a part-time player; he was also the Phils' manager; [5] Also managed the team, posting a 14-13 record; [6] Killebrew also finished in the top five in total bases, RBI, base on balls, and slugging average; [7] Howard also finished in the top five in total bases, on-base percentage, and slugging average; [8] NL Cy Young Award winner; [9] NL MVP Award winner; [10] AL Cy Young Award winner.

Sources: *Total Baseball*, 1999; *The Sports Encyclopedia: Baseball*, 1998.

Pitchers Who Could Hit

What a concept!

Marc Okkonen

Since the American League adopted the designated-hitter rule in the 1970s, the pitcher's role in providing offense has disappeared completely from the junior circuit. It is also dramatically diminished in the National League, where pitchers are still required to take their place in the batter's box. With the advent of so-called "set-up" men, "closers," etc. in modern baseball, complete games by a starting pitcher are extremely rare and pinch-hitting for the pitcher is so commonplace that little or nothing is expected of National League hurlers at the plate. This trend, if it continues, will eventually force the already rare hitting pitcher into extinction. Now, the only skill with a bat required for pitchers is the ability to bunt with runners on base. Otherwise, their meaningless ritual at bat is an exercise in orchestrated futility.

As anyone who has followed the game for several decades knows, this was not always the case. There was a time when some pitchers, if only a minority even then, could inflict damage on the opposition with the bat and many times could win their own ball game with a timely hit. This was an exciting element of baseball in the decades preceding the DH era, and its departure is sadly missed by those of us who remember how thrilling it was to see a pitcher like Fred Hutchinson thwart the opponent's strategy by delivering a key hit, sometimes even pinch-hitting for a

pitching teammate. Those pitchers with exceptional batting skills were usually among the fiercest competitors in the game and their ability to deliver in the clutch added a dramatic touch that is sadly absent in today's game. Lest their heroics be ignored and forgotten because of the nature of modern baseball, let us recall some of those gifted two-way athletes of decades past.

First, a quick summary of those pitchers with reasonably productive careers on the mound who stand out as the finest hitters among major league moundsmen in the past century. To no one's surprise, George Herman Ruth tops the list, even though he finished his long career as an outfielder. The Babe was a potential Hall of Fame pitcher in his first six seasons in the majors and, unlike many other pitchers-turned-position players, his mighty bat was explosive from the start. From 1914 to 1919, his last year as a regular pitcher, he hit around .315. Toward his final years in Boston he began to demonstrate his home run power along with his hitting average and was often put in the lineup as an outfielder to utilize his offensive skills on a more daily basis. Once he was traded to New York, the Yankees made the painful decision to convert him permanently to the outfield and the rest is history.

In the mid-1920s, the rival Giants under John McGraw shelled out big bucks to the powerful AAA Baltimore team for what they hoped would be their own Babe Ruth clone—a hard-hitting pitcher named Jack Bentley. For several seasons Bentley nearly lived

Marc Okkonen, *a SABRite since 1985, is a semiretired artist, writer, and researcher in Muskegon, Michigan. He is the author of* Baseball Uniforms of the 20th Century *and other historical books.*

up to that potential, enjoying modest winning success on the mound and hitting an astounding .424 in his first season at the Polo Grounds. But big Jack came nowhere near the numbers of the Bambino and the cruel comparison made him appear a colossal failure. Discarding the Ruth comparison, however, Bentley finished his brief career in 1927 with a 46-33 W-L record and a lifetime batting average of .291, ranking him right under the Babe among pitchers who could hit. In fact, considering pitchers with at least four productive seasons on the mound, Ruth and Bentley are the only two who hit better than .290 as pitchers.

Among pitchers with reasonably full careers as pitchers only, George Uhle, who won 200 games, mostly for Cleveland from 1919 to 1935, had a lofty career batting average of .289. His most productive season of combined pitching and batting was 1923, when he hit .361 while leading the league in victories with twenty-six. Back around the turn of the century, Win Mercer hit .286 along with 135 wins from 1894 up to his tragic suicide in 1902 at age twenty-eight. From 1908 to 1918, Doc Crandall hit .285 en route to 101 pitching victories, including two stellar years in the Federal League of 1914-15. George Mullin was Detroit's most consistent winning pitcher in the early 1900s, but he was also a fine hitter, finishing his career with the Federal League in 1915 with a lifetime batting mark of .262 to go along with 229 pitching victories. Red Lucas, who began his big league career as an infielder/pitcher in 1923, won 157 games, mostly with Cincinnati,

George Uhle

and hit .281 in his sixteen-year career. Schoolboy Rowe, the Tigers' pitching phenom of the mid-1930s, helped his own cause in leading Detroit to consecutive pennants in 1934-35. His twenty-four victories in '34 were accompanied by a .304 BA and in '35 he hit .312 in registering nineteen wins. He finished his injury-plagued career in 1949 with a .263 lifetime batting percentage.

One of the most dominant and combative right-handers in the American League during the Great Depression was Wes Ferrell, brother of Hall of Fame catcher Rick Ferrell. Wes, like George Uhle, is considered by many as Hall of Fame caliber, with an admirable total of 193 wins from 1927 to 1941. As impressive as his pitching credentials were, he is even better remembered for his prowess with the bat. Wes could hit and hit with power, establishing a major league record for home runs in a season by a pitcher, with nine in 1931. From 1931 to 1936, Ferrell hit thirty-four homers, an average of almost six per season. His lifetime BA of .280 ranks with the best among big league hurlers and he was feared at the plate as much as any hitter in the lineup. His most remarkable seasons were 1931 when he hit .319 (including his nine HR's) to go along with twenty-two wins, and 1935 when his twenty-five wins led the league and were aided by his seven HR's and a solid .347 average.

Jim Tobin, a journeyman pitcher during the 1940s, carried a creditable .230 lifetime average but also set a one-game slugging record for pitchers by belting three homers against the Cubs on May 13, 1942, at Braves Field. In fact, the Boston righthander had homered the previous day in a pinch-hitting role giving him four home runs in five at-bats, a mark that may never be equaled by a major league pitcher. Boston's Johnny Sain (.245 lifetime) and Detroit's Hutchinson (.263) were two of the most consistent hitting pitchers in the postwar era and were used frequently as pinch hitters.

Big Don Newcombe was the ace of the Brooklyn pitching corps in the early 1950s, and his lifetime .271 average also made him the premier batsman among the major league pitchers of his era. His most impressive season of combined hitting and pitching was 1955 when his .359 average, including seven home runs, went along with a fine record of 20-5. During the same period over in the American League, Bob Chakales, a journeyman reliever with several clubs, matched Newcombe's numbers with an identical .271 average. Mickey McDermott and Don Larsen (of World Series perfect game fame) were also creditable hitters in the 1950s.

Righthander Earl Wilson won 121 games for the Red Sox and Tigers from 1959 to 1970 and carried a solid .242 career average, but was best remembered for his home run output. A latter-day Wes Ferrell, Wilson reached the seats twenty-nine times from 1964 through 1968 including highs of seven in '66 and '68. The Braves' Tony Cloninger, only a .196 career hitter, startled the baseball world in 1966 by hitting two grand-slam home runs in the same game, a feat that eluded even career sluggers like Gehrig, Ruth, Foxx, Greenberg, and Aaron. During the same era, Hall of Famer Catfish Hunter garnered 201 pitching victories for the A's and Yankees and posted a respectable .226 career average in an age when team batting averages were at an all-time low. His finest season of combined hitting and pitching was 1971, when he backed up a fine 21-11 record with a .350 average.

The Cardinal's great Bob Gibson, also from this period of pitching dominance, was considered a dangerous hitter despite a less impressive .207 career average. In 1970 Gibson had his finest two-way season when he hit .303 to go along with a 23-7 record. The Dodgers' Don Drysdale, only a lifetime .186 hitter, also produced a dream season of hitting and pitching in 1965, with an even .300 average to complement a 23-12 pitching performance. The Dodgers' big righthander could also hit for distance, twice belting seven homers in a season.

The age of occasional hard-hitting pitchers was nearly over by this time as the DH era was about to dawn. Ken Brett, the pitching brother of Hall of Famer George, was one of the last of his breed—an effective AL pitcher who averaged .262 before the DH rule took the bat out of his hands at the peak of his career in the mid-'70s. Brother George, a three-time batting champion, often claimed that Ken was the better hitter of the two. National League pitchers of more recent times such as Fernando Valenzuela, Orel Hershiser, and Tom Glavine enjoyed a modest reputation as batsmen but their lowly averages around the .200 mark reflect the current de-emphasis of pitchers' hitting in contemporary major league baseball.

Among the pitchers enshrined in Cooperstown (aside from Ruth), Red Ruffing stands at the head of the class with a lifetime batting average of .269. In a twenty-one-year career from 1924 to 1947, the red-head hit over .300 no less than nine times, his top mark being .364 in 1930, the year he was acquired by the Yankees from Boston. Spitballer Burleigh Grimes also ranks high with a .248 career average. Ted Lyons and Bob Lemon, a converted infielder, retired with lifetime batting averages of .233 and .232 respectively. The great Walter Johnson was also no slouch at the plate, posting a .235 average during his fabulous twenty-one-year career. In 1925, at age thirty-seven, he led his Washington club to a second straight American League flag with the most spectacular hitting display that ever accompanied a twenty-win season by any pitcher. In ninety-seven at bats, the Big Train hit safely forty-two times for an astounding .433 average.

Dolf Luque and Dizzy Dean were also respectable batsmen, with lifetime averages of .227 and .225. The "Old Fox," Clark Griffith, was a premier pitcher in the 1890s and finished with a .233 career average; respectable but not so impressive during an era when batting averages were considerably higher all around. The legendary Cy Young, a Griffith contemporary, was even less effective at the plate with a career .210 average, but he did contribute both ways in the Boston championship season of 1903, batting .321 to complement his twenty-eight mound victories.

Seemingly in concert with the ups and downs of overall team batting averages, the shortage or abundance of good-hitting pitchers also occurred in cycles. The age of the "livelier" baseball, which took place from around 1920 on through the 1930s, seemed to produce a majority of the higher pitcher batting averages in the twentieth century. Wading through the player statistics of this period produces not only some remarkable individual pitcher batting averages, but even a few entire pitching staffs with extraordinary batting punch—this was truly the "golden age" of pitchers who could hit. The value of this welcome bonus of offensive potential is evident in that most of those clubs with a supply of hard-hitting hurlers were contenders or outright pennant winners.

The Cleveland Indians of 1920 won their first AL pennant and subsequent World Series championship with a team batting average of .303. Six of the eight regulars in the daily lineup hit over .300, but the pitchers also contributed with the bat. Sophomore righthander Uhle, whose prowess with the bat has already been discussed, led the staff with .344. The averages of the remaining "workhorses" in Tribe manager Tris Speaker's pitching corps are as follows: Jim Bagby, .252; Stan Coveleski, .225; Ray Caldwell, .213; Guy Morton, .217; Duster Mails, .200; and Dick Niehaus, .444.

Red Ruffing

Transcendental Graphics

era was that of the Chicago Cubs of 1930, a runner-up after a pennant year in '29. Since 1930 was the strongest hitter's year in the century, with the majority of clubs hitting over .300 as a team, a pitching staff with .200-plus batting averages is less impressive, but this was still one of those rare occasions when only one of the regularly used hurlers fell below that mark at the plate. Eight of the nine pitchers used with any regularity surpassed the .200 level with the bat, led by Guy Bush at .282. Only Bob Osborn, with a 10-6 record, failed to produce as a hitter, posting a .095 average. The Cubs of 1938 also had a fine hitting group of pitchers who averaged over .200 among their starters and delivered a pennant to Wrigley Field.

In my opinion, so long as major league pitchers continue to be pampered and discour-

The following year, it was the Yankees' turn to claim their first league pennant. The batting averages of their 1921 pitching staff were comparable to Cleveland's in 1920. Carl Mays, a .268 career batter, led the hurlers with .343, followed by Bob Shawkey's even .300. Alex Ferguson, Bill Piercy, Waite Hoyt, and Jack Quinn were all over .200, and only Rip Collins fell below that mark with .196. That same year, newly-appointed manager Ty Cobb transformed a .270 Tiger team average into a record-breaking .316, and the pitching staff made a major contribution to this metamorphosis. Three of the four starters hit well over .200—Ehmke at .284, Dauss at .261, and Oldham at .224.

Another hard-hitting pitching corps in this hitter's

aged, if not forbidden, to contribute any batting offense for the good of the team, the National League may as well throw in the towel and adopt the designated-hitter rule and make it universal for all baseball. Being a baseball purist and traditionalist, I would prefer a return to the old ways and restore the system that allows a talented and competitive athlete to put forth the maximum effort to win games and provide excitement for the fans. But given the newfound financial independence of players due to free agency and a powerful players' union, this yearning for the game of yesterday is not realistic. We may never see the likes of a Wes Ferrell or Freddie Hutchinson again—and the game will be the poorer for it.

Seasonal Records

As they were set

Scott Nelson

It was a rare event when Mark McGwire set a new individual season home run record in 1998. In fact, most major league individual season marks have stood for at least sixty-seven years.

Of the nineteen statistical categories in this study—which begins with the turn of the century—only seven have had new record holders since 1931, all of them in the past three decades. There are no existing major league recoreds that were set in the '40s, '50s, or '60s .

In the '90s, the only new major league records have been McGwire's seventy homers and Bobby Thigpen's fifty-seven saves for the Chicago White Sox in 1990. Big Mac's 162 walks in 1998 set a new NL standard.

Other than the home run drama of 1998, there have been few notable threats to a major league individual season record since 1990. McGwire threatened Rogers Hornsby's 1925 National League slugging record of .756 in 1998 with his .752, as Jeff Bagwell had in 1994 with his .750.

Nap Lajoie started the century by leading the American League in no fewer than eight categories, and Honus Wagner led in four in the National. While Lajoie's recently revised 1901 batting average of .426 is the only mark to stand since the year one, saves records have changed hands sixteen times in each league.

The chronological history of league individual season records brings to light some names and accomplishments long lost. As Tom Ruane pointed out in his chronological view of major league career hitting records in the 1998 *Baseball Research Journal*, record books tend to have a poor sense of history. Once a mark is broken, no matter how long it sat atop the heap, it's discarded and replaced by the new standard.

The major league season record that held up the longest before being broken was Rube Waddell's strikeout mark of 349, which he set in 1904. It was sixty-one years later that Sandy Koufax fanned 382 batters in 1965.

Among league records, Hack Wilson's National League home run peak of fifty-six in 1930 held up for sixty-eight years until McGwire came along.

Triples just haven't been all that popular since Chief Wilson recorded thirty-six of them in 1912. In fact, Willie Wilson, who holds the major league season record of 706 at-bats in 1980, and Lance Johnson are the only players with more than twenty triples in a season since 1949.

One player who might have had more triples if he wanted to was Earl Webb, who holds the major league record of sixty-seven doubles in 1931. Speculation has been that Webb purposely slowed down on potential triples in order to add to his total of two-baggers.

Since 1930, the only category to have a new record holder three years in a row is the unsought one of batter strikeouts—1961 to 1963.

Scott Nelson recently took time out from his baseball interests to compile a 278-page history of his immediate family. His ten grandchildren include players of golf, soccer, basketball, volleyball, and softball, but not baseball. There is hope, though: three boys are five or younger.

In recent decades, Nolan Ryan, with his record 383 strikeouts in 1973, took the top spot by the smallest margin possible—one strikeout over Koufax's 382 in 1965.

Probably the biggest record jump occurred in 1920 when Babe Ruth increased his own slugging mark by 190 points, from .657 to .847.

Ruth holds the most major league season records (four): runs scored (177), total bases (457), walks (170) and slugging (.847). These records were all set during the '20s, along with hits (257 by George Sisler in 1920) and singles (198 by Lloyd Waner in 1927), making the Roaring Twenties the most prolific decade for existing season records.

American Leaguers have broken major league records more than 63 percent of the time and hold thirteen of the nineteen all-time standards in the study. Starting in 1901, no National League player has held a major league record in seven categories.

Following most sets of statistics is the record existing at the turn of the century. Major league records are in bold.

Chronological history of individual season records (1900-98)

American League			National League			American League			National League		
At-bats						Sam Rice, Wash.	1925	**182**			
Jack Tobin, SL	1921	**671**	Rabbit Maranville, Pitt	1922	**672**	Willie Wilson, KC	1980	184			
Harvey Kuenn, Det.	1953	**679**	Lloyd Waner, Pitt.	1931	**681**	Wade Boggs, Bos.	1985	187			
Willie Wilson, KC	1980	**705**	Woody Jensen, Pitt.	1936	**696**	Pre-1900					
			Matty Alou, Pitt.	1969	**698**	Jesse Burkett, Cleveland (N), 1896, 191					
			Dave Cash, Phil.	1975	**699**						
			Juan Samuel, Phil.	1984	701						
Pre-1900						**Doubles**					
Tom Brown, Louisville (N), 1892, 660						Nap Lajoie, Phil.	1901	**48**	Honus Wagner, Pitt.	1900	45
						Nap Lajoie, Cle.	1904	**50**	Rogers Hornsby, SL	1922	46
Runs Scored						Nap Lajoie, Cle.	1910	**53**	R. Stephenson, Chi.	1927	46
			Roy Thomas, Phil.	1900	131	Tris Speaker, Bos.	1912	**53**	Paul Waner, Pitt.	1928	50
Nap Lajoie, Phil.	1901	**145**	Jesse Burkett, SL	1901	139	Tris Speaker, Cle.	1923	**59**	J. Frederick, Brk.	1929	52
Ty Cobb, Det.	1911	**147**	Rogers Hornsby, SL	1922	141	Geo. Burns, Cle.	1926	**64**	Chuck Klein, Phil.	1930	59
Babe Ruth, NY	1920	**158**	Kiki Cuyler, Pitt.	1925	144	Earl Webb, Bos.	1931	**67**	Paul Waner, Pitt.	1932	62
Babe Ruth, NY	1921	**177**	Rogers Hornsby, Chi.	1929	156				Joe Medwick, SL	1936	64
			Chuck Klein, Phil.	1930	158	Pre-1900					
Pre-1900						Ed Delahanty, Phil. (N), 1899, 55					
Billy Hamilton, Phil. (N), 1894, 192											
						Triples					
						Jimmy Williams, Bal.	1901	21			
Hits						Jimmy Williams, Bal.	1903	23	Honus Wagner, Pitt.	1900	**22**
			Willie Keeler, Brk.	1900	208	Sam Crawford, Det.	1903	**25**	Sam Crawford, Cin.	1902	23
Nap Lajoie, Phil.	1901	**232**	Jesse Burkett, SL	1901	228	Joe Jackson, Cle.	1912	26	Larry Doyle, NY	1911	**25**
Ty Cobb, Det.	1911	**248**	Rogers Hornsby, SL	1921	235	Sam Crawford, Det.	1914	26	Chief Wilson, Pitt.	1912	**36**
Geo. Sisler, SL	1920	**257**	Rogers Hornsby, SL	1922	250	Pre-1900					
			Lefty O'Doul, Phil.	1929	254	Heinie Reitz, Balt. (N), 1894, 31					
			Bill Terry, NY	1930	254						
Pre-1900						**Home Runs**					
Jesse Burkett, Cleveland (N), 1896, 240						Nap Lajoie, Phil.	1901	14	Herman Long, Bos.	1900	**12**
Singles						Socks Seybold, Phil.	1902	**16**	Sam Crawford, Cin.	1901	16
Nap Lajoie, Phil.	1901	154				Babe Ruth, Bos.	1919	**29**	Frank Schulte, Chi.	1911	21
P. Dougherty, Bos.	1903	161	Willie Keeler, Brk.	1900	**179**	Babe Ruth, NY	1920	**54**	Gavvy Gravath, Phil.	1915	24
Willie Keeler, NY	1904	164	Jesse Burkett, SL	1901	**180**	Babe Ruth, NY	1921	**59**	Rogers Hornsby, SL	1922	42
Willie Keeler, NY	1906	166	Lloyd Waner, Pitt	1927	**198**	Babe Ruth, NY	1927	**60**	Chuck Klein, Phil.	1929	43
Ty Cobb, Det.	1911	169				Roger Maris, NY	1961	**61**	Hack Wilson, Chi.	1930	56
Geo. Sisler, SL	1920	171							Mark McGwire, SL	1998	**70**
Jack Tobin, SL	1921	179				Pre-1900, Ned Williamson, Chi. (N), 1884, 27					

American League			National League		
Total Bases					
Nap Lajoie, Phil.	1901	**345**	Elmer Flick, Phil.	1900	**305**
Ty Cobb, Det.	1911	**367**	Jesse Burkett, SL	1901	313
George Sisler, SL	1920	**399**	Cy Seymour, Cin.	1905	325
Babe Ruth, NY	1921	**457**	R. Hornsby, SL	1920	329
			R. Hornsby, SL	1921	378
			R. Hornsby, SL	1922	450

Pre-1900

Hugh Duffy, Bos. (N), 1894, 372

Runs Batted In					
Nap Lajoie, Phil.	1901	125	Elmer Flick, Phil.	1900	**110**
Ty Cobb, Det.	1911	**144**	Honus Wagner, Pitt.	1901	**126**
Babe Ruth, NY	1921	**171**	Gavvy Cravath, Phil.	1913	128
Lou Gehrig, NY	1927	**175**	Rogers Hornsby, SL	1921	**126**
Lou Gehrig, NY	1931	**184**	Rogers Hornsby, SL	1922	152
			Hack Wilson, Chi.	1929	159
			Hack Wilson, Chi.	1930	**191**

Pre-1900

Sam Thompson, Detroit (N), 1887, 166

Walks					
Dummy Hoy, Chi.	1901	86	Roy Thomas, Phil.	1900	115
Topsy Hartsel, Phil.	1902	87	Miller Huggins, SL	1910	116
Topsy Hartsel, Phil.	1905	**121**	Jimmy Scheckard, Chi.	1911	**147**
Babe Ruth, NY	1920	**148**	Eddie Stanky, Brk.	1945	148
Babe Ruth, NY	1923	**170**	Jim Wynn, Houston	1969	148
			Barry Bonds, SF	1996	151
			Mark McGwire, SL	1998	162

Pre-1900

Jack Crooks, SL (N), 1892, 136

Batter Strikeouts (from available records)					
Danny Moeller, Wash.	1913	**106**	John Hummel, Brk.	1910	81
Gus Williams, SL	1914	**120**	Ed McDonald, Bos.	1912	**91**
Larry Doby, Cle.	1953	121	George Kelly, NY	1920	92
Jim Lemon, Wash.	1956	**138**	Frank Parkinson, Phil.	1922	93
Jake Wood, Det.	1961	**141**	Hack Wilson, Chi.	1928	94
Harmon Killebrew, Minn.	1962	**142**	D. Camilli, Chi./Phil.	1934	94
Dave Nicholson, Chi.	1963	**175**	Dolf Camilli, Phil.	1935	113
Gorman Thomas, Mil.	1979	175	Vince DiMaggio, Bos.	1938	**134**
Pete Incaviglia, Tex.	1986	185	Pancho Herrera, Phil.	1960	136
Rob Deer, Mil.	1987	186	Donn Clendenon, Pitt.	1963	136
			Dick Allen, Phil.	1964	138
			Dick Allen, Phil.	1965	150
			Donn Clendenon, Pitt	1968	163
			Bobby Bonds, SF	1969	**187**
			Bobby Bonds, SF	1970	**189**

Pre-1900

Sam Wise, Boston (N), 1884, 104

American League			National League		
Batting Average					
Nap Lajoie, Phil.	1901	**.426**	Honus Wagner, Pitt.	1900	.381
			Jesse Burkett, SL.	1901	.382
			Rogers Hornsby, SL	1921	.397
			Rogers Hornsby, SL	1922	.401
			Rogers Hornsby, SL	1924	.424

Pre-1900

Hugh Duffy, Bos. (N), 1894, .440

Slugging Percentage					
Nap Lajoie, Phil.	1901	**.635**	Honus Wagner, Pitt.	1900	.572
Babe Ruth, Bos.	1919	**.657**	Rogers Hornsby, SL	1921	.659
Babe Ruth, NY	1920	**.847**	Rogers Hornsby, SL	1922	.722
			Rogers Hornsby, SL	1925	.756

Pre-1900

Hugh Duffy, Bos. (N), 1894, .694

Stolen Bases					
Frank Isbell, Chi.	1901	48	Jimmy Barrett, Cin.	1900	46
Topsy Hartsel, Phil.	1902	54	Honus Wagner, Pitt.	1901	**48**
Ty Cobb, Det.	1909	76	J. Scheckard, Brk.	1903	67
Eddie Collins, Phil.	1910	81	Frank Chance, Chi.	1903	67
Ty Cobb, Det.	1911	83	Bob Bescher, Cin.	1910	70
Clyde Milan, Wash.	1912	88	Bob Bescher, Cin.	1911	81
Ty Cobb, Det.	1915	96	Maury Wills, LA	1962	**104**
R. Henderson, Oak.	1980	100	Lou Brock, SL	1974	**118**
R. Henderson, Oak.	1982	**130**			

Pre-1999

Three tied with 111 stolen bases

Pitching Wins					
Cy Young, Bos.	1901	33	Joe McGinnity, Brk.	1900	28
Jack Chesbro, NY	1904	41	Joe McGinnity, NY	1903	31
			Joe McGinnity, NY	1904	35
			Christy Mathewson, NY	1908	37

Pre-1900

Frank Killen, Pitt. (N), 1893, 36

Pitchers' Winning Percentage

(Starters with 16 or More Wins)

American League

Clark Griffith, Chi.	1901	24-7	.774
Bill Bernhard, Phil./Cle.	1902	18-5	.783
Bill Donovan, Det.	1907	25-4	**.862**
Joe Wood, Bos.	1912	34-5	**.872**
Lefty Grove, Bos.	1931	31-4	**.886**
Ron Guidry, NY	1978	25-3	**.893**
Randy Johnson, Sea.	1995	18-2	.900
*Johnny Allen, Cle.	1937	15-1	.938

National League

Joe McGinnity, Brk.	1900	29-9	.763
Jack Chesbro, Pitt.	1902	28-6	.824
Ed Reulbach, Chi.	1906	19-4	.826
King Cole, Chi.	1910	20-4	.833
Tom Hughes, Bos.	1916	16-3	.842
Emil Yde, Pitt.	1924	16-3	.842
Fred Fitzsimmons, Brk.	1940	16-2	**.889**
Rick Sutcliffe, Chi.	1984	16-1	**.941** (4-5 With Cle.)
*Roy Face, Pitt.	1959	18-1	**.947** (Relief)

* Significant records.

Pre-1900

Bill Hoffer, Balt. (N), 1895, 31-6, .838

Earned Run Average

American League			National League		
Cy Young, Bos.	1901	**1.62**	J.Tannehill, Pit.	1901	2.18
Addie Joss, Cle.	1904	1.59	Jack Taylor, Chi.	1902	**1.33**
Rube Waddell, Phil.	1905	1.48	C. Mathewson, NY	1905	**1.28**
Addie Joss, Cle.	1908	1.16	M. Brown, Chi.	1906	**1.04**
Walter Johnson, Wash.	1913	1.14	(300 or more innings)		
Hub Leonard, Bos.	1914	**1.00**	Bob Gibson, SL	1968	1.12

Pre-1900

Clark Griffith, Chi. (N), 1898, 1.88

Pitchers' Strikeouts

Cy Young, Bos.	1901	159	Rube Waddell, Pitt.	1900	133

Rube Waddell, Phil.	1902	210	Noodles Hahn, Cin.	1901	**233**
Rube Waddell, Phil.	1903	**301**	Christy Mathewson, NY	1903	267
Rube Waddell, Phil.	1904	**349**	Sandy Koufax, LA	1961	269
Nolan Ryan, Cal.	1973	**383**	Sandy Koufax, LA	1963	306
			Sandy Koufax, LA	1965	**382**

Pre-1900

Old Hoss Radbourne, Prov. (N), 1884, 441

Saves

Bill Hoffer, Cle.	1901	3	Frank Kitson, Brk.	1900	**4**
Rube Waddell, Phil.	1905	4	Joe McGinnity, NY	1904	**5**
Ed Walsh, Chi.	1908	6	Claude Elliott, NY	1905	**6**
Frank Arellanes, Bos.	1909	8	Geo. Ferguson, NY	1906	**7**
Ed Walsh, Chi.	1912	10	M. Brown, Chi.	1911	**13**
Chief Bender, Phil.	1913	13	Jack Quinn, Brk.	1931	**15**
Firpo Marberry, Wash.	1924	15	Andy Karl, Phil.	1945	**15**
Firpo Marberry, Wash.	1925	15	Ace Adams, NY	1945	**15**
Firpo Marberry, Wash.	1926	22	Hugh Casey, Brk.	1947	**18**
Joe Page, NY	1949	27	J. Konstanty, Phil.	1950	22
Ellis Kinder, Bos.	1953	27	Jim Hughes, Brk.	1954	24
Luis Arroyo, NY	1961	29	Lindy McDaniel, SL	1960	26
Dick Radatz, Bos.	1964	29	Roy Face, Pitt.	1962	28
Ron Kline, Wash.	1965	29	Ted Abernathy, Chi.	1965	**31**
Jack Aker, KC	1966	32	Wayne Granger, Cin.	1970	**35**
Ron Perranoski, Minn.	1970	34	Clay Carroll, Cin.	1972	**37**
Sparky Lyle, NY	1972	35	Rollie Fingers, SD	1978	**37**
John Hiller, Det.	1973	38	Bruce Sutter, Chi.	1979	**37**
Dan Quisenberry, KC	1983	45	Bruce Sutter, SL	1984	**45**
Dave Righetti, NY	1986	46	Lee Smith, SL	1991	47
Bobby Thigpen, Chi.	1990	57	Randy Myers, Chi.	1993	53
			Trevor Hoffman, SD	1998	53

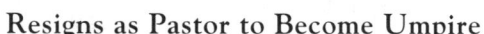

Resigns as Pastor to Become Umpire

PEORIA (Ill.), March 7.—Rev. George Schroeder, pastor of the First Congregational Church at Elmwood, has been signed as umpire in the Illinois and Michigan League. When his application for the position of umpire was accepted he tendered his resignation to the Congregational Church, feeling that his duties as umpire would conflict with those attending his ministry. The resignation was accepted. Rev. Schroeder received his contract while still serving his flock, but kept it unsigned until action was taken on his resignation.

—Joe Murphy, from the San Francisco *Chronicle*, March 7, 1910

Ranking Baseball's Dynasties

The cream of the crop

Sky Andrecheck

With all the talk of whether or not the Braves are a dynasty, I decided to explore the statistical meaning of the word. Before coming up with a formula I had to establish some basics.

Dynasties are all about performance over time, so longevity is vital; a couple of super seasons aren't sufficient. Likewise, a couple of mediocre seasons should not necessarily kill a dynasty. A dynasty must excel during both the regular season and postseason.

Once I had my general ground rules established, I had to decide how to evaluate teams. I decided that using the percentage of other teams in the sport that the focus team was better than would properly reward longevity and allow cross-era comparison by eliminating variables such as the number of games played, number of teams in the league, and different playoff formats.

So how good does a team have to be before we start saying, "There's another example of dominance," rather than "There's another mediocre year?" I decided that to start building a dynasty, a team has to be better than at least seventy-five percent of the teams in baseball. Why seventy-five percent? This will put a team in the top seven or eight teams in baseball in a thirty-team league. That will usually be good for around eighty-eight wins. Anything above this would add to a team's dynastic stature, while anything below

would detract from it. In my calculations, I decided to combine both leagues because I think the larger sample gives a better representation of excellence.

How much weight should we give to the postseason versus the regular season? On one hand, the regular season could be weighted more, because it has 162 games, whereas the playoffs are only fifteen or so games long. On the other hand, the ultimate goal of every team is to win the World Series, not to win the most games. Therefore, I decided it was logical to give equal weight to postseason and the regular season.

Now that I had established that being better than seventy-five percent of the teams was the benchmark for adding to a dynasty, and I had decided that the post-season and regular should be given equal weight, I was ready to implement a formula.

$$\frac{\dfrac{\text{Teams better than in regular season}}{\text{Teams in major leagues - 1}} - .75 + \dfrac{\text{Teams better than in post season}}{\text{Teams in major leagues -1}} - .75}{2}$$

We subtract .75 so that we get a positive score for teams better than seventy-five percent of all other teams, therefore adding to thier dynasty, while we get a negative score for teams below the benchmark.

Here's an example of how it works. The 1906 Cubs had a better record than every other team in baseball or 100 percent (15/15) of teams. Subtract .75 to get a score of .25 for the regular season. However, because they lost the World Series, the Cubs were only better than 93.3 percent (14/15) of teams in the post-season.

Sky Andrecheck *is a seventeen-year-old senior in high school. He is planning to major in statistics and become the greatest sabermetrician in the universe. And he's modest, too.*

Subtracting .75 gives a score of .183. Average the two scores to give the 1906 Cubs a score of .217.

Now that it is possible to get a score for a single season, it is easy to keep adding years together to find a team's total dynasty score. How can you tell when a dynasty is over? It is when the dynasty is at its peak score. (Remember, a team's score will decline when it is lnot better than seventy-five percent of the other teams.) However, a dynasty is not necessarily over after a year or two below the seventy-five percent mark. We need to wait a few years to see if the team can turn things around. I decided that for a team to qualify as a dynasty, it has to achieve a total score of 1.000, which can be achieved in four "perfect" seasons.

Using the these rules, here is the list of baseball dynasties and ratings:

Team	Year	Score
Yankees	21-64	6.434
Giants	03-25	2.050
Orioles	68-83	1.848
Braves	91-98	1.645
Cardinals	39-49	1.417
Cubs	03-12	1.300
Dodgers	45-56	1.283
Reds	72-81	1.164
A's	25-32	1.100

As you can see here, the Yankees top the list with an astonishing 6.434 score—roughly equivalent to a team that had the best record in baseball and won the World Series twenty-six years in a row. Their ability to put together strings of championships allowed them to overcome the few years in which they were not of championship quality. This allowed them to continue the dynasty for forty-four years, even though the team in 1921 bore no resemblance to the 1964 squad.

The surprise on the list is not of course, who is in first place, but who's in fourth. Not only do the Braves qualify as a dynasty, they rank fourth all-time. For each year of their eight-year run, the Braves were always at least the third best team in both the regular and postseasons.

A surprising omission on this list is the A's of the 1970's. Oakland's omission stems from the fact that even though it won three World Series in a row, the title-winning teams were only third, fourth, and fourth respectively in winning percentage. Good years in '71 and '75 almost got them to dynasty standing, but the '70 to '75 A's fall .011 short of the 1.000 mark.

A fun feature of this formula is that since it uses percentage-of-teams-better-than as its method of comparing dynasties, it is possible to compare baseball dynasties to dynasties of other sports. No team in any sport can match the dominance of the Yankees, but in the NBA, the Celtics of the '60s lead the way. No one was better than the Yankees, but the Celtics of the '60s lead the way, flooowed by the '80s Lakers and Celtics. Michael Jordan's Chicago Bulls have a 1.450 rating, the fourth best dynasty in the NBA, but trailing the Braves' score by .195.

The formula gives some interesting results and a strong vote of confidence for the Braves as a dynasty. It could be tinkered with by changing the weight of the playoffs versus the regular season, or by changing seventy-five percent to make it more or less focused on longevity, but I think the original formula defines a dynasty very well.

Bug bucks

A 1911 quote from Ren Mulford, Cincinnati sportswriter: "Scouting has been an expensive pastime for Cincinnati. Salaries, railroad fares, hotel bills, and purchase money for bloomers [promising players; also called "raws"] have probably cost Garry Herrmann $100,000 in the past decade."

—A. D. Suehsdorf

Home Run All Star Teams and the 1998 Home Run Parade

Top sluggers by position and decade

Alan S. Kaufman and James C. Kaufman

The home run dramatics of 1998 reverberated throughout the world. Some have tried to downplay the upsurge of the long ball in 1998 with statistical arguments that show "conclusively" that the home run rate was no different in 1998 from in the years preceding it, and that 1998 was no aberration. But it was. It was not just Mark McGwire and Sammy Sosa who surged, but the whole upper echelon of players. Never mind the "average" player in 1998 versus prior years. Global comparisons of one year to the next deal with the entire home run continuum. But who cares about the guy who might have improved from sixteen to eighteen home runs? What about the player who's selected to All Star teams and holds teams hostage during free-agent negotiations? This is the level that can help answer questions about the similarity or difference between 1998 and previous seasons.

To answer that question, and to explore home run prowess from years past, we selected All Star teams from each season where the sole criterion was to hit the most home runs in the majors at one's position. We didn't limit a player's home run total just to the home runs he hit at a particular position, but we included all home runs he hit that season. So, for example, Todd Hundley may have set the all-time record for home runs by a catcher when he hit forty-

one in 1996, but for our purposes, Johnny Bench's forty-five in 1970 set the standard for catchers. We know he hit home runs as an infielder or outfielder, and perhaps as a pinch hitter that season, but he also started 139 games behind the plate.

We arbitrarily decided that to be eligible a player had to play at least forty games at a position (about twenty-five percent of a team's games in either 154- or 162-game seasons). We chose nine-man teams, adding a Designated Hitter (DH) to round out the squad. Often, the DH slot went to a man who had a great season but was beaten out by someone else at his position. In 1998, for example, Al Belle and his forty-nine home runs made the team as the DH because he couldn't crack the Sosa-Griffey-Vaughn fifty-plus outfield. Sometimes the slot went to an actual DH. In all cases, we first selected the eight position players; the DH was the one "left over" whose home runs would maximize the nine-man team's home run total.

Table 1 shows the Home Run All Star team for 1998, a powerhouse team that produced 444 home runs, an average of 49.3 per man. This table also gives the second and third teams for 1998, impressive nines that averaged 39.0 and 32.3 home runs, respectively.

Table 2 gives the top Home Run All Star teams prior to 1998. The previous record was 388 home runs (average of 43.1), by both the 1997 and 1996 teams—impressive numbers, but a far cry from the output of the 1998 squad. Next came the 1961 Maris-Mantle season, with teams from 1969, 1987, 1955, 1953, and 1970 rounding out the leader board. The teams from

Alan S. Kaufman, *an author of psychological tests and texts, is Clinical Professor of Psychology at the Yale University School of Medicine.* **James C. Kaufman**, *a playwright, is completing his Ph.D. degree in Cognitive Psychology at Yale. They are authors of the 1995 Citadel Press book,* The Worst Baseball Pitchers of All Time, *and of numerous articles on baseball, including several that have appeared in* Baseball Research Journal.

1961 and 1969 both came during expansion years, but neither came close to the 1998 expansion-year team. A glance at Tables 1 and 2 indicates that the second team from 1998 ranks seventh all time, behind the number one 1998 team and only five teams from the past. Maybe the most interesting aspect of Table 2 is noting the second baseman on the 1955 squad: The gerbil, Don Zimmer, with fifteen. Also noteworthy, though, is a list of players who would never be expected to show up on any home run team, ever—players like Matt Nokes, Frank Bolling, Granny Hamner, and Mike Andrews.

What about 1994, when Matt Williams had forty-three home runs before the strike hit, Ken Griffey Jr. (forty) and Jeff Bagwell (thirty-nine) were close behind, and home runs were flying out of the park at a record pace? Would that season boast the most impressive Home Run All Star team of all time? The 1994 team hit 291 home runs in the shortened season in which teams played 112 to 117 games, averaging about a 114-garne season. Prorating the total of 291 to a 162-game season yields a team total of 414, an average of 46.0 per man. Impressive numbers, yes. Good enough to rank second all time, ahead of the 1996 and 1997 totals of 388, but still thirty home runs behind the vintage 1998 season. And the prorated total for 1994 is at least a little inflated because Bagwell's total would have remained at thirty-nine (not its prorated value of fifty-five) because of a season-ending wrist injury just before the strike. If the 1994 team is limited to healthy players, then Frank Thomas' thirty-eight home runs replaces Bagwell's thirty-nine at first base, and Fred McGriff (with thirty-four) takes over the DH slot from Thomas. That Bagwell-less 1994 squad hit 286 home runs; its prorated total of 406 is a more realistic estimate of what would have happened without the strike—good enough for second place all time, nothing more.

The shortened 1995 season is a similar story. The '95 Home Run All Star team hit 325 home runs in 144 games. That prorates to a total of 366, or about what the 1961 season produced. Again, among the best of all time, but no threat to the sluggers of 1998.

In Table 3, the all-decade teams are shown for each decade between the 1920s and the 1990s. The players with the best single seasons of each decade, by position, were chosen for these Home Run All Star teams. We started with 1920 for selecting teams, the year that the Babe signaled the end of the Dead Ball Era by increasing his personal best of the previous year (and the ML record) from twenty-nine to fifty-four. (In 1918, the NL leader was Gavvy Cravath with

eight.) The one stipulation was that a player could only be selected once for each all-decade team; it was fine for a player to be selected to two different all-decade teams (as several were, such as Ruth and McGwire), but not twice for the same team. As expected, the decade of the 1990s—led by five players from 1998—was the runaway leader with 461 homers, an average of 51.2, followed by the decade of the 1960s with 418 (average = 46.4). The 1920s, naturally, pulled up the rear with a 338 total, the only decade to average fewer than forty home runs (37.6). However, the 1930s, led by Hank Greenberg's and Jimmie Foxx's fifty-eight and Hack Wilson's fifty-six, outranked the 1980s.

The most unlikely decade leader was second baseman Felix Mantilla, who paced the 1960s with the thirty homers he hit for the Red Sox in 1964. Mantilla, who played 133 games that year (forty-five at second), had never hit more than seven home runs during any of his six seasons with the Milwaukee Braves, but found Fenway Park's Green Monster to his liking. And if Mantilla is the most unlikely player of a decade, Marty McManus, who led 1920s shortstops with eighteen homers for the Tigers in 1929, is probably the most unknown to today's fans. Also interesting is the fact that Hank Aaron made the teams of the 1950s and 1970s, but not the 1960s when he hit the bulk of his 755 home runs. And note the third baseman for the 1940s; it is Ken Keltner whose previous claim to fame was his defensive gems that stopped DiMaggio's hitting streak at fifty-six.

Table 4 shows the All Time Home Run All Star team from 1920 to 1998. This team, headed by McGwire's seventy and Sosa's sixty-six, includes players from all decades except the 1940s and 1980s. Its total of 499 (and impressive average of 55.4) is tantalizingly close to 500. That magic number could be reached if we dropped the stipulation that a player can make the team only once. Then the DH would be filled by Ruth's fifty-nine home runs in 1921 instead of the Foxx-Greenberg fifty-eight. However, we preferred to keep the one-time rule. Otherwise, Griffey Jr.'s fifty-six in consecutive seasons would have placed him in two of the outfield positions for the team of the 1990s. Worse yet, the 1920s outfield would have been composed of Ruth (sixty in '27), Ruth (fifty-nine in '21), and Ruth (fifty-four in '20)—and the DH would have been Ruth (fifty-four in '28)! Also, we'd like to see the 500 mark reached in 2000 by Griffey Jr. raising his standard to fifty-nine, by A-Rod or Nomar topping Banks' shortstop standard of forty-seven, or by Vinny Castilla becoming the first third baseman to reach the fifty mark. (See update, below.)

Table 5 presents All Star teams composed of the players who were selected to the most single-season teams between 1920 and 1998. The first team is an awesome array of Hall of Famers accompanied by a future Famer (Ripken Jr.). Schmidt, named to 12 teams, finished well ahead of Eddie Mathews (8), although most other races were quite close. Killebrew also finished well ahead of the field for DH and he was the quintessential DH, the player without a position: He made ten teams—three at third base, three in the outfield, two at first base, and two at DH. Mel Ott's twelve selections ties him with Schmidt for second place to the Babe's fourteen. An outfield of Ruth, Aaron, and Ott may surprise some (except those who were fans during the 1930s), and underscores the notion that Ott's achievements far outweigh his legacy.

The three All Star teams in Table 5 include all players who made six or more single-season teams, plus some players who made the third team with fewer than six: the unheralded Whitey Kurowski who dominated third base on the Home Run All Star teams of the 1940s (despite a career total of 106), and the probability-defying eight-way tie among catchers who were named to four teams. (Mike Piazza would have made it a nine-way tie if he hadn't finished a close second to Javy Lopez in 1998—see Table 1.) Joe Cronin was the only player selected for a DH spot in Table 5 who was consistently named at only one position (shortstop), but the DH position was the only way to include this six-time team member on an All Star squad. Among players who just missed the top teams in Table 5 are the following players selected for five single-season teams: Belle, Griffey Jr., Travis Jackson, Chuck Klein, Dick McAuliffe, Joe Morgan,

Dale Murphy, Duke Snider, Cy Williams, and Hack Wilson. The only real surprise here is the Tigers' McAuliffe who paced second basemen three times and shortstops twice between 1964 and 1971 with home run totals of sixteen to twenty-two. Williams is less well known to contemporary fans, but was a popular slugger who played for the Cubs and Phillies from 1912 to 1930. He led the NL in home runs four times, both during the Dead Ball Era (with twelve in 1916) and after (with totals of fifteen, thirty, and forty-one). He hit 251 career home runs and tied Ruth for the ML best in 1923 when he clouted forty-one for the Phillies. Hall of Famer Jackson, the Giants' shortstop from 1922 to 1936, was not known for his power, but neither were the shortstops (or third basemen) of his day. His twenty-one home runs in 1929 was a decade-best for the left side of the infield (see Table 3), and he led shortstops with totals of eight to fourteen during four other seasons in the 1920s.

From Table 5, it is evident that Ripken Jr. (nine) and McGwire (eight) are the leaders at their respective positions among players active in 1999. Other active leaders are catcher Piazza (three), second baseman Jeff Kent (three), third baseman Matt Williams (four), and outfielders Belle (five), Griffey Jr. (five), Juan Gonzalez (four), and Jose Canseco (four).

These Home Run All Star teams demonstrate rather decisively that 1998 was not the same as the years that preceded it, or any other year in baseball history. Yes, the mid- to late1990s represent the apex of home run hitting; but 1998 stands tall in this company, setting a standard that may not be reached for years to come. Yet, noteworthy as well is the player named to the most single-season Home Run All Star teams: the Babe with fourteen.

1999 Update

Like McGwire and Sosa, the other sluggers of 1998 nearly maintained their torrid pace in '99, but when the dust cleared, 1998 remained the undisputed Home Run All Star team champion of the century.

The 1999 team: C—Piazza (40), 1B—McGwire (65), 2B—Jay Bell (38), 3B—Chipper Jones (45), SS—Alex Rodriguez (42), OF—Sosa (63), OF—Griffey, Jr. (48), OF—Greg Vaughn (45), DH—Rafael Palmeiro (47). The '99 squad's total of 433 (average = 48.1) soared into second place all time, but trailed the '98 team by nearly a dozen homers. A-Rod matched his own decade-high home run total, but the team of the 1990s remained unchanged (see Table 3). The '99 results do shuffle the three all-time teams shown in Table 5. Piazza creates a nine-way tie for the third-team catcher. Griffey, Jr. joins the outfield on the third team by virtue of making his sixth team. And Big Mac's ninth team ties him with Gehrig on the first team, instead of with Foxx on the second team. McGwire also joined Ripken as the active players who made the most Home Run All Star teams.

Table 1

1998 Home Run All Star Teams

	First Team			Second Team			Third Team	
C	J. Lopez	34		M. Piazza	32		I. Rodriguez	21
1B	M. McGwire	70		A. Galarraga	44		M. Vaughn	40
2B	J. Kent	31		D. Easley	27		B. Boone	24
3B	V. Castilla	46		C. Jones	34		D. Palmer	34
SS	A. Rodriguez	42		N. Garciaparra	35		J. Bell	20
OF	S. Sosa	66		J. Canseco	46		V. Guerrero	38
OF	K. Griffey, Jr.	56		J. Gonzalez	45		M. Alou	38
OF	G. Vaughn	50		M. Ramirez	45		J. Burnitz	38
DH	A. Belle	49		R. Palmeiro	43		C. Delgado	38
Total		444			351			291
Average		49.3			39.0			32.3

Table 2

Top Home Run All Star Teams Before 1998 (1920 to 1997)

	#1 (tie)-1997		#1 (tie)-1996		#3-1961		#4-1969	
C	M. Piazza	40	T. Hundley	41	Four-way tie*	21	J. Bench	26
1B	M. McGwire	58	M. McGwire	52	J. Gentile	46	W. McCovey	45
2B	J. Kent	29	R. Sandberg	25	F. Bolling	15	J. Morgan	15
							M. Andrews	15
3B	V. Castilla	40	V. Castilla	40	H. Killebrew	46	H. Killebrew	49
			K. Caminiti	40				
SS	N. Garciaparra	30	A. Rodriguez	36	E. Banks	29	R. Petrocelli	40
OF	K. Griffey, Jr.	56	B. Anderson	50	R. Maris	61	F. Howard	48
OF	L. Walker	49	K. Griffey Jr.	49	M. Mantle	54	R. Jackson	47
OF	J. Gonzalez	42	A. Belle	48	O. Cepeda	46	H. Aaron	44
DH	T. Martinez	44	J. Gonzalez	47	R. Colavito	45	C.Yastrzemski	40
			A. Galarraga	47				
Total		388		388		363		354
Average		43.1		43.1		40.3		39.3

	#5-1987		#6-1955		#7 (tie)-1953		#7 (tie)=1970	
C	M. Nokes	32	R. Campy	32	R. Campy	41	J. Bench	45
1B	M. McGwire	49	T. Klu.	47	T. Klu.	40	W. McCovey	39
2B	J. Samuel	28	D. Zimmer	15	G. Hamner	21	M. Andrews	17
3B	H. Johnson	36	E. Mathews	41	E. Mathews	47	H. Killebrew	41
SS	A. Trammell	28	E. Banks	44	R. Boone	26	R. Petrocelli	29
OF	A. Dawson	49	W. Mays	51	G. Zernial	42	F. Howard	44
OF	G. Bell	47	D. Snider	42	D. Snider	42	B. Williams	42
OF	D. Murphy	44	W. Post	40	R. Kiner	35	C. Yastrzemski	40
DH	D. Straw.	39	M. Mantle	37	A. Rosen	43	T. Perez	40
Total		352		349		337		337
Average		39.1		38.8		37.4		37.4

*E. Howard, J. Blanchard, E. Averill, & J. Romano tied for the lead with 21 home runs apiece.

Table 3

Top Home Run All Star Teams By Decade, 1920s to 1990s

	1990s		1980s		1970s		1960s	
C	T. Hund.-96	41	C. Fisk-85	37	J. Bench-70	45	J. Torre-66	36
1B	M. Mac.-98	70	M. McG-87	49	H. Aaron-71	47	J. Gentile-61	46
2B	R. Sdbg.-90	40	R. Sdbg.-89	30	D. Johnson-73	43	F.Mantilla-64	30
3B	V. Cstlla.-98	46	M. Schm.-80	48	M. Schm.-79	45	H. Killeb.-69	49
SS	A. Rod.-98	42	R. Yount-82	29	R. Petro.-70	29	E. Banks-60	41
OF	S. Sosa-98	66	A. Daw.-87	49	G. Foster-77	52	R. Maris-61	61
OF	K. Grf. Jr.-98	56	G. Bell-87	47	D. King.-79	48	M. Mantle-61	54
OF	B. Ander.-96	50	K. Mitch.-89	47	W. Starg.-71	48	W. Mays-65	52
DH	G. Vaughn-98	50	D. Murph.-87	44	J. Rice-78	46	F. Robby-66	49
	A. Belle-95	50						
Total		461		380		403		418
Average		51.2		42.2		44.8		46.4

	1950s		1940s		1930s		1920s	
C	R. Campy-53	41	W. Coop.-47	35	G. Hartn.-30	37	G. Hartn.-25	24
1B	T. Klu.-54	49	J. Mize-47	51	H. Greenb.-38	58	L. Gehrig-27	47
2B	B. Doerr-50	27	J. Gordon-48	32	J. Gordon-39	28	R. Horns.-22	42
3B	E. Math.-53	47	K. Keltner-48	31	M. Ott-38	36	M. McM.-29	18
SS	E. Banks-58	47	V. Steph.-49	39	G. Wright-30	20	T. Jacksn.-29	21
OF	M. Mantle-56	52	R. Kiner-49	54	H. Wilson-30	56	B. Ruth-27	60
OF	W. Mays-55	51	T. Will.-49	43	B. Ruth-30	49	C. Klein-29	43
OF	R. Kiner-50	47	H. Grnbg.-40	41	J. DiMag.-37	46	M. Ott-29	42
DH	H. Aaron-57	44	J. DiMag.-48	39	J. Foxx-32	58	C. Will.-23	41
			S. Musial-48	39				
Total		405		365		390		338
Average		45.0		40.6		43.3		37.6

Note: The year in which the player hit the decade-leading number of home runs follows his name. Griffey, Jr. hit 56 in '97 and '98.

Table 4

Top Home Run All Star Team, 1920 to 1998

	Player	Year	HR
C	Johnny Bench	1970	45
IB	Mark McGwire	1998	70
2B	Davey Johnson	1973	43
3B	Harmon Killebrew	1969	49
SS	Ernie Banks	1958	47
OF	Sammy Sosa	1998	66
OF	Roger Maris	1961	61
OF	Babe Ruth	1927	60
DH	Jimmie Foxx	1932	58
	Hank Greenberg	1938	58
Total	499		
Average	55.4		

Table 5

Home Run All Star Tearns, 1920 to 1998—Number of Teams Made

	First Team		Second Team		Third Team	
	Player	Teams	Player	Teams	Player	Teams
C	G. Hartnett	7	J. Bench	6	Eight-way Tie*	4
1B	L. Gehrig	9	M. McGwire	8	H. Greenberg	6
			J. Foxx	8		
2B	R. Hornsby	10	J. Gordon	9	R. Sandberg	8
3B	M. Schmidt	12	E. Mathews	8	W. Kurowski	5
SS	C. Ripken	9	V. Stephens	8	E. Banks	7
OF	B. Ruth	14	W. Mays	9	R. Kiner	7
OF	M. Ott	12	J. DiMaggio	9	M. Mantle	6
OF	H. Aaron	10	R. Jackson	8	H. Sauer	6
			T. Williams	8		
DH	H. Killebrew	10	D. Kingman	7	F. Robinson	6
			W. McCovey	7	J. Cronin	6

*Y. Berra, R. Campanella, G. Carter, M. Cochrane, B. Dickey, C. Fisk, L. Parrish, J. Torre.

Note: The number of teams made includes all of the Home Run AllStar teams that a player made regardless of position. For example, Mel Ott (twelve) made eleven teams as an outfielder and one as a third baseman; Hank Aaron (ten) made nine teams as an outfielder and one as a first baseman; Joe DiMaggio (nine) made seven teams as an outfielder and two as the designated hitter.

The Expansion Effect

'27 or '98?

Phil Nichols

Listening to the broadcasters of the 1998 World Series proclaim that the New York Yankees of '98 were a better team than that of '27, I thought they were ignoring something: a statistical boost from "the expansion effect."

In short, I thought that winning teams generally win more games in years of expansion. To test this theory, I began by picking the top three teams in each league in the year immediately preceding each expansion and in the year of expansion. See Table 1 on the next page, which shows the standings of these teams, their records, and their winning percentages.

I adjusted the table for the 1962 NL playoff and the 1978 AL East playoff. These results are in parentheses in the table. For the 1961 AL and the 1962 NL, I adjusted the 154 vs. 162 game disparity by accounting for extra wins at the rate of each team's won-lost percentage. These adjustments are in brackets.

I did not adjust if a team played fewer games than a full schedule. The exception is 1976, when the Yankees were three games short. I used their .610 percentage to assume two more wins. The results are in parentheses in the table. Such an adjustment for 1976 actually diminishes the expansion effect slightly. The 1968 Cleveland result and the 1977 results for Baltimore and Boston tend to balance one another, because 1968 yields one fewer game pre-expansion and 1977 yields one fewer game post-expansion.

Phil Nichols *is an attorney in Stephenville, Texas, and has been a SABR member since 1994. This is his first SABR publication. He is still waiting in line for Houston Astros World Series tickets.*

I subtracted games won before expansion from games won during the expansion year, and compared. Table 2 shows that, adjusted for the change in the length of the schedule, the first-place teams in each expansion year won a total of forty-nine more games than the first-place teams in the preceding year. Second-place teams gained forty-eight wins and third-place teams gained forty-seven wins.

The mean increased wins per year was 6.125 for first-place teams, six wins even for second-place teams, and 5.875 wins for third-place teams.

Taking all three finishes into consideration, the mean first, second, or third place team gained six wins in an expansion year. That is a significant number over a 162-game schedule. Every first-place team in an expansion year has won more games than the team with the best record in the preceding year. There is an expansion effect.

Back to the comparison of the '27 and '98 Yankees. The 1927 Yankees won 110 games in a 154-game schedule. At the same .714 won-lost percentage, that would be about 115 wins (115.71) in 162 games. Discounting the "expansion effect" on the '98 Yankees, their 114 wins translate to about 109 wins (109.04). So, in my analysis, the '27 Yanks beat the '98 edition by six wins (6.67). However, Table 1 shows that the '98 Yankees had the greatest increase of victories for any of the top three teams in an expansion year (+sixteen). That is impressive enough not to be accounted for solely by the expansion effect. Which team was better? Maybe we're right back where we started!

Table 1

Expansion effect

	'60 AL							'61 AL					
1	NY	97	57	.630				NY	109	53	.673	+12	[+7]
2	Bal	89	65	.578				Det	101	61	.623	+12	[+7]
3	Chi	87	67	.565				Bal	95	67	.586	+8	[+3]

	'76 AL						'77 AL				
1	NY²	97 (99)	62	.610			KC	102	60	.642+5 (+3)	
2	KC	90	72	.556			NY	100	62	.590	+10
3	Bal	88	74	.543			Bal² Bos²	97	64	.569	+9

	'61 NL						'62 NL				
1	Cin	93	61	.604			SF¹	103 (101)	62 (61)	.624 +10 (+8) [+3]	
2	LA	89	65	.578			LA¹	102 (101)	63 (61)	.618 +13 (+12) [+7]	
3	SF	85	69	.552			Cin	98	64	.605+13 [+9]	

	'92 NL					'93 NL				
1	Atl	98	64	.605		Atl	104	58	.642	+6
2	Pit	96	66	.593		SF	103	59	.636	+7
3	Cin	90	72	.556		Phi	97	65	.599	+7

	'68 AL					'69 AL				
1	Det	103	59	.636		Bal	109	53	.673	+6
2	Bal	91	71	.562		Min	97	65	.599	+6
3	Cle²	86	75	.534		Det	90	72	.556	+4

	'97 AL					'98 AL				
1	Bal	98	64	.605		NY	114	48	.704	+16
2	NY	96	66	.593		Bos	92	70	.568	-4
3	Sea	90	72	.556		Cle	89	73	.549	-1

	'68 NL					'69 NL				
1	SL	97	65	.599		NY	100	62	.617	+3
2	SF	88	74	.543		Atl	93	69	.574	+5
3	Chi	84	78	.510		Chi	92	70	.568	+8

	'97 NL					'98 NL				
1	Atl	101	61	.623		Atl	106	56	.654	+5
2	Fla	92	70	.568		Hou	102	60	.630	+10
3	SF	90	72	.556		SD	98	64	.605	+8

Notes: [1] In '62 SF beat LA 2-1 in playoff

[2] Teams playing fewer than 162 games: '68 Cleveland and '76 New York (pre-expansion), and '77 Baltimore and Boston (expansion).

Table 2

Expansion effect summary

	First place	Second place	Third place	
60-61 AL	+7	+7	+3	
61-62 NL	+3	+7	+9	
68-69 AL	+6	+6	+4	
68-69 NL	+3	+5	+8	
76-77 AL	+3	+10	+9	
92-93 NL	+6	+7	+7	
97-98 AL	+16	-4	-1	
97-98 NL	+5	+10	+8	
Totals	**+49**	**+48**	**+47**	(Total +144)
Mean	**+6.125**	**+6.00**	**+5.875**	

Mean for all three places: 6.00

Umpire Bias Revisited

Home teams are not favored, but strike zones vary

Bob Boynton

In the lead article of the 1991 issue of this journal, Richard Kitchin showed that home-team winning percentages of major league teams varied considerably depending upon who was umpiring behind the plate. (The subtitle characterized the article as a "disturbing report on a hush-hush subject.") Two years later, also leading off in *BRJ*, Willie Runquist argued that the bulk of Kitchin's findings were statistically insignificant. Runquist also examined an additional season and found a negligible correlation between his statistics and those from an earlier season analyzed by Kitchin.

Typically, a full-time major league umpire works behind the plate only about thirty-five times during a season. Many factors, most of which have nothing to do with the decisions of the home-plate umpire, combine to determine the outcome of a baseball game. Runquist convincingly demonstrated that large variations in home-team winning percentages will occur by chance when as few as thirty-five games are involved.

The period under study here is the nine-year span 1988-96. The criterion for inclusion is that an umpire must have worked at least fifteen games behind the plate in no less than eight of these nine seasons. Fifty-two umpires met this criterion (twenty-nine in the AL and twenty-three in the NL). For both the AL and NL, the average number of games per season was

thirty-two (less than it would have been except for strike-shortened seasons). Data from 14,349 games were analyzed.[1]

A well-known statistical principle applies: the larger the sample, the more likely it becomes that evidence of umpire bias, if it exists, can be extracted from a mass of data randomly influenced by other factors. Combining the data from nine seasons increased the number of games in which a typical umpire called balls and strikes from the single-game value of thirty-two to nearly 300.

Home Team Winning Percentages—To illustrate the method of analysis, consider the record of Greg Bonin of the National League. The table below shows the percentage of home-team wins for games in which Bonin was behind the plate, compared to the league average for each of the nine seasons.[2]

Year	Home Games	Winning Pct Bonin	Winning Pct League	Direction Diff.
1988	26	.577	.532	+
1989	35	.472	.543	-
1990	34	.676	.542	+
1991	34	.647	.549	+
1992	31	.557	.531	+
1993	33	.455	.531	-
1994	23	.696	.507	+
1995	26	.346	.527	-
1996	34	.618	.565	+
	276	.559	.536	6-3

This is **Bob Boynton**'s *fifth article to have appeared in SABR journals since 1995. At age seventy-five, he does not plan to undertake any further baseball research during the new millennium.*

In some seasons (e.g. 1988) the home-team winning percentage for Bonin's games was greater than the league average, and a plus sign—indicating the direction of this difference—is placed in the rightmost column. When the difference is in the other direction, as in 1989, a negative sign is indicated. For each umpire, a sign test[3] is used to assess the odds that something other than chance could be responsible for the distributions of plus and minus signs.

The chance that the home-team winning percentage will exceed that of the league for all nine seasons is one in 2^9, or one chance in 512—the same likelihood as for a tossed coin coming up heads nine times in a row. The corresponding probability (p) is .002. For the most unbalanced nine-season splits, the associated probabilities are: 9-0, p =.002; 8-1, p =.020; and 7-2, p =.090. For eight seasons: 8-0, p =.004; 7-1, p =.035; 6-2, p =.145.

To define significance, statisticians often choose the five-percent level of confidence, which implies that there is no more than one chance in twenty that a result would occur by chance alone. For this study, the 9-0, 8-1, 8-0, and 7-1 splits meet this criterion and will be used to define statistical significance. In Bonin's case, the split is 6-3, implying that the difference between the average home-team winning percentage of Bonin's games and that of the league—.559 vs. .536—is insignificant. Note the substantial variability of Bonin's data from year to year, ranging from .696 in 1994 to .346 the following year. This kind of year-to-year fluctuation is typical of all umpires.

The table below shows the distribution of the splits when home-team winning percentages are examined with the data of both leagues combined. N is the number of umpires in each category (Bonin's split is one of sixteen shown in the "6-3 & 3-6" category for nine-season umpires.)

9 seasons		8 seasons	
Split	N	Split	N
9-0 & 0-9	0	8-0 & 0-8	0
8-1 & 1-8	0	7-1 & 1-7	0
7-2 & 2-7	9	6-2 & 2-6	3
6-3 & 3-6	16	5-3 & 3-5	5
5-4 & 4-5	15	4-4	4

There is no significant split for any of the fifty-two umpires (all values are zero above the line). Therefore it may be concluded that, where any possible influence on home-team winning percentage is concerned, no umpire stands significantly apart from the mean of the group.

Strike Zones—Anecdotal evidence indicates that strike zones vary considerably from umpire to umpire. If this is true, an analysis such as that just described might be able to show it objectively. It is hypothesized that umpires with small strike zones will grant the most bases on balls,[4] and it is expected that, when these men are behind the plate, more walks will be issued than average and these added baserunners will result in more runs being scored. For large strike zones, there should be a scoring disadvantage because some batters who otherwise would walk are forced to swing at bad pitches or be called out on strikes.

That walks and runs are correlated is clear in Figures 1 and 2 (following spread), which plot the averages for all seasons for each umpire. (The product-moment coefficient of correlation between runs per game and walks per game is .72 for the American League and .57 for the National.) To examine which of the home plate umpires are associated with significantly more or fewer bases on balls than average, the sign test of statistical significance has again been applied, this time with the following results.

For bases on balls:

9 seasons		8 seasons	
Split	N	Split	N
9-0 & 0-9	2	8-0 & 0-8	1
8-1 & 1-8	5	7-1 & 1-7	2
7-2 & 2-7	8	6-2 & 2-6	1
6-3 & 3-6	12	5-3 & 3-5	5
5-4 & 4-5	14	4-4	2

For runs scored:

9 seasons		8 seasons	
Split	N	Split	N
9-0 & 0-9	1	8-0 & 0-8	0
8-1 & 1-8	1	7-1 & 1-7	1
7-2 & 2-7	5	6-2 & 2-6	2
6-3 & 3-6	18	5-3 & 3-5	5
5-4 & 4-5	17	4-4	2

For bases on balls, ten of the fifty-two umpires show a significant result (values above the line), and for runs scored, there are three such cases. The umpires involved, with their season splits, are:

Bases on Balls: Cousins (AL) 8-1; Kosc (AL) 1-8; Froemming (NL) 9-0; Gregg (NL) 1-7; Hallion (NL) 8-1; Marsh (NL) 9-0; McCoy (AL) 0-8; McKean (AL) 1-8. McSherry (NL) 7-1; Young (AL) (8-1).

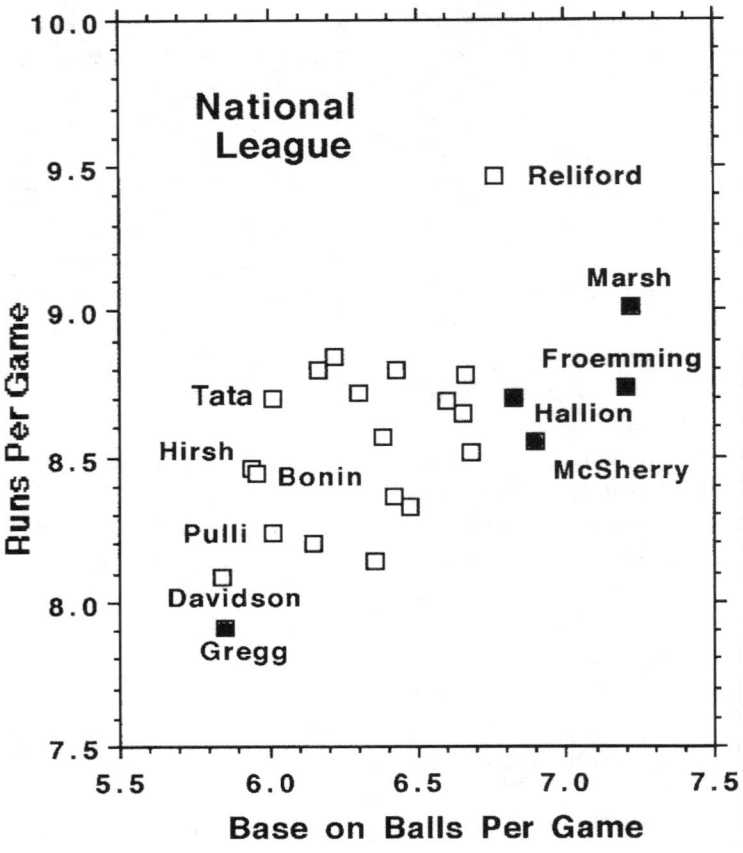

Figure 1. Runs verses Bases on Balls (per game) for National League umpires, 1988-1996. Data squares for umpires whose values differ from the league mean (on either dimension) are highlighted (filled). The data of these umpires, and a few others, are identified.

Runs Scored: Gregg (NL) 1-7; Reed (AL) 9-0; Roe (AL) 8-1.

These umpires, along with a few others, are identified in the figures. Symbols are highlighted for umpires who show statistically significant effects on either axis.

What it means—Responding to a survey undertaken by *Baseball Weekly*, a player remarked, referring to called strikes by Eric Gregg, that "a lot of the pitches he calls are unhittable." In Figure 1, Gregg's name will be found at the extreme lower-left corner of the chart, consistent with the idea that his unusually large strike zone tends to reduce the likelihood of walks, which in turn reduces the numbers of runs scored. The American League's Larry McCoy is similarly located in Figure 2. At the other extreme, where tight strike zones lead to more walks and more runs being scored, Randy Marsh leads the National League and Rocky Roe and Derryl Cousins are tops in the American. In both leagues, the mean number of runs scored per game varies by at least a run, depending upon who is calling balls and strikes.

The correlations of .72 for the AL and .57 for the NL correspond to variances r^2 of .512 and .327 respec-

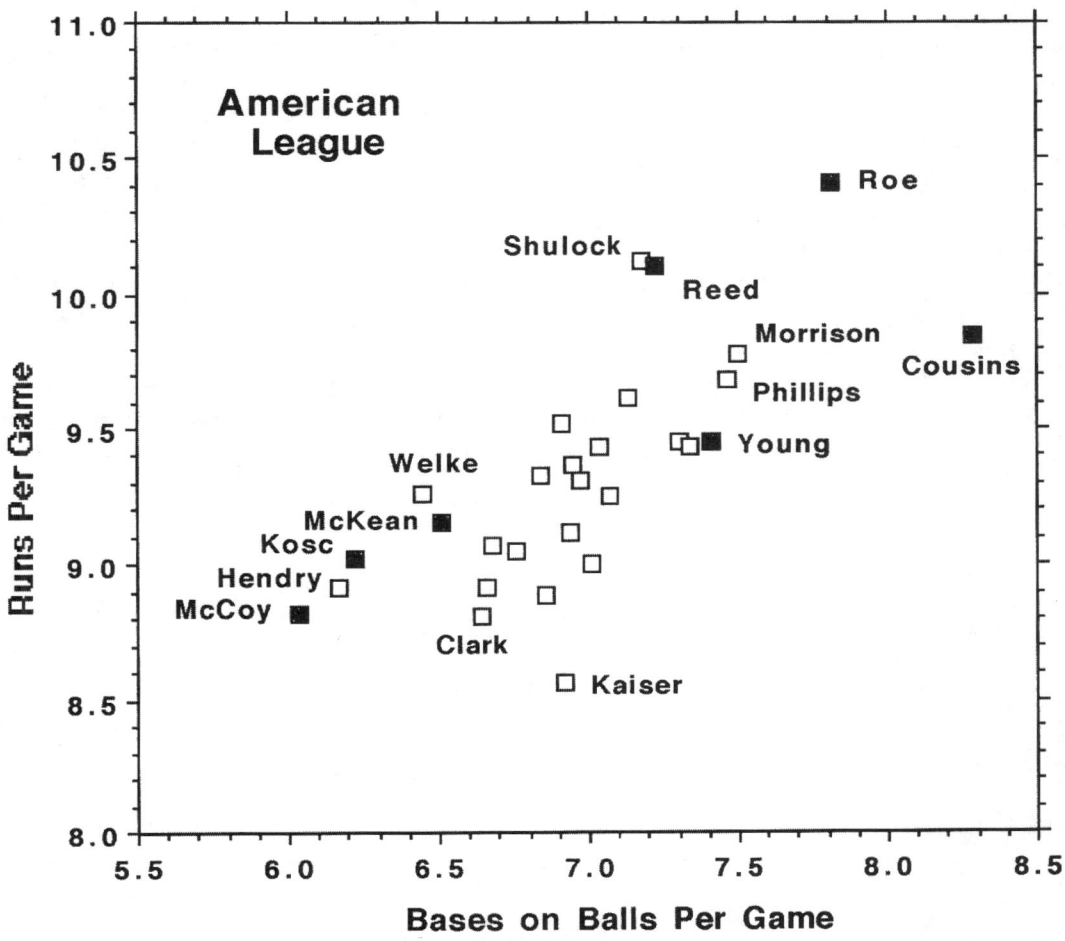

Figure 2. Same as Figure 1, for American League umpires

tively. These values imply that at least a third of the variance in the number of runs scored per game is associated with the differing numbers of bases on balls per game issued by the various umpires.

In the summary of his critique of Kitchin, Runquist wrote:

"If umpiring differences exist, and the players adjust to those differences, no statistical differences are likely to be obtained. This, in fact, is the most likely scenario. Umpires that are wildly variant in their calls do not reach the major leagues, and even amateur players can adjust to small but consistent differences. Moreover, a larger strike zone does not necessarily lead to more strikeouts and fewer hits and walks. In fact it may lead to more balls in play and more offense because batters will not take close pitches if they are likely to be called strikes."

Runquist's speculative comments are wrong on all counts. The results presented in this paper indicate that some umpires *are* rather "wildly variant in their calls," and that they *do* reach the major leagues. Also, despite whatever adjustments players may be able to make, a larger strike zone leads to fewer walks and fewer runs scored.

Runquist also wrote: "If genuine differences among umpires are so small that it takes 25,000 at bats and 400 games to detect them, they are unlikely to be of much practical significance." This is definitely not so.

For any single game, the numbers of walks and runs scored depend on a vast number of factors, most of which are unrelated to the decisions of the home plate umpire. Consequently the influence of varying sizes of umpires' strike zones is undetectable in a single game and is not reliably detectable even for a whole season. Not even the 400 games mentioned by Runquist are enough. More than 14,000 games were analyzed here to reveal the differences among umpires.

These differences definitely *are* of practical significance. They lead to a variation of at least one run per game, which is similar to the DH-inspired difference in runs scored between the leagues in recent years.

If half the major league games were played every day with Eric Gregg behind the plate, and the remaining contests were umpired by Rocky Roe, the influence of their differing strike zones would, like the higher scores in the American League, become apparent in fairly short order. Instead, the strikezone

influence of each home plate umpire is disguised during a season by being spread over relatively few games that involve a variety of teams.

The lack of any evidence of selective bias favoring the home team underscores the excellent work of major league umpires. Still, the home team wins about 54 percent of the time, no matter who is calling balls and strikes. This home-team advantage is very well known, and has persisted over the years. If umpire bias were an important cause, the data reported in this paper would imply that all umpires are biased toward the home team to about the same extent, which seems unlikely, especially because there are so many other reasonable explanations.[5] To the contrary, although major league umpires differ in their perceptions of the strike zone, and probably in other ways not examined in this paper, the important conclusion to draw is that on the whole they are unbiased arbiters who, despite their varying strike zones, call the game in the same way for both teams.

Notes

(1) I am indebted to Tom Ruane for his remarkable ability—known to all who subscribe to SABR-L—to quickly sort Project Scoresheet data any way he chooses, and for his generosity in supplying the season statistics, broken down according to umpire, that I used to begin my analysis.

Project Scoresheet had failed to record the names of umpires for 182 games in the 1988-90 period. Tom sent me a list of these games and I was pleased to look up the box scores and complete the roster.

2. The mean value of .559 is the average of the unweighted values shown for each year.

3. The sign test (see Guilford in the Reference list) is the simplest of statistical tests and the most conservative one that could have been used. As with any test, some real differences may not show up as statistically significant. That is, it is impossible to prove the null hypothesis, which in this context would be that there is no home-away bias on the part of any umpire. All that can be safely said is that, by the test used (which proved to be sufficiently sensitive to show strike-zone differences), no significant bias was revealed for home-team winning percentages.

4. Strikeouts were also examined. Initially, it was thought that the ratio of walks to strikeouts would provide the best index of strike zone, but the inclusion of strikeouts did not improve the analysis, or alter it in any significant way.

5. See the 1989 edition of *Total Baseball*, where home-team advantage is discussed on page 2,197, and the September 21, 1998, issue of *Sports Illustrated*, which describes tricks that have been used by the Bossard family to tailor ballpark grounds to favor their home teams. Contributing to the SABR-L listserver on August 25, 1998, Jeff Angus provided a good list of factors that might contribute to the home-team advantage: 1) Teams tend to be optimized, both offensively and defensively, to take advantage of the idiosyncrasies of their home ballparks. 2) An emotional

lift, provided by the support of home-town fans, could improve performance. 3) Physiological advantages may accrue to the players on the home team because they a) are less likely to have travelled the day before first game of a home series; b) tend to sleep better at home than in a hotel; c) are less likely to engage in extra-curricular activities that can reduce sleep, deplete nutrition, and lead to reduced attention to duty next day. 4) The advantage of batting last allows selective applications of strategy in the late innings. Angus's list was triggered by the finding that the home-team advantage tends to disappear for games in which unusually large numbers of runs are scored. He argued, reasonably enough, that the strategic home-team advantage of batting last tends to be lost in such games because the scores tend to be lopsided.

References

Guilford, J.P., *Fundamental Statistics in Psychology and Education*, McGraw-Hill, 1956, pp.248-49.

Kitchen, Richard, "Do the Umps Give A Level Field?" *Baseball Research Journal*, Vol. 20, 1991, pp. 2-5.

Runquist, Willie, "How Much Does the Umpire Affect the Game?" *Baseball Research Journal*, Vol. 22, 1993, pp. 3-8.

Smith, Gary, "Diamond Cutters." *Sports Illustrated* Vol. 21, No. 12, 1998, pp.100-114.

Thorn, John and Palmer, Pete, *Total Baseball*, Warner Communications, 1989.

Williams, Pete, "The Umpires: Zoned out—or on the ball?" *USA Today Baseball Weekly*, Vol. 8 No. 4, April 15-21, 1998, pp. 8-13.

Minor League Slugging Champions

List and commentary, 1900-1997

Ron Selter

When minor-league star Joe Bauman hit an incredible seventy-two home runs for the Roswell Rockets of the Longhorn League in 1954, he also had the highest slugging percentage in minor league history—.916. In the more than 3,000 league/seasons in the twentieth century the .900 mark has been bettered only two other times. The prior minor league slugging record (.907) was set in 1929 by Edward Kallina with Midland in the West Texas League. The third player to join this very exclusive club was Nicolas Castaneda, who had a slugging average of .904 with San Luis Potosi in the 1986 Mexican League. No major leaguer has come closer to .900 than Babe Ruth's .847 in 1920.

In the period 1900-1997, eighty-six players had the highest minor league slugging percentage for one or more seasons. Hector Espino was the only three-time champion. Eight others topped the minors two times: Buzz Arlett, Randy Bass, Joe Bauman, Ramiro Caballero, Derek Bryant, Frank Huelsman, Ron Kittle, and D.C. Miller.

Forty-one of the eighty-six appeared in the majors, but only ten went on to have significant major league careers (500 or more games). These were Willie Aikens, John Freeman, Joe Hauser, Charlie Hemphill, Ron Kittle, Sherm Lollar, Willie McCovey, Kevin McReynolds, Tony Solita, and George Stone. Stone, who had the highest minor league slugging average in

1904, led the National League in both batting and slugging two years later. McCovey, minor league slugging champ in 1959, was one of the majors' top sluggers between 1960 and 1980, and hit 521 home runs in his major league career.

A number of the lesser-known players had impressive minor league careers. The lifetime records of thirty-eight of the eighty-six are included in the *Minor League Register*.[1] One is Huelsman, the top twentieth-century minor league slugger in the era before 1920. He led all minor leagues in batting five times and slugging twice before the first World War.

Espino, the only three-time champ, is the all-time career minor league home run leader. Bauman's minor league *career* slugging percentage was .702, and Hauser was, until 1999, the only player in baseball history with two sixty-home-run seasons.

Minor league slugging champions have come from as far north as Edmonton, Alberta, and as far south as Yucatan, Mexico. Many leagues produced champs, but some leagues produced many. Despite being included in organized baseball only since 1955, the Mexican League produced the minors' slugging champion thirteen times, including ten straight years (1984-93). The American Association finished a close second with eleven leaders during the century.

The Mexican League had the advantage of more teams, higher average elevations, and in some years a lively ball. In 1986, the Mexican League used what was called the Rocket Ball. It was appropriately named. Hitting, slugging, and home runs reached as-

Ron Selter *has written for SABR on the WTNM League. A graduate of Cal State University, Long Beach and UCLA, he is an economist in the space program. He has been a SABR member since 1989.*

tounding heights. Five players achieved slugging marks above .700.

Also notable is the record of the Mexican Center League. While a long-season league for only eleven years (1960-70), it produced six minor league slugging champions. In fact, in four of these years the champ played for the little-known city of Guanajuato in central Mexico. Other leagues with more than two slugging champions are the Pacific Coast with seven; the Western with six; the Eastern with four, and the International, West Texas-New Mexico, and Western Association, with three each.

Standards—Determining the minor league slugging champion required me to set some standards. First, I considered only league slugging leaders. Thus, if a player qualified as the slugging leader for a given league, his record in another league in that same season would not affect his league-leading performance. Second, I set the minimum number of at-bats to qualify as the league slugging leader at 2.6 per game played (the average number of games played per team), with a maximum of 400. For the overall minor league slugging leader, I set the minimum number of at bats at 350.

As with the rules for batting championships, when batters had fewer than the minimum number of at-bats, I added at-bats to reach the minimum for the league championship and for the overall minor league leadership. Slugging percentages I figured this way are in *italics* in the table. I omitted leagues with schedules shorter than eighty games because their players could not achieve the required 350 at-bats. I made exceptions for the war-shortened 1917 and 1918 seasons, for which I set the minimums at 250 and 175, respectively.

Modern minors—Since the rise of comprehensive farm systems controlled by the major league teams in the early 1960s, the opportunity for any minor league player to achieve an outstanding slugging mark has been greatly diminished. If a farm system player is tearing up a minor league he stands a good chance of being moved in midseason to a higher minor league or to the parent club. As a result, in two recent seasons the player with the top minor league slugging mark split his time between two minor leagues and thus failed to qualify in either league. In 1993, the Cleveland organization's Manny Ramirez had a .581 slugging percentage in 344 at-bats in the Class AA Eastern League and a .690 slugging percentage in 145 at-bats in the Class AAA International League for a combined mark of .613, which topped the best marks of any league leader that year. In 1997, Oakland's Ben Grieve split his 1997 season between Huntsville of the Southern League and Edmonton of the Pacific Coast League. His overall slugging percentage of .640 was better than the mark set by champion Paul Konerko (.621). Grieve did qualify with 372 at-bats in Huntsville, but he was only second best in the league to Luis Raven (.612 to .610).

In a similar manner, Jose Canseco was having a monster season (slugging at a .739 pace after fifty-eight games) with Huntsville in 1985, when he was promoted to Tacoma in the PCL. He did not get enough at-bats in either league to qualify as slugging champion. A more recent case is Todd Green. After sixty-four games in 1997, Green was leading the PCL in home runs and slugging at a .727 pace when the Anaheim Angels called him up. He did not qualify for the slugging championship. Current organizational practices make it most unlikely that any future minor league will produce a slugging percentage in the .750-.800 range or better.

During the period 1900-1997, the minor league slugging champion was also the minor league batting champion thirteen times.[2][3] In 1901-1919 the same player led the minors in both batting and slugging five times, with Huelsman alone accomplishing this feat twice (1911, 1913). This has happened only twice since 1962: by Willie Aikens in 1989 and Nelson Simmons in 1993—both in the Mexican League. Slugging champs led the minors in home runs thirty-three times, their leagues sixty-nine times.

The composite batting record for the minor league slugging champions: batting average .369; slugging percentage .710; twenty-nine doubles; six triples; thirty-six home runs, and 130 RBI. The minor league champ surpassed the major league leader eighty-three times, 1900-1997. Minor league champs topped Ruth's .847 major league record eight times. Except for a few isolated seasons, the majors posted better top slugging percentages than the minors only in two unique four-year eras. The first was 1918-21 when the Babe changed how baseball was played. The second was 1994-97, and is a reflection of the accelerated movement of top hitters through the minors by the parent major league organizations.

Notes:

1. *Minor League Register*, Lloyd Johnson Editor, 1st Edition.

2. "Unknown and Phenomenal: Minor League Batting Champions," John E Spaulding, *Baseball Research Journal*.

3. *Baseball America Almanac* 1990-98.

Minor League Slugging Champions, 1900-1997

Yr.	Player, team, and league	AB	R	H	D	T	HR	RBI	SB	BA	SA	TB
1901	Frank Roth, Evansville (Three I)	430	102	141	22	9	27	NA	11	.328	.609	262
1902	Emil Frisk, Denver (Western)	450	89	168	23	21	15	NA	2	.373	.618	278
1903	Joe Marshall, San Francisco (Pac. National)	469	102	161	30	8	25	NA	17	.343	.601	282
1904	George Stone, Milwaukee (Amer. Assn.)	627	153	254	36	19	7	NA	21	.405	.557	349
1905	Charlie Hemphill, St. Paul (Amer. Assn.)	560	122	204	38	12	5	NA	40	.364	.502	281
1906	Henry Melchoir, Pueblo (Western)	622	108	220	NA	NA	<11	NA	30	.354	.531	330
1907	Buck Freeman, Minneapolis (Amer. Assn.)	528	80	177	38	10	18	NA	21	.335	.547	289
1908	R. Miller, McKeesport (Ohio-Penn.)	342	60	111	NA	NA	<8	NA	7	.325	.600	210
1909	Harry Welch, Omaha (Western)	527	81	196	41	15	7	NA	51	.372	.546	288
1910	Joe Riggert, Lyons (Kansas State)	384	88	139	20	15	13	NA	38	.362	.594	228
1911	Frank Huelsman, Salt Lake (Union Assn.)	451	93	160	28	11	29	125	17	.355	.661	297
1912	Larry Lejune, Grand Rapids (Central)	465	97	168	32	8	25	NA	49	.361	.626	291
1913	Frank Huelsman, Salt Lake (Union Assn.)	473	123	200	36	20	22	126	16	.423	.723	342
1914	Bill Bankston, Cordele (Georgia State)	401	82	144	14	14	31	NA	8	.359	.696	279
1915	Otto Beese, McAlester (Western Assn.)	430	78	121	24	6	34	NA	6	.281	.602	259
1916	Hank Butcher, Denver (Western)	541	116	204	31	20	15	NA	32	.377	.591	320
1917	Harry Harper, Tacoma (Northwest)	296	67	113	29	8	11	NA	21	.382	.645	191
1918	Art Griggs, Sacramento (Pac. Coast)	344	49	130	16	4	12	NA	22	.378	.552	190
1919	Al Nixon, Beaumont (Texas)	494	99	215	47	15	9	NA	49	.435	.646	319
1920	Yam Yaryan, Wichita (Western)	577	124	206	39	4	41	NA	7	.357	.652	376
1921	Ollie Tucker, Cedartown (Georgia State)	349	76	146	25	10	22	NA	7	.418	.734	257
1922	Frank Reiger, Enid (Western Assn.)	479	125	188	39	6	31	NA	6	.392	.693	332
1923	Moses Solomon, Hutchinson (Southwestern)	527	143	222	40	15	49	NA	12	.421	.833	439
1924	Wilbur Davis, Okmulgee (Western Assn.)	650	151	260	50	11	51	190	6	.400	.746	485
1925	Joe Munson, Harrisburg (NY-Penn.)	470	132	188	34	17	33	129	29	.400	.755	355
1926	Moose Clabaugh, Tyler (East Texas)	444	106	167	23	1	62	NA	16	.376	.851	378
1927	William Barrett, Knoxville (South Atl.)	442	106	159	29	7	39	100	9	.360	.722	319
1928	Danny Boone, High Point (Piedmont)	468	123	196	40	11	38	131	11	.419	.795	372
1929	Ed Kallina, Midland (West Texas)	367	126	159	28	7	44	NA	16	.433	.907	333
1930	Ken Strong, Hazelton (NY-Penn)	450	114	168	31	16	41	130	10	.373	.787	354
1931	Stan Keyes, Des Moines (Western)	550	144	203	36	24	38	160	8	.369	.729	401
1932	Buzz Arlett, Baltimore (Intl.)	516	141	175	33	4	54	144	11	.339	.733	378
1933	Joe Hauser, Minneapolis (Amer. Assn.)	570	153	189	35	4	69	182	1	.332	.770	439
1934	Buzz Arlett, Minneapolis (Amer. Assn.)	430	106	137	32	1	41	132	8	.319	.684	294
1935	George Puccinelli, Baltimore (Intl.)	582	135	209	49	9	53	172	4	.359	.747	435
1936	Cal Lahman, Jamestown (Northern)	466	154	182	30	9	48	162	20	.391	.803	374
1937	Maurice Van Robays, Ogdensburg (Can-Amer)	432	135	159	28	9	43	150	14	.368	.773	334
1938	Murray Franklin, Beckley (Mountian State)	385	91	169	31	13	26	110	13	.439	.790	304
1939	Tommy Robello, Pocatello (Pioneer)	507	168	205	33	7	58	179	5	.404	.840	426
1940	Gordon Nell, Borger (West Texas-New Mex.)	529	137	206	48	15	40	175	15	.389	.764	404
1941	Les Fleming, Nashville (Southern Assn.)	374	99	155	34	8	29	103	5	.414	.781	292
1942	Norm Small, Mooresville (NC State)	383	91	144	35	6	32	107	7	.376	.749	287
1943	Thomas Astbury, Allentown (Interstate)	349	75	121	23	7	18	70	22	.347	.606	212
1944	John Cappa, Allentown (Interstate)	525	117	168	36	7	30	106	7	.320	.587	308
1945	Sherm Lollar, Baltimore (Intl.)	464	104	169	27	4	34	111	5	.364	.659	306
1946	Willie Duke, Clinton (Tobacco State)	328	106	129	29	6	27	109	15	.393	.717	251
1947	Bill Serena, Lubbock (West Texas-New Mex.)	506	183	189	43	9	57	190	26	.374	.832	421
1948	Floyd Yount, Newton-Conover (W. Carolina)	402	139	169	30	7	43	140	26	.420	.851	342
1949	D.C. Miller, LaMesa (West Texas-New Mex.)	389	103	157	22	1	52	135	2	.404	.866	337

Yr.	Player, team, and league	AB	R	H	D	T	HR	RBI	SB	BA	SA	TB
1950	Manuel Salviterra, Laredo (Rio Grande V.)	387	126	138	23	2	49	138	33	.357	.806	312
1951	D. C. Miller, Hickory (NC State)	426	115	181	32	1	40	136	2	**.425**	.786	**335**
1952	Marv Williams, Chihuahua (Arizona-Texas)	397	136	159	27	9	45	131	10	**.401**	.854	339
1953	Joe Bauman, Artesia (Longhorn)	463	**135**	172	43	1	53	141	4	.371	.812	**376**
1954	Joe Bauman, Roswell (Longhorn)	498	**188**	199	35	3	72	224	4	**.400**	.916	**456**
1955	Keith Little, Corpus Christi (Big State)	364	83	112	16	1	47	116	2	.308	.745	271
1956	Leonard Tucker, Pampa (Southwestern)	565	**181**	228	40	13	51	181	47	**.404**	.791	**447**
1957	Claudio Solano, Cananea (Arizona-Mex.)	468	140	188	39	3	41	159	6	**.402**	.761	356
1958	Jose Echeverria, Chihuahua (Arizona-Mex.)	399	103	152	22	3	35	126	3	.381	.714	285
1959	Willie McCovey, Phoenix (Pac. Coast)	349	84	130	26	11	29	92	0	.372	.757	265
1960	Ray Reed, Boise (Pioneer)	401	86	139	22	2	37	134	2	.347	.688	276
1961	Jorge Calvo, Guanajuato (Mex. Center)	418	98	154	31	9	29	130	19	**.368**	.694	290
1962	Ramiro Caballero, Guanajuato (Mex. Center)	423	123	**175**	25	0	59	170	3	**.414**	.891	377
1963	Guillermo Frayde, Guanajuato (Mex. Center)	320	85	114	24	9	28	98	21	.356	.686	240
1964	Hector Espino, Monterrey (Mexican)	448	**118**	166	22	3	46	115	5	**.371**	.741	332
1965	Ramiro Caballero, Leon (Mex. Center)	425	133	151	18	3	34	113	5	.355	.652	277
1966	Heriberto Vargas, Guanajuato (Mex. Center)	481	168	214	33	1	55	174	3	**.445**	.861	**414**
1967	Hector Espino, Monterrey (Mexican)	419	106	159	29	3	34	80	6	**.379**	.706	296
1968	Tony Solita, H P-Thomasville (Carolina)	467	**106**	141	20	3	49	122	1	.302	.672	314
1969	Juan Herrera, Carmen (Mexican Southeast)	380	87	125	16	1	39	106	5	.329	.684	260
1970	Trinidad Cardona, Cuid. Madero (Mex. Ct.)	370	89	141	24	0	29	101	5	.381	.681	252
1971	Richard Scheinblum, Denver (Amer. Assn.)	374	83	145	31	10	25	108	1	**.388**	.725	**271**
1972	Hector Espino, Tampico (Mexican)	433	101	154	23	1	37	101	0	.356	.670	290
1973	Tom Robson, Pittsfield (Eastern)	418	83	132	20	2	38	126	4	.316	.646	270
1974	Bill McNulty, Sacramento (Pac. Coast)	526	**135**	173	25	0	55	135	0	.329	.690	363
1975	Gary Alexander, Lafayette (Texas)	346	80	114	24	1	23	81	5	.329	.597	209
1976	Roger Freed, Denver (Amer. Assn.)	398	88	123	21	2	42	102	7	.309	.688	**274**
1977	Kelly Snider, Lodi (California)	530	124	183	34	9	36	139	5	.345	.647	343
1978	Champ Summers, Indianapolis (Amer. Assn.)	462	98	**170**	25	5	34	124	11	.368	.665	307
1979	Randy Bass, Denver (American Assn.)	421	91	146	28	1	36	105	2	.347	.675	284
1980	Randy Bass, Denver (American Assn)	450	**106**	150	25	2	37	143	3	.333	.644	290
1981	Ron Kittle, Glen Falls (Eastern)	389	97	127	17	3	40	103	0	.326	.694	270
1982	Ron Kittle, Edmonton (Pac. Coast)	472	**121**	163	22	10	50	144	5	.345	.752	355
1983	Kevin McReynolds, Las Vegas (Pac. Coast)	446	98	168	**46**	9	28	116	14	**.377**	.709	316
1984	Derek Bryant, Tampico (Mexican)	355	98	138	19	3	41	99	6	.389	.806	286
1985	Derek Bryant, Tampico (Mexican)	446	92	164	**38**	1	38	121	8	.368	.713	318
1986	Nicolas Castaneda, San Luis P. (Mexican)	396	**141**	163	36	0	53	147	3	.412	.904	358
1987	Nelson Barrera, Mex. City Reds (Mexican)	438	97	153	26	2	42	134	6	.349	.705	309
1988	Enrique Aguliar, Aguacalientes (Mexican)	452	104	155	27	2	35	115	8	.343	.644	291
1989	Willie Aikens, Leon (Mexican)	423	**108**	167	40	1	37	131	1	**.395**	.757	320
1990	Nicolas Castaneda, Yucatan (Mexican)	330	67	128	24	3	22	80	0	**.388**	.640	224
1991	Ron Shepherd, Leon (Mexican)	354	97	131	26	2	34	98	5	.370	.743	263
1992	Ty Gainey, Mex. City Reds (Mexican)	405	114	146	18	3	47	133	13	.360	.768	311
1993	Nelson Simmons, Jalisco (Mexican)	369	91	141	27	0	34	95	1	**.382**	.732	270
1994	Billy Ashley, Albuquerque (Pac. Coast)	388	**93**	134	19	4	37	105	6	.345	.701	272
1995	Jose Ibarra, Burlington (Midwest)	437	72	144	30	1	34	96	1	.330	.636	**278**
1996	Lee Stevens, Oklahoma City (Amer. Assn)	431	84	140	**37**	2	32	94	3	.325	.643	277
1997	Paul Konerko, Albuquerque (Pac. Coast)	483	97	156	31	1	37	127	2	.323	.621	300

Bold: Led or tied for league lead in categories other than slugging percentage.

World Series Versus Career Pitching

At World Series time, do pitchers' ERAs fall like the leaves?

Eugene E. Heaton, Jr. and Alan W. Heaton

A previous paper focused on the batting performance of major league baseball players in the World Series, comparing that performance with their career batting records. (See "World Series vs. Career Batting," Baseball Research Journal 26, page 63.)

In brief, the research showed that there is a decline in World Series batting performance (across all levels of Series experience) compared with batters' career results, as measured by the Total Production Average (TPA) and other statistics such as batting and alugging averages. (For detailed information on the TPA, see "Total Production Average," *Baseball Research Journal* 24, page 127.)

This paper presents a similar analysis of how pitchers' World Series performance has compared with their career efforts.

The Research—We studied a total of ninety-two World Series from 1903 through 1996, which included 541 games. (Between 1903 and 1996, there were two years in which there was no World Series: 1904, when John McGraw, the New York Giants manager, refused to play the Boston Pilgrims, and 1994, when a players' strike cut the season short.)

Our data were drawn from the Eighth Edition of the *Baseball Encyclopedia*, for records through 1989, and the Fifth Edition of *Total Baseball*, for data from 1990

to 1996. Career records of some recent World Series performers will therefore be incomplete, though they will include data through 1996.

We classified World Series pitchers into two groups: Group A included those who had pitched the equivalent of a complete (nine-inning) game, or who had appeared in a total of six innings or more in three or more games. Group B includes those who had pitched less than that.

Group A—A total of 378 men pitched the equivalent of a complete game, or an average of two innings in three games. This group was on the mound for the vast majority—an estimated 86 percent—of innings, and were involved in 88 percent of the decisions. Eighty-seven percent of the group—328 pitchers— had one or more decisions.

Group B—There were 391 pitchers who pitched fewer than nine World Series innings, or less than a total of six innings in three or more games.

Of these, only 112 (29 percent) had any World Series decisions. Almost all of these had just one; eleven had two or more, and George Frazier of the 1981 Yankees had three—all defeats—to set a World Series standard for futility among this group.

As another measure of the relative World Series involvement of the two groups, the 378 in Group A pitched an average of 22.1 World Series innings, while those in Group B pitched an average of only 3.3 innings.

Eugene E. Heaton *is a retired market and opinion researcher.*
Alan W. Heaton *is Consumer Research manager at Merck & Co. Both father and son regularly field simulated baseball teams, with all the "ups and downs" that entails.*

Pitchers omitted from the analysis—Seven pitchers were not included in the research, either because they did not retire a batter and did not have a run scored on them, (Howie Krist, 1943 Cardinals, and Joe Klink, 1990 Athletics), or because they accumulated an infinite ERA by having one or more runs scored on them without registering an out (Russ Christopher and Eddie Klieman of the 1948 Indians; Dick Pole, 1975 Red Sox; Art Reinhart, 1926 Cardinals, who also recorded a loss, the only one of this group to do so; and Reb Russell, 1917 White Sox).

In addition, two pitchers who would have fallen into Group A were barred from this analysis, just as they were barred from baseball in 1920, for their role in the notorious Black Sox scandal in the 1919 World Series. (The Chicago hitters who participated in the scandal were similarly omitted from our paper on career vs. World Series batting.)

Claude "Lefty" Williams, who in a career of 189 games achieved an 82-48 record and an ERA of 3.13, lost all three of his starts in the 1919 fix, and in 17.1 innings recorded an ERA of 6.75.

Eddie Cicotte, who had a career record of 208-149, lost two of his three 1919 Series starts, including a 2-0 loss in which Cincinnati scored both their runs on Cicotte errors.

Career versus World Series ERA—For their total careers, the 378 pitchers in Group A had an average earned run average of 3.44. In World Series, they averaged 3.07. (We prefer to use the average of each pitcher's performance, rather than a composite figure representing overall pitching performance.) On this basis, they gave up about 11 percent fewer runs per nine innings than they did in their careers.

Not surprisingly, this figure is very nearly the mirror opposite of the fall-off in productivity found in our previous analysis of batters' career versus World Series performance. Baseball is close to a zero-sum game in the contest between batter and pitcher. If the batter drives in or scores a run, his TPA is enhanced, while the pitcher's ERA is increased (if no error is involved).

The 391 members of Group B compiled an average ERA of 3.72 over their careers—about 8 percent less effective than the members of Group A. In the World Series, however, these pitchers performed atrociously. Their average ERA during the average of 3.3 innings in which they appeared was 6.62.

Just as in the analysis of career versus World Series batting performance, those pitchers who played relatively little (Group B) were much less effective than those who played a reasonable amount (Group A).

The main finding of this analysis, however, is that, compared to the regular season, when the chips are down in World Series competition the edge is with the pitcher over the hitter.

World Series versus Career Effectiveness by era—The figures presented and discussed in this paper are not "contaminated" by changes that have taken place in baseball statistics over time, since in each case a pitcher's World Series record is being compared with his own career record. Nevertheless, it is worth asking whether the overall pattern of about an 11 percent improvement in World Series pitching effectiveness, among the Group A pitchers who accounted for nearly 90 percent of all World Series innings played has held true throughout the years.

To examine this issue, we grouped the World Series into five eras: 1903-20; 1921-40; 1941-60; 1961-80; and 1981-96. These five groupings roughly parallel the Dead Ball Era; the advent of the livelier ball and the emphasis on slugging in the '20s and '30s; the wartime and early postwar years of baseball; the pre-free-agent part of the modern "expansion" era, and the most recent part of the modern era.

In the analysis, we have categorized each of the 378 Group A pitchers into the period in which he pitched most regular-season games.

Results of this analysis by era are shown below.

	# Pitchers	Career ERA	W.S. ERA	Percent Improvement
1903-20	54	2.69	2.18	19%
1921-40	73	3.72	3.03	19%
1941-60	88	3.57	3.29	8%
1961-80	89	3.44	3.07	11%
1981-96	74	3.56	3.50	2%

It is no great surprise that, in the Dead Ball Era (1903-1920), fewer runs were scored in both regular season and World Series competition than in later periods. There are some genuine surprises in the rest of the findings, however.

First, the *career* ERAs of Group A World Series pitchers do not differ much from period to period, from the 1920s on. It may be that these pitchers, the cream of the crop in their respective times, are always going to hold hitters down.

Second, it is evident that pitchers in the early days of the World Series (1903-20 and 1921-40) were extremely dominating, improving their performance by 19 percent in the fall classic, compared to their career performance. In contrast, since 1941, batters and pitchers look more evenly matched, though the edge still has gone to the pitcher. In the most modern period, though, the pitcher's advantage has nearly vanished. Expansion, greater player movement, a (probably) livelier ball, a shrinking strike zone, better scouting, regular study of game videotapes by players, and bigger, stronger batters have closed the gap dramatically.

It will be very interesting to follow the relative performance of pitchers and batters in future World Series, to see whether the trend toward batters "catching up" with pitchers in the tense postseason confrontation continues.

Levels of improvement—Which pitchers improved most during the World Series? To answer this question, we focused on the 104 pitchers who pitched the equivalent of three complete games or more in the Series. Fully 75 percent of this group had a World Series ERA lower than their career ERA.

Among the ten World Series pitchers who showed the most improvement in their ERAs, all shaved 50 percent or more off their career figure. Following are the ten pitchers who improved most.

	Career ERA	W.S. ERA	Percent Improvement
Monte Pearson	4.00	1.01	75%
Sherry Smith	3.32	0.89	73%
Harry Brecheen	2.92	0.83	72%
Bill Hallahan	4.03	1.36	66%
Sandy Koufax	2.76	0.95	66%
George Earnshaw	4.38	1.58	64%
Babe Ruth	2.28	0.87	62%
Hippo Vaughn	2.49	1.00	60%
Jesse Haines	3.64	1.67	54%
Rollie Fingers	2.90	1.35	54%

Looking ahead—Based on the results of our two analyses it is clear that over most of modern baseball history pitchers have had an extra edge on batters in the postseason classic. However, the data on more recent World Series suggest that edge has shrunk to the point where World Series pitchers and hitters are performing very similarly to their regular-season records.

As the twenty-first century arrives, it will be intriguing to see whether this recent trend continues, accelerates, or is reversed.

Southern Bans Broadcasting

Broadcasting of the games in the Southern League has been done away with.

The club owners by agreement last week decided that the radio was a hindrance rather than a boon to interest in the game. In the communities where the games were being put on the air it was found that broadcasting was making stay-at-homes of fans who might ordinarily go to the parks, and eating into the attendance figures.

That, gentlemen of the baseball audience, is the story of the radio and baseball in the Southern League which embraces the largest population centers below the Mason and Dixon line, West of Atlanta, Ga., and East of Texas. It is a story that might well be dissected and studied by other leagues where the radio has become a part of the daily baseball menu.

There can be no doubt that sooner or later broadcasting of the games will be found to be a boomerang. It breeds and indolence which keeps fans away from the parks at the slightest provocation and will be found in time to have other drawbacks once started.

The Southern League acted wisely in making a league issue of it, thereby relieving any local strain that might otherwise have developed in throwing the microphones out. It is easy to give the people something for nothing, but not so easy to take it away from them.

A situation in St. Louis, wherein one broadcaster who was shut out of Sportsman's Park because another broadcasting firm paid a sum of money for the exclusive privileges, showed what kind of a situation might arise. This broadcaster inferentially has tried to bring the club into disfavor with the fans.

In San Francisco the club officials recently conducted a test of the effects of broadcasting and the conclusion was that the attendance was off 12 per cent when the games were being put on the air.

Other baseball men may soon be taking stock.

—Joe Murphy, from a *Sporting News* editorial, May 16, 1929

The Intentional Walk

Strategic gem or blunder?

David F. Riggs

Conventional baseball wisdom calls for an intentional walk in several situations. With first base unoccupied a menacing batter is given a free pass to get to an easier opponent, to set up a double play, or to increase the number of options for a force-out. This strategy is used routinely by managers who have divergent approaches to the game. Does it really work?

While baseball's practitioners and commentators have remained faithful to the intentional walk, a few analysts have questioned its practicality. Earnshaw Cook, who collaborated with Wendell R. Garner in the 1960s, employed formulas that applied the laws of chance to the national pastime. Cook went beyond the obvious criticism that the intentional walk gives the opposition baserunners who become potential runs. His calculations showed that the chances were increased for scoring multiple runs, and he believed that a free pass should be issued only to face a significantly weaker hitter in the ninth or extra innings of a close game.[1]

Two decades later John Thorn, Pete Palmer, and David Reuther used computer simulations to reach similar conclusions with a new twist. They reasoned that while an intentional walk never reduces the expected number of runs scored, it can help in late innings to decrease the opposition's chance of winning the game. However, when the eighth hitter in the lineup is walked with two outs and the strategy succeeds by retiring the number nine batter, the opposition's run potential is increased the next inning because the top of the order is coming to the plate.[2]

There is also the psychological element of the intentional base on balls. Is the incentive increased for the batter whom the fielding team prefers to face because he is considered weaker or more apt to hit into a force-out or double play? Is pressure increased on the pitcher who now has the burden of an extra baserunner? Is his control or concentration dulled by tossing four balls so wide of the plate?

But instead of theory, let's consider reality. What has happened on the playing field to suggest the wisdom or folly of intentionally increasing the number of baserunners in order to face the subsequent batter? As a step toward answering that question, I examined fifty years of postwar World Series games. The teams in these contests mastered their leagues with the strategy, physical skills, and tenacity to finish first. They therefore make interesting studies.

What constitutes the "success" or "failure" of an intentional base on balls can be a complex matter in its own right. If the batter who follows the walk makes an out and the next hitter drives in a run, it is fair to argue that the strategy failed by extending the inning and enabling the successful hitter to bat in more favorable circumstances. Conversely, if the batter who follows the walk reaches base but no runs ultimately score, we might consider the walk worthwhile since it bypassed the hitter who was considered more dangerous.

David F. Riggs *is a museum curator with the National Park Service at Colonial National Historical Park, Jamestown, Virginia.*

In this study, "success" and "failure" are defined by the results of the batter who followed the intentional pass. If the batter made an out and no runs scored during his at-bat, I consider the intentional walk a success, with the exception of a sacrifice or sacrifice fly, which can have runner advancement rather than run production as its immediate objective. If the batter reached base by way of a hit, a walk, being hit by the pitcher, or an error, I deem the strategy a failure, whether or not a runner scores on that at-bat. I consider a fielder's choice or a double play a failure for the fielding team if a run scored on the play.

During the period 1946-1996, there were 301 World Series games. Intentional walks were issued 240 times. Ninety were failures and 150 were successes—a success rate of sixty-two percent. Furthermore, eighteen of the successful efforts were double plays, and 109 of the outs were the final out of the inning. Upon scrutiny, though, the positive results were less rewarding.[3]

Intentional Walks Per Inning

Inning	IW	Inning	IW
		1	17
6	34		
2	12	7	34
3	13	8	40
4	20	9	29
5	25	10+	16

Number of Outs When IW Occurred

0	1	2
12	90	138

Runners on Base When IW Occurred

1	2
139	101

Score When IW Occurred

Fielding Team Ahead	Batting Team Ahead	Tied
21	138	81

Almost fifty percent of the intentional walks came in the seventh inning or later. Most of them occurred with two outs, with one runner on base, and with the lead held by the team that was batting. Many free passes occurred with one out, with two runners on base, and with the score tied, but surprisingly few materialized when the fielding team was ahead.

The success rate of sixty-two percent sounds good, since we know a thirty percent rate is great hitting, but remember that we are talking here about the suc-

cess of the fielding team, which means that the offensive team prevails thirty-eight percent of the time—a good offensive rate.

As might be expected when facing quality pitchers, most batting averages are not especially high in the World Series. During the 1946-1996 period, the aggregate batting average was .242. In comparison, the 240 hitters who came to the plate following an intentional walk batted .261—twenty-one points higher. These 240 at bats included fifty by pitchers—clearly good targets for the intentional walk strategy—whose collective batting average was .140. The average for regular position players was .273.

Batters who followed intentional walks produced fifty-five hits and a slugging average of .393. The variety of plate appearances and the run production that resulted in the fielding team's thirty-eight percent failure rate is shown at the top of the next page.

During the fifty-year period of this study there were thirteen grand slams—three of them by batters who followed an intentional pass (Gil McDougald in 1951, Bill Skowron in 1956, and Lonnie Smith in 1992). Bases-loaded homers are an excellent example of how the free pass can prolong an inning and invite further damage. In three other instances the intentional pass was a success and resulted in an out by the next batter, but the following hitter tagged a four-run four-bagger (Chuck Hiller in 1962, pitcher Dave McNally in 1970, and Kent Hrbek in 1987). Therefore, the intentional base on balls set the table for six of these thirteen grand slams.

An astounding number of failed intentional walks resulted in runs scored by the next at-bat, sometimes costing the game. A run scored seventy-one times—a failure rate of thirty percent. Nineteen of these runs decided the game. This means that on 8 percent of the occasions that a free pass was issued in World Series games, the direct result was that the fielding team lost.

Here are just a few games during this period in which the intentional walk played a role in World Series history:

1947 Everyone remembers that Cookie Lavagetto's pinch-hit double in the bottom of the ninth won Game 4 for Brooklyn and was the only hit against the Yankees' Bill Bevens, but it is frequently forgotten that the preceding batter, Pete Reiser, was intentionally walked.

1954 Dusty Rhodes launched the Giants on their surprise sweep of the Indians with a three-run homer in the tenth inning of Game 1 after a free pass to Hank Thompson. Undaunted, Cleveland intention-

Intentional Walks in World Series Games, 1946-1996

Success and Failure

Games	Total IW	Successful	Failed
301	240	150	90

What has happened when the strategy has failed

Home Runs, 4 RBIs	3
Home Runs, 3 RBIs	3
Triples, 3 RBIs	1
Doubles, 3 RBIs	1
Doubles, 2 RBIs	5
Doubles, 1 RBI	2
Singles, 2 RBIs	7
Singles, 1 RBI	29
Singles, 0 RBIs	4
Base on Balls, 1 RBI	4
Base on Balls, 0 RBIs	10
Intentional Walks, 0 RBIs	2
Hit By Pitcher, 0 RBIs	1
Sacrifice Flies, 1 RBI	1
Sacrifice Flies, 0 RBIs	9
Sacrifice and Error, Run Scored	1
Sacrifice, No Runs Scored	1
Fielder's Choice, 1 RBI	2
Error, 2 Runs Scored	1
Error, 1 Run Scored	1
Error, No Runs Scored	1
Double Play, 1 Run Scored	1

ally walked Thompson two games later and Rhodes's heroics continued with a pinch-hit, two-run single.

1956 The Dodgers were down three games to two and attempting to recover from Don Larsen's perfect game of the previous day. With two outs, one runner on, and the game scoreless in the bottom of the tenth, Duke Snider received his second free pass of the day. Jackie Robinson then singled home the winning tally in the last Series game the Dodgers won in Brooklyn.

1967 Leading three games to two and trailing by a mere run in the top of the ninth, the Cardinals passed Rico Petrocelli to load the sacks with Bosox. Elston Howard responded with a single that scored two runs. Roger Maris blasted a bases-empty round tripper in the Cardinals' home half that would have tied the game at 1-1 had it not been for Howard's clutch hit. Fortunately for St. Louis, the Cardinals had Bob Gibson for Game 7.

1969 The Miracle Mets accepted gifts, as demonstrated in Game 4. The score was tied in the bottom of the tenth whÅÚ§...n intentional walk put runners at first and second for pinch hitter J.C. Martin, who bunted. Oriole pitcher Pete Richert fielded the ball,

hit Martin with his throw, and the lead runner scampered home with the winning run and a commanding Series lead of three games to one.

1976 Sparky Anderson's well-oiled machine needed little assistance but received it anyway in Game 2. Joe Morgan's free pass with two outs in the bottom of the ninth merely replaced one superstar with another as Tony Perez's single scored Ken Griffey from second.

1980 Philadelphia lost the opportunity for a lead of three games to none. With a runner on second and two outs in the tenth, George Brett received a complimentary ticket and Willie Aikens did the honors with a game-winning single.

1985 Umpire Don Denkinger's missed call received the spotlight in the Cardinals' loss of Game 6, which St. Louis led, 1-0, in the bottom of that fateful ninth inning. Little is said of Jack Clark misplaying a foul pop one batter later or Darrell Porter's subsequent passed ball, and even less attention is given to the intentional walk Hal McRae received to load the bases. The next batter, Dane Iorg, singled in two runs for the win, and the Redbirds never recovered.

1986 Why should Bill Buckner receive all the blame for Boston's famous tenth-inning loss in Game 6? An intentional pass set the stage in the bottom of the eighth when the Red Sox led, 3-2. With one out and runners on second and third, Keith Hernandez was intentionally sent to first, and Gary Carter drove in the tying run with a sacrifice fly. Two innings later, the Mets staged their famous rally.

1991 Not one but two intentional walks in the tenth inning led to the climactic ending of the scoreless seventh game between the Twins and Braves. Minnesota's leadoff hitter, Dan Gladden, doubled and was sacrificed to third, at which point Kirby Puckett and Kent Hrbek were awarded four balls apiece. With the outfielders drawn in, pinch-hitter Gene Larkin obliged with a shot over their heads. Could Atlanta have done worse facing Puckett and Hrbek?

1996 Five years later, Braves manager Bobby Cox still retained faith in the intentional walk. Atlanta had two wins under its belt, but lost its commanding 6-0 lead over the Yankees in Game 4, going into the tenth inning knotted at six runs apiece. The first two men in pinstripes were retired, but then Tim Raines walked, Derek Jeter singled him to second, and the Braves elected to intentionally walk Bernie Williams and load the bases, even though first base was occupied. Wade Boggs came to the plate, eyed each pitch carefully, and drew a walk, forcing in the lead run. An error produced an insurance run, the Braves lost, 8-6, and Atlanta never had the Series lead for the remainder of the Series.

As one might expect, given the Yankee dynasty, New Yorkers are the record holders for individual intentional walks. Mickey Mantle and Yogi Berra are tied with six each, followed by Joe DiMaggio at five. The Yankee Clipper was so highly respected that he received two free passes in the final game of his career despite batting only .263 during the 1951 season and .261 in the Series. The Giants chose to face rookie Gil McDougald, who followed all three Series intentional walks. In Game 5, he followed Johnny Mize and responded with a grand slam. When he followed DiMaggio in Game 6, he had an RBI sacrifice fly and lined to third. However, the intentional walk paid Yankee dividends even on McDougald's liner as Mize followed him with a walk and Hank Bauer hit a bases-loaded triple. Another example of respect for a batter occurred in 1946, when Rudy York was intentionally walked three times in the same game. The strategy backfired once when Pinky Higgins doubled in a run.

The greatest number of intentional walks in a World Series is thirteen, in both 1946 and 1972. In contrast, six Series have had only one (1957, 1974, 1977, 1978, 1984, 1988). Excluding fall classics where there have been only a few free passes, the Series with the highest success rates have been 1975 (eight, seven successful), 1973 (nine, seven successful), and 1979 and 1991 (ten, seven successful). Uncontested for the highest failure rate is the 1961 World Series, with eight intentional walks—all failures. On eleven occasions there have been two free passes in the same half-inning, of which two were back-to-back.

Managers also are an interesting study. During the period 1946-1996, ten managers appeared in three or more World Series. Tony LaRussa authorized only one intentional walk, so Casey Stengel and Sparky Anderson are better indicators with considerably

above average success rates of 79 percent and 75 percent, respectively.

Manager	Percentage	Total IW	Success	Failure
LaRussa	100	1	1	0
Stengel	79	19	15	4
Anderson	75	12	9	3
Herzog	73	11	8	3
Lasorda	70	10	7	3
Alston	67	12	8	4
Weaver	67	12	8	4
Cox	63	16	10	6
Williams	60	15	9	6
Houk	50	6	3	3

So what conclusions can we draw from this limited study? Analysts can point to numerous success stories, and they can argue that the intentional walk should be used discreetly and only in specific situations. But regardless of the inning, the number of outs, the number of base runners, or the score, the standard failure rate is 38 percent. A manager can expect the offensive team to succeed at the rate of .380, and who can afford to insert Ted Williams into his opponent's lineup!

Notes:

1. Earnshaw Cook, *Percentage Baseball* (Cambridge, Massachusetts: M.I.T. Press, 1964), 90.

2. John Thorn and Pete Palmer, *The Hidden Game of Baseball: A Revolutionary Approach to Baseball and Its Statistics* (Garden City, New York: Doubleday & Co., 1984), 159-60.

3. Statistics and calculations in this and subsequent paragraphs came from numerous sources, including the Macmillan *Baseball Encyclopedia*, Thorn and Palmer's *Total Baseball*, Cohen and Neft's *The World Series*, Sporting News *Official World Series Records*, data provided by Retrosheet courtesy of David W. Smith, and the author's personal scorebooks. Guidance also came from SABR's Baseball Records Committee courtesy of Lyle Spatz and from David P. Mamuscia at the 1997 SABR Convention.

For a complete listing of all World Series intentional walks, 1946-1996, including year, game, inning, outs, runners on base, runs scored by each team before the walk, pitcher, the batter who was walked , the batter the pitcher then faced, and what happened, send a 55-cent SASE to:
SABR Publications Office
P.O. Box 736
Woodbury, CT 06798

Most Valuable Offensive Seasons

A theory of relativity

Joseph D'Aniello

The argument is one generation younger than baseball itself: my heroes are better than your heroes. While growing up, if I said the name Mickey Mantle, my father said Joe DiMaggio. If I said Willie Mays, he said Mel Ott. When Carl Yastrzemski won the triple crown, my father reminded me that Ted Williams won two of them, narrowly missed a third, and batted .406 in another season. My father even called Tom Tresh "Tom Trash."

But baseball statistics must be examined in their context. It's easy to be awed by a .325 season with forty-three home runs and 125 RBIs, but are the statistics truly significant? Take a look at the following pairs of seasons:

	Runs	HR	RBI	BA
Player A	149	47	175	.373
Player B	100	10	109	.354
Player C	89	24	115	.285
Player D	141	36	123	.358
Player E	127	45	128	.323
Player F	121	44	130	.319

In the first pair, Player A, Lou Gehrig in 1927, appears to have buried Player B, Honus Wagner in 1908.

Joe D'Aniello *out-hit Ty Cobb in a little league career that spanned 1965-1971, batting .370 (78 for 211) with six home runs. He lives in Rocky Hill, Connecticut, with wife Ellen, daughter Lisa, and son Michael.*

Yet, relatively speaking, Wagner's 1908 season had slightly more value to his team and league than Gehrig's did in 1927.

In the second example, Player C appears to fall far short of Player D. However, Player C, Gavvy Cravath in 1915, was such a feared righthanded slugger that the Red Sox refused to pitch southpaw Babe Ruth against him in the World Series. Cravath's season in its context had the same value as George Sisler's .407 season in 1920. Player D is Alex Rodriguez in 1996. Great numbers, yes, but only marginally better than the mass of sluggers that 1996 produced. Rodriguez's season had as much value to the Mariners in 1996 as Darryl Strawberry's seemingly modest (101 runs, 39 HR, 101 RBI's .269) 1988 season had to the Mets.

Hank Aaron's 1962 and 1963 seasons comprise Players E and F. The numbers look similar, but in fact his 1963 season is far superior. In 1962, the National League expanded. Pitching faltered. Aaron was the fourth-best offensive threat in the National League behind Frank Robinson, Willie Mays, and Tommy Davis. By 1963, the strike zone had expanded and young pitchers like Sandy Koufax, Juan Marichal, Jim Maloney, and Dick Ellsworth blossomed. Aaron narrowly missed winning the triple crown in 1963. In my study, Aaron's 1962 season wasn't even in the top 100 seasons of all time. His 1963 season, however, ranked thirty-third, between triple crown seasons by Mickey Mantle and Frank Robinson.

This article grabs the bat[on] from Bill Szepanski's

"Best Offensive Statistical Years" (*BRJ* 1996). Szepanski compared the batting statistics of players with bulging stats using eleven categories (runs, hits, 2B, 3B, HR, RBI, W, Avg, OBP, Slugging, SB), to determine percentage values. For example, Hack Wilson's 190 (now 191) RBIs is the major league record. Wilson received 100 points for RBIs (190/190), while Babe Ruth's 1921 season earned 90 points (171/190). The points for the eleven categories were then added together to get a total percentage.

Even before I saw the results of Szepanski's analysis, I knew what to expect: all those monster seasons from the 1920s and 1930s would dominate his results. Sure enough, of the top thirty seasons, only Ty Cobb in 1911, Stan Musial in 1948, and Ted Williams in 1949 broke the 1920-1939 juggernaut. But we know that a hit in 1968, when the major leagues batted .237, had much more value than a hit in 1930, when the two leagues combined for .296. Likewise, a home run today, when a dozen players can blast forty, has less value than a 1945 homer when the major league leader had just twenty-eight. Szepanzki's article sparked my interest. I wanted to know more than which seasons had the greatest *quantity*. I wanted to know which seasons had the greatest *quality*.

Quadruple crown—While Szepanski used eleven categories, I used just four. The question I asked myself is, what is really important in baseball? The answer: winning games. Well, what wins games? Runs. Runs and RBIs are the two statistics that lead to winning games, but certainly other categories are important. Batting average shows a player's ability to hit safely and move runners around. On Base Percentage often parallels batting average, but since nobody with a low batting average and a high OBP (e.g. Eddie Yost) will ever be considered great, and the public has yet to embrace OBP, I went with batting average. I included home runs because they always produce at least one run, they bring a necessary ingredient of intimidation to the game, and people like them.

Adjusted statistics: the George Brett rule—I was nearly a quarter done with my analysis when I realized that I kept seeing a paradox. If two players in the same league with similar statistics in the same season played a different number of games, the player with the fewer games ranked higher. I rationalized by saying, "Well, sure, I'd much rather have a player hit thirty home runs in 120 games than thirty home runs in 162 games because the substitutes for those forty-two games are bound to produce something." Then I

came across George Brett's 1980 season. Brett's career year (.390, twenty-four HR, 118 RBI, eighty-seven runs) was interrupted by forty-five missed games—more than 25 percent of the season. This persuaded me that I had to make an adjustment for players who missed games. Remember, the purpose of this study is to determine which players had the most value to their team and league in a season, and a player who bats .390 over 162 games is certainly more valuable than a player who bats .390 over 117 games.

Typically, when a starter—especially a star—is injured, nobody expects the replacement to perform at the star's level. Under these circumstances, I added to the player's stats the team averages minus the player's statistics. George Brett will serve as the example.

Each team has nine offensive positions. A team that plays 162 games has 1,458 (162 times 9) Man Games. For the Royals in 1980 we have the following stats:

	Man Games	AB	R	Hits	HR	RBI	BA
Royals	1,458	5,704	809	1,633	115	766	.286
Brett	117	449	87	175	24	118	.390
Brett~	1,341	5,255	722	1,458	91	648	.277

Now that we know the "Royals without Brett" (Brett~) statistics, we have to break them down to a per-game basis. If every statistic (except batting average) is divided by Man Games played by Brett~ (1,341), the per-game figures are 3.919 at bats; .5384 runs; 1.0872 hits; .0679 home runs, and .4832 runs batted in. The .277 batting average stands.

The final step in determining Brett's adjusted statistics is to multiply the Brett~ per game statistics by the number of games Brett missed—forty-five. The results are 176 at bats, twenty-four runs, three home runs, and twenty-two runs batted in. We add these totals to his statistics to find his true value to the team in 1980.

	Man Games	AB	R	HR	RBI	BA
Brett	117	449	87	24	118	.390
Brett~	45	176	24	3	22	.277
Adjusted	162	645	111	27	140	.358

Recognize that these adjusted statistics do not represent what Brett would have done in 162 games. They represent the value that his 117-game season had to his team that year normalized to 162 games. While it's not as impressive as .390, it's still better than Cecil Cooper's adjusted statistics of 101 runs, twenty-six HR, 126 RBIs, .347 batting average. Despite missing forty-five games, Brett was still the most potent offensive force in the American League in 1980, and given that he led the Royals to a pennant, his MVP award was more than justified.

Relativity—Once we compare the adjusted figures of the Quadruple Crown against the league averages, we assign players a set of relative numbers. We determine league averages by dividing the statistic in question (other than batting average) by the number of lineup positions in the league, which is nine times the number of teams in the league. In Brett's case, the AL's twelve teams in 1980 scored 10,201 runs, so the average lineup position scored 87.457 runs (10,201 divided by the product of twelve times nine. To get Brett's relative run ratio, we divide his adjusted runs (111.23) by 87.457. The result is 1.3739. We treat RBIs the same way (for Brett, 139.74 divided by 75.98, or 1.8391). Batting average is easier—just divide Brett's adjusted average .358 by the league average of .269, which gives him a relative batting average of 1.332. A relative average of one indicates a player who performed at the league average.

Home runs—Home runs presented a special case. Runs, RBIs, and batting average have had stable fluctuations throughout baseball history. That is, no player has ever batted twice as high as the league average or been 2-1/2 times better than the league average in runs or runs batted in. Since World War II, though, the home run leader has usually had three to four times the league average. Before 1945 and especially between 1900 and 1930, the relative numbers were all over the place.

For home runs, I had to give precedence to common sense over relative numbers. Otherwise I would be forced to deem Harry Davis's eight homers in 1905 (relative HR rating of 3.704) nearly as valuable as Mark McGwire's seventy in 1998 (3.991). When Babe Ruth first came along, his relative number soared into double digits (10.651) in 1920. While his fifty-four home runs in 1920 had more value than Mark McGwire's seventy in 1998, it didn't have 2-1/2 times the value. Relativity is significant, but its raw form needed an adjustment.

When I plotted the values of batting average, runs, and RBIs, I got a normal bell curve. That is, most of the players were bunched near the midpoint. For home runs, the bell curve peaked, not at the midpoint, but at the base 10 logarithm.[1] That is, home run relativity didn't increase in a linear manner like runs, RBIs, and batting average. It increased exponentially. The solution was to use the base 10 logarithm of the relative number. While the formula for Runs, RBIs, and batting average is Adjusted / League Average, the Relative Home Runs Logarithm (HR-L) is calculated like this:

HR-L = Logarithm(Adjusted HR / League Average HR)

It should also be noted that unlike the other categories, where a value of one means the player batted at the league average, in this logarithmic calculation, a HR-L value of zero indicates the league average. This is because the log of one is zero.

Back to George Brett and his 27.05 Adjusted Home Runs. The league average was 14.63. First, divide 27.05 by 14.63 to get 1.8489. Brett's HR-L, the logarithm of 1.8489, is .2669 (i.e. $10^{.2669}$ = 1.8489). Ruth in 1920 had a HR-L of 1.027 based on the logarithm of his adjusted home runs of 54.59 divided by the league average of 5.13. Using this calculation, Ruth's fifty-four home runs in 1920 were 1.71 times as valuable as McGwire's seventy home runs in 1998.

Still, no matter how I tweaked the relative number, Harry Davis still nipped at Mark McGwire's cleats. I needed another calculation. So in addition to the logarithm of relative home runs, I also weighed the home run differential—the difference between the player's adjusted home run amount and the league average home run amount.

But now the pendulum swung toward the modern players, leaving the Dead Ball sluggers in the diamond dust. To compensate, I added a Dead Ball adjustment. Since Babe Ruth's twenty-nine home runs in 1919 were approximately half (at least it was before 1998) the record total of the subsequent years, I used a 2-1 differential adjustment for pre-1920 hitters.

Finally, since home run differential is affected by the number of games played (relative numbers are not), I adjusted the differential based on a 162-game season. It would have been unfair to penalize Mike Schmidt's 1981 home run differential of a relatively modest 24.6 because of a player strike.

Here is the formula for Home Run Differential (HR-D):

HR-D = ((Adj HR-League Avg HR) x Dead Ball factor x (162/Team Games)

Compare the home run differentials for both Brett in 1980 and Gavvy Cravath in 1915. Both players hit twenty-four home runs, and although Brett's adjusted home runs are higher, Cravath's differential (HR-D) had almost a four-fold increase over Brett's.

G.Brett's HR-D = ((27.05-14.63) x 1 x (162/162) = 12.42

Cravath's HR-D = ((24.08-3.13) x 2 x (162/153) = 44.38

Cravath's HR-D, which puts him in the Babe Ruth category where he belongs, means that had he played a 162-game season in the lively ball era, he would have hit 44.38 more home runs than the average player.

Normalization—Based on the player's relative numbers, he is awarded a maximum of 250 points in each of the four quadruple crown categories with home runs being split between HR-L and HR-D. The player with the all-time highest relative number in a category gets 250 points (125 for the two home run categories). The player at the league average gets no points (if the relative number was below the league average, then he gets negative points). For example, since Ty Cobb's 1909 .375 adjusted batting average (.377 actual) gave him the highest relative batting average of 1.54, he gets 250 points for Normalized Batting Average.

The formula for Normalized Value—for batting average, runs and RBIs—is as follows:

(Player's Relative Number - 1) / (Best Player's Relative Number - 1) x 250

For George Brett, whose adjusted batting average of .358 was 1.332 times the league average of .269, the formula is:

(1.332 - 1) / (1.540 - 1) x 250 = 154

If Brett had been able extend his .390 batting average over 162 games, his normalized points for batting average would have jumped from 154 to 207. The other relative highs used for normalization are Runs 2.106 (Ty Cobb, 1915); HR-L 1.0274 (Babe Ruth, 1920); HR-D 60.382 (Babe Ruth, 1919), and RBI 2.348 (Honus Wagner, 1908).

Two calculations are required for Home Run normalization:

1) Normalized HR-L = HR-L / 1.02740668998 * 125

2) Normalized HR-D = HR-D / 60.3824329058 * 125

For George Brett, his normalized home run total becomes:

Normalized HR-L = .2669 / 1.0274 [Babe Ruth in 1920] x 125 = 32.4

Normalized HR-D = 12.42 / 60.382 [Babe Ruth in 1919] x 125 = 25.7

At last, George Brett's normalized figures are Runs 84, HR-L 32, HR-D 26, RBIs 156, and batting average 154 for a total of 452, slightly below Jose Canseco's 40-40 MVP season in 1988.

1998 Crop—Between 1920 and 1994, fifty or more home runs had been hit eighteen times, or about once every four seasons. Since 1995, it has been done nine times, and this excessiveness does diminish the historic totals of McGwire and Sammy Sosa a bit. McGwire's seventy home runs were four times and fifty-three more than the league average. Roger Maris's sixty-one home runs were 3-1/2 times and only forty-three more than the league average. In every way—quantity and quality—McGwire passed Maris. In quality, McGwire had the best home run season since Jimmie Foxx hit fifty-eight in 1932. Foxx hit six times as many home runs and fifty more than the average player (based on 162 games). Foxx totaled 199 normalized home run points, McGwire 183, Sosa 170, and Maris 159.

Overall, Sosa had the best offensive season in 1998, rating 50th all-time. McGwire ranked 70th. No other 1998 player made it into my top 200.

Results—Whereas Szepanski's top thirty had one player from 1901 through 1919, twenty-seven players from 1920 through 1939, and two from the 1940s, my top thirty was spread out a bit more: ten before 1920, twelve from 1920 through 1939, five from 1940 through 1959, one from 1960 through 1979, and two from 1980 through 1998.

It makes sense that most of the greatest relative seasons came from the first four decades. As baseball has evolved, the difference between the best and worst players has grown closer to the mean.

And the winner is—Ty Cobb's 1909 edged Szepanski's winner, Babe Ruth's 1921, 830.52 to 819.11. Ironically, Cobb's 1909 failed to make Szepanski's top thirty. But Ruth fans need not despair. In addition to second place, the Babe also captured third, fourth, thirteenth, fourteenth, fifteenth, eighteenth, twentieth, forty-third, forty-fourth and fourty-eighth. The biggest decline from Szepanski's top thirty was Lou Gehrig's 1937, twenty-eighth in Szepanski's study, but 103rd in mine. Here is my all-time Most Valuable Offensive Seasons lineup:

		Normalized best	Seasons in top 100
1b	Lou Gehrig	746	6
2b	Rogers Hornsby	666	6
ss	Honus Wagner	757	3
3b	Mike Schmidt	642	1
of	Ted Williams	740	6
of	Ty Cobb	831	10
of	Babe Ruth	819	11
c	Too close to call between Bench, Campanella and Piazza.		

Fun stuff—Now that I had a normalized number, I could play a little bit. I wondered where Brett would rank if he had been able to stretch his torrid hitting over the entire 1980 season. I divided his team's games (162) by his games (117) and multiplied his stats (save batting average) by the quotient (1.3846). This time Brett had 609 points, which would have placed him in thirty-ninth place all-time.

Larry Walker of the 1997 Colorado Rockies finished in thirty-eighth place with 612 points, based on his 143 runs, 49 home runs, 130 RBIs, and .366 batting average. What would he have needed to place first? This would have done it: 166 runs, 61 home runs, 166 RBIs, and .400 batting average.

I could also see how some of our famous sluggers performed in their final, usually dismal, seasons. Mickey Mantle didn't do too badly, with an above-average 68. But Willie Mays had -111 and Hank Aaron had -79. I checked out the dreaded Mendoza line. In 1979, Mario Mendoza played 148 games and batted .198, good (!) for -476 points. Only Dal Maxvill's -469 points in 1970 approached Mendoza's level of ignominy.

Finally, what would it have taken in super offensive 1930 and pitching-dominated 1968 to have the all-time most valuable seasons?

	Runs	HR	RBI	BA
1930 NL	180	61	206	.442
1968 AL	121	46	133	.343

It's all relative.

Missing pieces—After completing this study, I wondered if any player was unfairly penalized by my system. I was concerned, for example, that the study was dependent on lineup position, and that certain players might be penalized for batting outside the meat of the order where they would have maximum opportunities to knock in runs.

Rickey Henderson is such a player. His batting average and power figures are very good, his runs scored outstanding, but his RBI totals are low because he bats leadoff. Yet, unlike Pete Rose, Lou Brock, or Maury Wills, Henderson would have performed splendidly in the middle of the lineup. Henderson's best offensive season, 1985, netted him just 338.55 points. My apologies to Mr. Henderson.

I also left ballpark fluctuations out. *Total Baseball* says "The computation for PF [Park Factor] is admittedly daunting …," and after a full page of calculations in six-point type, I had to agree. I also must say that I disagree with the spirit of the *Total Baseball* formulas, which suggest that a ballpark like the old Fulton County Stadium in Atlanta can change from a hitter's park to a pitcher's park. In Fulton's case, I'm inclined to give more credit to Greg Maddux, Tom Glavine, and John Smoltz than I am to the ballpark. Players change, but absent significant modifications, parks are constants. However, since nearly every hitter who goes to Colorado turns in a career year, I do have to acknowledge the presence of ballpark factor even if I can't determine its significance.

Final word—I'll have to call it a draw with my father. Mays was better than Ott (Mays had four seasons better than Ott's best), Williams easily bested Yaz, and DiMaggio and Mantle were about even. But I don't have time to worry about those guys. I have to set my kids straight. They think that Ken Griffey Jr., Frank Thomas, and Mike Pizza [sic] are better than Hank Aaron, Mike Schmidt and Johnny Bench. Now I know better.

Table keys—In the tables on the next few pages, TG = team games, NP = normalized points, and Sz = Bill Szepanski's rankings.

Sources:

Total Baseball, Fifth Edition, John Thorn, Pete Palmer, Michael Gershman and David Pietrusza, 1997.

The Sports Encyclopedia Baseball, Neft & Cohen 1993.

Sporting News Baseball Guide, The Sporting News, various years 1941-1998.

USA Today, September 29-30, 1998.

Note:

1. The base 10 logarithm is 10 raised to the x power will give you y. Since $10^2 = 100$, then the log off 100 is 2. Also, the log of 10 is 1, the log of 3.162 (square root of 10) is .5, and the log of 1 is 0.

Greatest Seasons—Relatively Speaking

				Player Stats							Adjusted				Relative					Normalized						
Player	Yr	Lg	G	AB	R	H	HR	RBI	BA	TG	R	HR	RBI	BA	R	HR-L	HR-D	RBI	BA	R	HR-L	HR-D	RBI	BA	NP	Sz
1 Cobb	1909	AL	156	573	116	216	9	107	.377	158	117	9	108	.375	1.973	.775	15.4	2.264	1.540	220	94	32	234	250	830.52	
2 Ruth	1921	AL	152	540	177	204	59	171	.378	153	178	59	172	.377	2.029	.950	55.5	2.195	1.290	233	116	115	222	134	819.11	1
3 Ruth	1920	AL	142	458	158	172	54	137	.376	154	165	55	143	.367	2.019	1.027	52.0	2.001	1.296	230	125	108	186	137	785.79	4
4 Ruth	1927	AL	151	540	158	192	60	164	.356	155	161	60	166	.354	1.898	.995	56.7	2.155	1.241	203	121	117	214	111	767.11	6
5 Wagner	1908	NL	151	568	100	201	10	109	.354	155	102	10	110	.351	1.767	.680	16.6	2.348	1.468	173	83	34	250	217	757.27	
6 Gehrig	1927	AL	155	584	149	218	47	175	.373	155	149	47	175	.373	1.760	.887	42.8	2.267	1.308	172	108	89	235	142	745.75	2
7 T. Williams	1942	AL	150	522	141	186	36	137	.356	152	142	36	138	.355	1.962	.688	30.6	2.070	1.382	217	84	63	199	177	739.87	
8 Lajoie	1901	AL	131	544	145	232	14	125	.426	137	149	14	128	.420	1.821	.649	25.9	1.922	1.516	186	79	54	171	239	728.14	
9 Cobb	1911	AL	146	591	147	248	8	127	.420	154	151	8	130	.412	1.927	.471	11.3	2.031	1.509	209	57	24	191	236	717.46	10
10 T. Williams	1946	AL	150	514	142	176	38	123	.342	156	145	38	126	.339	2.074	.626	30.4	1.950	1.328	243	76	63	176	152	710.13	
11 Bagwell	1994	NL	110	400	104	147	39	116	.368	115	107	39	118	.363	1.811	.511	38.4	2.141	1.361	183	62	80	212	167	703.93	
12 Gehrig	1931	AL	155	619	163	211	46	184	.341	155	163	46	184	.341	1.847	.760	39.7	2.255	1.225	191	92	82	233	104	703.05	7
13 Ruth	1931	AL	145	534	149	199	46	163	.373	155	156	47	170	.367	1.771	.768	40.6	2.079	1.320	174	93	84	200	148	700.16	22
14 Ruth	1923	AL	152	522	151	205	41	131	.393	152	151	41	131	.393	1.847	.825	37.2	1.792	1.391	191	100	77	147	181	696.81	3
15 Ruth	1926	AL	152	495	139	184	47	145	.372	155	141	47	147	.370	1.737	.904	43.2	1.995	1.315	167	110	89	185	146	696.50	18
16 Foxx	1932	AL	154	585	151	213	58	169	.364	154	151	58	169	.364	1.689	.771	50.7	2.030	1.316	156	94	105	191	146	691.97	8
17 T. Williams	1949	AL	155	566	150	194	43	159	.343	155	150	43	159	.343	1.870	.605	33.8	2.126	1.303	197	74	70	209	140	689.44	19
18 Ruth	1919	AL	130	432	103	139	29	114	.322	138	106	29	117	.318	1.669	.940	60.3	2.117	1.186	151	114	125	207	86	683.97	
19 Cobb	1910	AL	140	508	106	194	8	91	.382	155	113	8	96	.369	1.777	.605	12.9	1.898	1.518	176	74	27	167	240	682.32	
20 Ruth	1928	AL	154	536	163	173	54	142	.323	154	163	54	142	.323	1.997	.906	49.7	1.894	1.149	225	110	103	166	69	673.56	24
21 Hornsby	1922	NL	154	623	141	250	42	152	.401	154	141	42	152	.401	1.639	.756	36.4	1.975	1.373	144	92	75	181	173	665.77	9
22 Cobb	1917	AL	152	588	107	225	6	102	.383	154	108	6	103	.381	1.711	.514	8.8	1.941	1.537	161	63	18	175	249	664.82	
23 F. Baker	1913	AL	149	564	116	190	12	117	.337	153	118	12	119	.335	1.765	.738	20.9	2.147	1.310	173	90	43	213	144	662.38	
24 Musial	1948	NL	155	611	135	230	39	131	.376	155	135	39	131	.376	1.771	.522	28.5	1.853	1.443	174	63	59	158	205	660.45	21
25 Cobb	1907	AL	150	605	97	212	5	119	.350	153	98	5	120	.349	1.572	.541	7.6	2.341	1.409	129	66	16	249	189	648.88	
26 T. Williams	1941	AL	143	456	135	185	37	120	.406	155	142	38	127	.395	1.732	.570	28.9	1.668	1.484	165	69	60	124	224	642.50	
27 M. Schmidt	1981	NL	102	354	78	112	31	91	.316	107	80	31	93	.314	1.725	.671	37.2	2.145	1.231	164	82	77	212	107	641.81	
28 Yastrzemski	1967	AL	161	579	112	189	44	121	.326	162	112	44	121	.326	1.689	.520	30.8	1.975	1.383	156	63	64	181	178	641.37	
29 Lajoie,	1904	AL	140	554	92	211	6	102	.381	154	98	6	107	.369	1.596	.459	8.6	2.048	1.508	135	56	18	194	235	637.93	
30 Foxx	1933	AL	149	573	125	204	48	163	.356	152	127	48	165	.354	1.502	.757	42.4	2.097	1.300	113	92	88	204	139	635.94	30
31 Mantle	1956	AL	150	533	132	188	52	130	.353	154	134	52	132	.350	1.680	.546	39.5	1.762	1.415	154	66	82	141	192	635.82	
32 Cobb	1915	AL	156	563	144	208	3	99	.369	156	144	3	99	.369	2.106	.130	1.6	1.747	1.488	250	16	3	139	226	634.11	
33 Aaron	1963	NL	161	631	121	201	44	130	.319	163	122	44	131	.318	1.774	.515	30.5	2.056	1.295	175	63	63	196	137	633.32	
34 A. Simmons	1930	AL	138	554	152	211	36	165	.381	154	162	37	174	.371	1.751	.599	29.2	2.039	1.289	170	73	61	193	134	629.82	
35 Klein	1932	NL	154	650	152	226	38	137	.348	154	152	38	137	.348	1.927	.624	30.5	1.866	1.258	209	76	63	161	120	628.86	26
36 F. Robinson	1966	AL	155	576	122	182	49	122	.316	160	124	49	124	.314	1.785	.514	34.8	1.916	1.306	177	62	72	170	142	623.26	
37 Hornsby	1925	NL	138	504	133	203	39	143	.403	153	141	40	150	.392	1.644	.654	32.8	1.922	1.343	145	80	68	171	159	622.92	25
38 L. Walker	1997	NL	153	568	143	208	49	130	.366	162	148	50	135	.361	1.791	.467	33.1	1.724	1.374	179	57	69	134	173	611.77	
39 Gehrig	1930	AL	154	581	143	220	41	174	.379	143	143	41	174	.379	1.544	.642	33.3	2.035	1.316	123	78	69	192	146	608.34	5
40 Gehrig	1934	AL	154	579	128	210	49	165	.363	154	128	49	165	.363	1.462	.710	41.5	2.026	1.301	104	86	86	190	139	606.41	20
41 J. DiMaggio	1937	AL	151	621	151	215	46	167	.346	157	155	47	171	.344	1.715	.619	36.5	2.025	1.221	162	75	76	190	103	605.43	29
42 Medwick	1937	NL	156	633	111	237	31	154	.374	156	111	31	154	.374	1.436	.554	23.2	2.156	1.378	98	67	48	215	175	603.46	
43 Ruth	1924	AL	153	529	143	200	46	121	.378	153	143	46	121	.378	1.677	.921	42.9	1.579	1.305	153	112	89	107	141	602.23	14
44 Ruth	1930	AL	145	518	150	186	49	153	.359	157	157	50	159	.356	1.691	.726	42.5	1.860	1.237	156	88	88	159	110	601.62	16
45 Wagner	1907	NL	142	515	98	180	6	82	.350	157	104	6	87	.339	1.794	.497	8.7	1.846	1.396	179	60	18	157	183	598.12	
46 Gehrig	1928	AL	154	562	139	210	27	142	.374	154	139	27	142	.374	1.703	.605	21.3	1.894	1.330	159	74	44	166	153	595.60	
47 Seymour	1905	NL	149	581	95	219	8	121	.377	155	98	8	123	.372	1.387	.505	11.6	2.130	1.459	87	61	24	210	213	595.51	
48 Ruth	1929	AL	135	499	121	172	46	154	.345	154	133	47	164	.338	1.558	.759	41.2	2.091	1.190	126	92	85	202	88	594.41	

#	Name	Year	Lg																											
49	Cravath	1915	NL	150	522	89	149	24	115	.285	153	90	24	116	.285	1.437	.887	44.4	2.202	1.148	99	108	92	223	68	589.79	
50	Sosa	1998	NL	159	643	134	198	66	158	.308	163	136	66	160	.307	1.643	.573	48.4	2.036	1.172	145	70	100	192	80	587.15	
51	G. Sisler	1920	AL	154	631	137	257	19	122	.407	154	137	19	122	.407	1.681	.569	14.6	1.709	1.437	154	69	30	132	202	587.06	27
52	Foxx	1938	AL	149	565	139	197	50	175	.349	150	140	50	176	.348	1.528	.620	41.1	2.039	1.240	119	75	85	193	111	583.80	17
53	Speaker	1912	AL	153	580	136	222	10	90	.383	154	137	10	90	.382	1.789	.665	16.5	1.452	1.443	178	81	34	84	205	582.29	
54	Klein	1933	NL	152	606	101	223	28	120	.368	152	101	28	120	.368	1.482	.642	23.0	1.897	1.382	109	78	48	166	177	578.00	
55	K. Williams	1922	AL	153	585	128	194	39	155	.332	154	129	39	156	.331	1.579	.729	33.4	2.136	1.164	131	89	69	211	76	575.27	
56	T. Williams	1947	AL	156	528	125	181	32	114	.343	157	125	32	114	.342	1.750	.531	23.3	1.714	1.339	170	65	48	132	157	571.96	
57	Allen	1972	AL	148	506	90	156	37	113	.308	154	92	37	115	.305	1.548	.536	27.8	2.062	1.277	124	65	58	197	128	571.90	
58	Cobb	1908	AL	150	581	88	188	4	108	.324	153	89	4	109	.322	1.502	.399	5.1	2.281	1.349	113	49	11	238	162	571.70	
59	Foster	1977	NL	158	615	124	197	52	149	.320	162	126	52	151	.319	1.592	.540	37.3	2.040	1.218	134	66	77	193	101	570.80	
60	Wilson	1930	NL	155	585	146	208	56	190	.356	156	147	56	191	.355	1.503	.656	45.4	2.085	1.170	114	80	94	201	79	567.82	11
61	Hornsby	1921	NL	154	592	131	235	21	126	.397	154	131	21	126	.397	1.675	.517	15.4	1.793	1.371	152	63	32	147	172	566.34	
62	Hornsby	1929	NL	156	602	156	229	39	149	.380	156	156	39	149	.380	1.700	.571	29.6	1.750	1.292	158	69	61	139	135	563.35	23
63	Rosen	1953	AL	155	599	115	201	43	145	.336	155	115	43	145	.336	1.502	.547	32.2	2.009	1.279	113	67	67	187	129	562.88	
64	Stargell	1971	NL	141	511	104	151	48	125	.295	162	115	50	135	.292	1.633	.590	36.9	2.056	1.162	143	72	77	196	75	562.05	
65	Wagner	1909	NL	137	495	92	168	5	100	.339	154	100	5	107	.330	1.590	.403	6.7	2.073	1.353	133	49	14	199	163	558.67	
66	Greenberg	1937	AL	154	594	137	200	40	183	.337	155	138	40	184	.336	1.524	.554	30.2	2.179	1.196	118	67	63	219	91	557.88	15
67	Mize	1947	NL	154	586	137	177	51	138	.302	155	138	51	139	.302	1.748	.619	40.6	1.885	1.137	169	75	84	164	63	555.97	
68	Gehrig	1936	AL	155	579	167	205	49	152	.354	155	167	49	152	.354	1.716	.668	40.2	1.679	1.224	162	81	83	126	104	555.78	12
69	Musial	1946	NL	156	624	124	228	16	103	.365	156	124	16	103	.365	1.816	.312	8.5	1.630	1.429	184	38	18	117	199	555.58	
70	McGwire	1998	NL	155	509	130	152	70	147	.299	162	134	71	150	.297	1.613	.601	53.1	1.914	1.134	138	73	110	170	62	553.22	
71	J. Torre	1971	NL	161	634	97	230	24	137	.363	163	98	24	138	.362	1.392	.276	11.3	2.101	1.436	89	34	23	204	202	551.97	
72	B. Williams	1972	NL	150	574	95	191	37	122	.333	156	98	37	124	.329	1.454	.474	25.8	1.999	1.326	103	58	54	185	151	550.04	
73	Burkett	1901	NL	142	601	142	226	10	75	.376	142	142	10	75	.376	1.968	.501	15.6	1.243	1.409	219	61	32	45	190	546.94	
74	Klein	1930	NL	156	648	158	250	40	170	.386	156	158	40	170	.386	1.619	.509	28.7	1.860	1.271	140	62	59	159	126	546.43	13
75	Aaron	1971	NL	139	495	95	162	47	118	.327	162	105	49	126	.316	1.486	.583	36.1	1.926	1.257	110	71	75	172	119	546.10	
76	A. Simmons	1929	AL	143	581	114	212	34	157	.365	151	119	35	162	.361	1.398	.622	28.2	2.057	1.271	90	76	58	196	125	545.45	
77	T. Williams	1948	AL	137	509	124	188	25	127	.369	155	135	26	137	.357	1.667	.427	17.3	1.798	1.343	151	52	36	148	159	545.31	
78	Mays	1965	NL	157	558	118	177	52	112	.317	163	121	52	114	.315	1.655	.554	37.6	1.696	1.263	148	67	78	129	122	544.15	
79	Rice	1978	AL	163	677	121	213	46	139	.315	163	121	46	139	.315	1.603	.538	32.5	1.971	1.205	136	65	67	180	95	544.01	
80	Greenberg	1940	AL	148	573	129	195	41	150	.340	155	133	42	154	.338	1.561	.530	30.6	1.946	1.244	127	64	63	175	113	543.01	
81	Hornsby	1924	NL	143	536	121	227	25	94	.424	154	126	25	99	.413	1.632	.564	19.4	1.408	1.459	143	69	40	76	213	540.13	
82	Mantle	1961	AL	153	514	132	163	54	128	.317	163	137	55	133	.313	1.683	.512	38.1	1.749	1.226	154	62	79	139	105	539.32	
83	Cobb	1912	AL	140	553	119	227	7	83	.410	153	126	7	88	.396	1.648	.518	10.5	1.420	1.495	146	63	22	78	229	538.32	
84	F. Robinson	1962	NL	162	609	134	208	39	136	.342	162	134	39	136	.342	1.657	.384	22.9	1.811	1.310	148	47	47	150	144	536.82	
85	Hornsby	1927	NL	155	568	133	205	26	125	.361	155	133	26	125	.361	1.695	.588	20.2	1.734	1.280	157	72	42	136	130	536.50	
86	Cobb	1918	AL	111	421	83	161	3	64	.382	128	89	3	69	.363	1.738	.375	4.6	1.608	1.431	167	46	10	113	200	534.38	
87	Cash	1961	AL	159	535	119	193	41	132	.361	163	121	41	134	.358	1.486	.386	24.2	1.762	1.401	110	47	50	141	186	534.11	
88	Cravath	1913	NL	147	525	78	179	19	128	.341	159	84	20	132	.335	1.173	.656	31.0	2.183	1.278	39	80	64	219	129	531.38	
89	Clemente	1967	NL	147	585	103	209	23	110	.357	163	110	24	116	.348	1.592	.289	11.5	1.823	1.400	134	35	24	153	185	530.69	
90	Speaker	1923	AL	150	574	133	218	17	130	.380	153	135	17	132	.378	1.649	.445	11.6	1.801	1.339	147	54	24	149	157	530.65	
91	Crawford	1908	AL	152	591	102	184	7	80	.311	153	102	7	80	.311	1.722	.639	11.4	1.681	1.301	163	78	24	126	140	530.54	
92	Mize	1940	NL	155	579	111	182	43	137	.314	156	112	43	137	.314	1.481	.654	34.8	1.976	1.192	109	80	72	181	89	530.19	
93	Magee	1910	NL	154	519	110	172	6	123	.331	157	111	6	124	.330	1.601	.308	6.3	2.128	1.290	136	37	13	209	134	529.97	
94	Cobb	1916	AL	145	542	113	201	5	68	.371	155	117	5	72	.363	1.839	.406	6.5	1.338	1.462	190	49	13	63	214	529.06	
95	Mantle	1957	AL	144	474	121	173	34	94	.365	154	126	35	99	.358	1.739	.390	21.7	1.440	1.405	167	47	45	82	187	528.62	
96	Holmes	1945	NL	154	636	125	224	28	117	.352	154	125	28	117	.352	1.633	.543	21.0	1.658	1.330	143	66	44	122	153	527.38	
97	McCovey	1969	NL	149	491	101	157	45	126	.320	162	107	46	131	.313	1.466	.528	32.3	1.943	1.250	105	64	67	175	116	527.10	
98	J. Morgan	1976	NL	141	472	113	151	27	111	.320	162	125	29	122	.314	1.743	.447	18.5	1.836	1.233	168	54	38	155	108	523.48	
99	J. DiMaggio	1941	AL	139	541	122	193	30	125	.357	156	132	32	134	.346	1.604	.492	22.3	1.762	1.299	137	60	46	141	138	522.33	
100	Aaron	1959	NL	154	629	116	223	39	123	.355	157	117	39	124	.353	1.548	.388	24.0	1.739	1.355	124	47	50	137	164	522.28	

Best Seasons of Other Players

Player	Yr	NP	Player	Yr	NP	Player	Yr	NP
B. Anderson	1996	259.62	Goslin	1924	310.75	Parker	1978	491.01
Averill	1931	488.91	Griffey Jr.	1997	435.09	Perez	1970	417.96
Geo. Bell	1987	359.26	Groh	1919	320.63	Piazza	1997	447.39
Belle	1994	477.80	Gywnn	1997	350.19	Pinson	1963	385.03
Bench	1972	433.79	Hartnett	1930	240.64	Powell	1969	400.67
Berra	1954	365.73	Heilmann	1923	513.75	Puckett	1988	435.47
Bichette	1995	500.72	Henderson	1985	338.55	Raines	1987	272.68
Boggs	1987	280.51	Babe Herman	1930	425.39	Reiser	1941	402.62
Br. Bonds	1993	504.71	Billy Herman	1935	198.87	Ripken Jr.	1991	334.63
Bonilla	1990	365.51	C. Hickman	1903	456.55	Rizzuto	1950	106.01
Bonura	1936	238.47	Hodges	1954	401.46	B. Robinson	1964	338.03
Bottomley	1928	478.15	E. Howard	1963	246.54	J. Robinson	1949	413.65
Boudreau	1948	384.41	F. Howard	1969	454.72	A. Rodriguez	1996	394.75
Brett	1980	452.16	J. Jackson	1911	496.46	Rose	1968	304.79
Brock	1967	324.62	R. Jackson	1969	491.83	Roush	1918	382.25
Burks	1996	519.82	Jensen	1958	336.46	Sandberg	1990	409.62
Burroughs	1974	324.24	B. Johnson	1944	451.91	Sauer	1952	357.24
Camilli	1941	405.23	H. Johnson	1991	369.57	Santo	1964	382.49
Caminiti	1996	417.80	Kaline	1955	430.19	Sosa	1998	481.28
Campanella	1953	433.78	Kauff	1914	505.88	Sheffield	1992	424.76
Canseco	1988	455.15	Killebrew	1969	481.74	Sierra	1989	341.69
Carew	1977	400.86	Kiner	1947	498.55	Snider	1954	510.76
Cepeda	1961	469.02	Kingman	1979	408.77	T. Simmons	1975	286.82
Cochrane	1930	228.91	Kluszewski	1954	495.94	V. Stephens	1949	478.77
Colavito	1961	458.33	Kuenn	1959	254.09	R. Stephenson	1929	257.18
E. Collins	1914	511.89	Lazzeri	1929	308.48	Strawberry	1988	382.29
R. Collins	1934	457.11	Lombardi	1938	270.42	Terry	1930	377.32
C. Cooper	1980	368.56	Luzinski	1975	387.00	Thomas	1994	511.00
Cronin	1930	290.60	Lynn	1979	428.76	Traynor	1923	253.00
Cuyler	1925	369.57	Magee	1914	511.34	Trosky	1936	449.31
H. Davis	1906	506.13	Manush	1928	352.15	A. Vaughan	1935	402.60
T. Davis	1962	506.85	Maris	1961	489.57	M. Vaughn	1996	319.68
Dawson	1987	364.11	E. Mathews	1953	400.53	P. Waner	1928	327.94
E. Delahanty	1902	455.23	Mattingly	1985	421.66	Wheat	1916	345.95
Dickey	1936	346.70	McCormick	1939	376.76	B. Williams	1970	510.66
Doby	1954	363.52	McGriff	1994	425.57	C. Williams	1920	313.62
Dougherty	1903	349.58	McGwire	1998	450.96	M. Williams	1994	326.06
Dropo	1950	422.68	Meusel	1921	337.00	Wills	1962	155.70
Fielder	1990	413.70	K. Mitchell	1989	482.50	Winfield	1979	367.26
Fisk	1977	291.58	Munson	1976	273.15	York	1943	442.24
Freeman	1903	408.60	Murcer	1971	406.54	Yount	1982	420.77
Frisch	1923	319.24	D. Murphy	1983	500.89	Zimmerman	1912	425.29
Gallaraga	1997	465.18	E. Murray	1981	346.21			
Garvey	1974	343.37	Nicholson	1943	507.31			
Gehringer	1934	362.59	O'Doul	1929	497.66			
Gentile	1961	422.84	Oglivie	1980	325.29			
Gibson	1988	317.99	Olerud	1993	339.66			
Gonzalez	1996	403.74	Oliva	1965	393.86			
Gordon	1942	356.84	Ott	1942	487.85			

Hit by Pitched Balls

Historical trends and all-time records

Bill Rubinstein

Until recently, comprehensive historical data has never been published on batters hit by a pitched ball (HPB). With the publication of STATS, Inc.'s two-volume baseball encyclopedia, *The All-Time Baseball Handbook* and *The All-Time Baseball Sourcebook* (both 1998), it is now possible to highlight trends and point out historical leaders in this category. So far as I am aware, there has never before been such a study. (Data on the HPB was supplied to STATS by Pete Palmer.)

Data for HPB has been collected from 1884 in the American Association and from 1887 in the National League. It also exists for the Players League of 1890 and the Federal League of 1914-15, but not for earlier periods of baseball history.

The modern status of HPB—that a batter is awarded first base when hit by a pitch, and not charged with an at-bat—came into existence in the mid-1880s. Under what is currently Rule 6.08, there are two exceptions to this: if the ball is in the strike zone or if "the batter makes no attempt to avoid being touched by the ball." In these cases, the batter is not awarded first base. In practice, batters hit by pitched balls are almost automatically awarded first base. As David Nemec points out in *The Rules of Baseball* (1994), probably the most famous example of a batter not being awarded his base occurred on May 31, 1968. Don Drysdale, near breaking Walter Johnson's consecutive scoreless inning streak, hit

Dick Dietz with bases loaded. Normally, Dietz would have been awarded first base and knocked in a run, but plate umpire Harry Wendelstedt ruled that Dietz hadn't made a sufficient effort to avoid the pitch, and called it a ball. Drysdale went on to break Johnson's record. It is quite possible that Drysdale would not have been elected to the Hall of Fame had Wendelstedt made the normal ruling and ended Drysdale's pursuit of the record.

Being hit by a pitched ball really comprises the actions of two men, the pitcher and the batter. Some pitchers have become famous (or notorious) for hitting batters or trying to, usually to intimidate them. However, the data presented here suggests that among batters who are most likely to be hit by pitched balls, the occurance is a result of the batter's own actions. Being hit by pitches is often due to where and how the batter stands at the plate, but it is difficult to see why a very small number of players account for disproportionate numbers of HPB, unless there is an element of deliberation in their actions.

Because this relatively minor category of offensive action has received so little attention, only a handful of players in history have become known for being hit by pitches. Most accounts of the career of Hughie Jennings, the Hall of Fame shortstop of the great Baltimore Orioles teams of the 1890s, mention the fact that he was hit more than any other player in history. Ron Hunt (1963-1974), the second baseman who was hit by a pitched ball 243 times, said that "some people give their bodies to science, but I gave mine to base-

Bill Rubinstein *is professor of Modern History at the University of Wales, Aberystwyth. He has been a member of SABR since 1979.*

ball." Don Baylor and Frank Robinson (better known for slugging) were also noted for getting hit. Jason Kendall, the young catcher who has been hit by pitches seventy-seven times in his first three seasons (1996-8), has also become well-known for this ability. "The scouting report on me is to pitch inside. That's how I get hit so much" is his reasoning (*Baseball Digest*, January 1999, p.50), not explaining why the hundreds of other players for whom the pitchers' "book" is to pitch inside aren't hit so frequently. Apart from these three players, however, few others in baseball history have been well-known for being hit by pitches.

Table 1 sets out the batter with the most lifetime HPBs, arbitrarily arranged by the era in which they played most of their games. Table 2 presents the top ten single-season leaders in each era, while Table 3 gives the all-time teams in HPB, including all teams with ninety or more HPBs. Table 4 gives HPB data by league by decade, according to the average number of HPBs per ball club per year.

Table 1: **Batters with most hits by pitched balls, by era.**

1884/7-99

1.	Hughie Jennings	(1891-1912)	287
2.	Tommy Tucker	(1887-99)	272
3.	Jake Beckley	(1888-1907)	183
4.	Curt Welch	(1884-93)	173
5.	Fred Clarke	(1894-1915)	153
6.	Bill Dahlen	(1891-1911)	140
7.	Dummy Hoy	(1888-1902)	133
8.	John McGraw	(1891-1906)	132
9.	Steve Brodie	(1890-1902)	132
10.	Willie Keeler	(1892-1910)	129
11.	Bill Joyce	(1890-98)	108
12.	Dan Brouthers	(1879-1904)	105

1900-19

1.	Dan McGann	(1896-1908	173
2.	Kid Elberfeld	(1898-1914)	165
3.	Art Fletcher	(1909-22)	141
4.	Frank Chance	(1898-1914)	137
5.	Nap Lajoie	(1896-1916)	134
6.	Honus Wagner	(1897-1917)	124
7.	Buck Herzog	(1908-20)	120
8.	Steve Evans	(1908-15)	111
9.	George Burns	(1911-25)	110
10.	Sherry Magee	(1904-19)	109
11.	Wally Schang	(1913-31)	107
12.	Tris Speaker	(1907-28)	103

1920-45

1.	Frank Crosetti	(1932-48)	114
2.	Jimmy Dykes	(1918-39)	109
3.	Bucky Harris	(1919-31)	99
4.	Dick Bartell	(1927-46)	97
5.	Jack Fournier	(1912-27)	89
6.	Cy Williams	(1912-30)	86
7.	Kiki Cuyler	(1921-38)	85
8.	Bing Miller	(1921-36)	80
9.	Joe Sewell	(1920-33)	79

(10-12 Below 100th top all-time)

1946-68

1.	Frank Robinson	(1956-76)	198
2.	Minnie Minoso	(1949-80)	192
3.	Nellie Fox	(1947-65)	142
4.	Sherm Lollar	(1946-63)	115
5.	Bill Freehan	(1961-76)	114
6.	Orlando Cepeda	(1958-74)	102
7.	Norm Cash	(1958-74)	90

(8-12 Below 100th top all-time)

1969-82

1.	Don Baylor	(1970-88)	267
2.	Ron Hunt	(1963-74)	243
3.	Chet Lemon	(1975-90)	151
4.	Carlton Fisk	(1969-93)	143
5.	Brian Downing	(1973-92)	129
6.	Andre Dawson	(1976-96)	111
7.	Pete Rose	(1963-86)	107
8.	Reggie Jackson	(1967-87)	96
9.	Lonnie Smith	(1978-94)	92
10.	Gene Tenace	(1969-93)	91
11.	Cesar Tovar	(1965-)	88
12.	Bobby Grich	(1970-86)	86

1993-98

1.	Craig Biggio	(1988-98)	142
2.	Andres Galarraga	(1985-98)	137
3.	Brady Anderson	(1988-98)	112
4.	Mike MacFarlane	(1987-98)	96
5.	Gary Gaetti	(1981-88)	98
6.	Chuck Knoblauch	(1991-98)	92
7.	Joe Carter	(1983-98)	90
8.	Rickey Henderson	(1979-98)	84
9.	Jeff Blauser	(1987-98)	83
10.	Jason Kendall	(1996-98)	77

Table 2: **Top single season hpbs arranged by era**

	Through 1899				1900-19		
1.	Jennings	51	(1896)	1.	S. Evans	31	(1910)
2.	Jennings	46	(1897)	2.	Elberfeld	25	(1911)
3.	Jennings	46	(1898)	3.	McGann	24	(1900)
4.	McGann	39	(1898)	4.	McGraw	23	(1900)
5.	McGann	27	(1897)	5.	McGann	23	(1901)
6.	C. Welsh	36	(1891)	6.	J. Stahl	23	(1908)
7.	T. Tucker	33	(1889)	7.	Babb	22	(1903)

8.	Jennings	32	(1895)		8.	Jennings	20	(1900)
9.	T. Tucker	29	(1887)		9.	B. Gilbert	20	(1903)
	C. Welsh	29	(1888)		10.	Gessler	20	(1911)
	Roseman	29	(1890)					
	T. Tucker	29	(1891)					

1920-45					1946-68			
1.	B. Harris	21	(1920)	1.	Freehan	24	(1968)
2.	B. Harris	18	(1921)	2.	Minoso	23	(1956)
3.	Manush	17	(1923)	3.	Minoso	21	(1957)
4.	Manush	16	(1929)	4.	Hemus	20	(1952)
5.	G. Burns	15	(1924)	5.	Hemus	20	(1956)
6.	Crosetti	15	(1938)	6.	F. Robinson	20	(1957)
7.	I. Goodman	15	(1938)	7.	Freehan	20	(1965)
8.	B. Harris	14	(1992)	8.	F. Robinson	18	(1968)
9.	Mostil	14	(1922)	9.	Reichardt	18	(1966)
10.	4 players	17		10.	4 players	17	

1969-92					1993-98			
1.	Hunt	25	(1968)	1.	Biggio	34	(1997)
2.	Baylor	35	(1986)	2.	Kendall	31	(1997)
3.	Baylor	28	(1987)	3.	Kendall	31	(1998)
4.	Hunt	26	(1970)	4.	Biggio	27	(1996)
5.	Hunt	26	(1970)	5.	Santangelo	25	(1999)
6.	Hunt	26	(1972)	6.	Galaragga	25	(1998)
7.	Hunt	25	(1969)	7.	Santangelo	25	(1998)
8.	Hunt	24	(1973)	8.	Vina	25	(1998)
9.	Baylor	24	(1985)	9.	Biggio	22	(1995)
10.	Baylor	23	(1984)	10.	B. And'son	22	(1996)

Table 3: Teams with 90 or more HPBs

159	Baltimore NL	1898
125	Brooklyn NL	1899
122	Baltimore NL	1899
120	Baltimore NL	1896
115	Baltimore NL	1897
111	Philadelphia AA	1891
106	Baltimore NL	1895
100	Houston NL	1897
98	Baltimore NL	1894
96	Buffalo PL	1890
95	St. Louis AA	1890
92	Toronto AL	1896
91	New York NL	1903
91	Pittsburgh NL	1998
90	St. Louis NL	1901
90	New York NL	1905

Table 4: Hit by pitched balls—average HBP per team per decade

| | NL | AL | AA | PL | FL |
			(1884-91)	(1890)	(1914-15)
1887-89	39	-	51	51	37
1890-91	57	-			
1900-09	50	47			
1910-19	40	44			
1920-29	30	35			
1930-39	25	21			
1940-49	23	20			
1950-59	29	31			
1960-69	35	36			
1970-79	30	33			
1980-89	24	31			
1889-97	39	42			

(Note: No account here is taken of changes in schedule lengths. Since the season was shorter in the 1890s than now, the average of HPBs would be even higher in today's schedule.)

Some of the major conclusions about the HPB data can be summarised as follows:

1. The frequency of a player getting hit by a pitched ball is not random. Some batters are far more likely to get hit than others, with a few batters consistently leading the league in this category. Being hit by a pitched ball also represented a far higher percentage of plate activity for these players than for others. For instance, Hughie Jennings compiled 1,874 hits or walks in his career. His 287 HPBs represented 6.5 per cent of this total. In contrast, Ty Cobb compiled 5,439 hits and walks, compared with ninety-four HPBs (1.7 per cent). Babe Ruth compiled 4,929 hits or walks, compared with only forty-two HPBs (0.9 per cent). While Ron Hunt's 243 HPBs compared with his 1,984 hits plus walks (12.2 per cent), Mickey Mantle was hit only thirteen times in his career, compared with 4,148 hits plus walks (0.3 percent).

2. By and large, the players (in modern baseball, at least) most likely to figure as HPB leaders were middle infielders and catchers, often good but not great hitters. It is difficult to avoid the conclusion that some batters deliberately tried to be hit as an offensive weapon.

Very few great post-1920 sluggers figure among the all-time HPB leaders, Frank Robinson (198) and Don Baylor (an amazing 267) being the most notable exceptions. There are several explanations for this. First, sluggers are at the plate to hit, not to be hit. They are also usually big men and big stars, whose retaliation might be serious.

3. Batters were far more likely to be hit by a pitch in the nineteenth century. The frequency with which

batters were hit by pitchers declined sharply after the deadball era, but rose again from the 1960s on. This parallels the frequency of stolen bases, which are always relatively high when the number of runs per game is low, and then decline (given a readjustment interval) when the number of runs per game rises. Trends in stolen bases and HPB appear to parallel each other, and the idea that some batters deliberately try to get hit in a more run-scarce environment makes sense. There is, however, little overlap between the stolen base leaders and HPB leaders.

Several other reasons might be given for the decline of HPBs after 1920. As a result of the beaning death of Ray Chapman, umpires were instructed to change balls frequently, so the one in play was always clean and white. This is held by some historians to be the chief reason that all hitting went through the stratosphere in the 1920s: batters could see the ball. It also obviously helped batters to see the ball coming at them, and get out of the way. The Chapman tragedy might also have made some pitchers reluctant to brush batters back.

4. Did unpopular and controversial players get hit more often than others? There seems to be no evidence of this. For instance, neither Ty Cobb nor Rogers Hornsby, players who were regarded as unpopular, were among the leaders of their time in HPB. Among those on the all-time list, in fact, many were very popular players like Honus Wagner, Nap Lajoie, and Nellie Fox.

During the first few years of baseball integration, black players appeared to be hit slightly more than others. Jackie Robinson was second in HPBs (but with only nine) in 1947, his rookie season. He led the league (with seven), in 1948, and figured among the top five in the NL in 1949, 1951, 1952, 1953, and 1954. Other early black players—Larry Doby, Luke Easter, Sam Jethro, and Monte Irvin—also were among the league lead-ers, although their seasonal totals were very low. Despite the high totals of Minnie Minoso and Frank Robinson, however, by the 1960s it is difficult to see any racial patterns.

5. The team data clearly shows the predominance of the old Baltimore Orioles of the 1890s in this category. The old Orioles were, of course, renowned for their slashing, aggressive style of play, and may deliberately have dared opposing pitchers to hit them. Ned Hanlon, their manager, may also have deliberately used HPBs as an offensive weapon. When Hanlon went with many of the Orioles to the 1899 Brooklyn Superbas, that team produced one of the highest HPB totals in history. The Orioles that year, managed by John McGraw, were also among the highest ever.

In the early years of McGraw's managerial reign with the New York Giants, his teams also figured among the highest HPB totals ever, with the 1903 Giants being hit ninety-one times and the 1905 Giants ninety times. Thereafter, the Giants totals declined. Interestingly, none of the teams managed by Hughie Jennings or Wilbert Robinson of the old Orioles had high HPB totals. In the 1950s, the "Go Go" White Sox had unusually high HPB totals for their time—fifty-eight in 1955, seventy-five in 1956, sixty-eight in 1957—with Minnie Minoso, Nellie Fox, and Sherm Lollar among league leaders.

In very recent years there has been an increase in team totals, with the 1997 Houston Astros (100), the 1996 Toronto Blue Jays (ninety-two), and the 1998 Pittsburgh Pirates (ninety-one), producing the highest team totals since early in the century.

Any study of this subject must also take into account the role of pitchers and differences among pitchers in their likelihood of hitting batters, but this must await another discussion.

Hughie Jennings

Transcendental Graphics

Probablity of Performance

General relativity for the baseball fan

Michael Sluss

The probability of performance statistic may answer the age-old (or at least since 1876) question: how best to compare individual baseball players' performances from year to year and from league to league, while considering both the rate of success (Ty Cobb's batting average) and the amount of success (Pete Rose's hits). Whose performances were less probable and more outstanding:

- Ted Williams' .406 BA in 1941 or Rod Carew's .388 BA in 1977?
- George Sisler's 257 hits in 1920 or Hugh Duffy's .440 BA in 1894?
- Roger Maris' sixty-one home runs in 1961 or Mark McGwire's seventy in 1998?
- Hank Aaron's career 755 HR or Babe Ruth's 8.5 lifetime HR percentage?

To assess batting average, the probability of performance statistic (POP) determines the probability of an average league player hitting at least that batting average in a specific number of at-bats. POP uses the number of hits, at-bats, and the league average to measure just how good a player's batting average is. A less probable batting average is a more outstanding performance, resulting in a higher POP. A batter's POP is higher if his batting average is higher, if his number of hits is higher, or if the league batting average is lower.

Mike Sluss *is a neurologist in Green Bay, Wisconsin. A member of SABR since 1983, he has never forgiven Frank Lane for trading away Rocky Colavito.*

Season POP—To better understand the interaction of hits, at-bats, batting average, and league batting average, consider the three batters who achieved a season batting probability of performance (BA POP) of 8.61:

	BA POP	BA	H	AB	LG BA
Ty Cobb, 1918	8.61	.382	161	421	.252
Roberto Clemente, 1967	8.61	.357	209	585	.248
Tony Gwynn, 1987	8.61	.370	218	589	.260

Of the three players, Cobb has the best batting average .382, but he has the lowest total of hits. Clemente has the lowest personal batting average .357, but he achieved this in the league with the lowest league average: .248. Gwynn has the most hits 218, but he performed in a league with the highest league average: .260.

Because BA POP incorporates at-bats in its calculation, there is no need for an arbitrary cutoff level of at-bats in order to qualify for the best average. In the same league and year, the hitter with a better combination of batting average and hits earns a higher BA POP. POP takes into account that with more at bats it is more difficult (and less probable) to hit above average. For example, in 1910 Nap Lajoie and Ty Cobb virtually tied for the American League batting championship, but Lajoie's performance earns a BA POP of 14.09 compared to Cobb's 12.36, on the basis of Lajoie having substantially more hits than Cobb. POP is the optimal way to determine the sea-

POP

Calculation of POP is a two step process:

By using the binomial probability function, the probability that an average player (with an average league batting average of $L=$(league hits - H)/(league at-bats - A)) would get at least H hits in A at-bats (for a personal batting average of H/A) is P, where

$$P = \sum_{h=H}^{A} ((A! / (h! \times (A - h)!)) \times L^h \times (1 - L)^{(A - h)}$$

and

$$POP = - \log_{10}P$$

so that the actual probability of doing at least as well can be calculated from POP as

$$10^{(- POP)}$$

son batting champ.

The best batting season was Tip O'Neill's BA POP of 15.21 in 1887 in the American Association. Cobb's 14.31 in 1911 has been the best batting season in the American League. Hornsby's 11.91 in 1924 has been the best in the National League. The best batting season since 1924 has been Rod Carew's BA POP of 10.67 in 1977. In the POP Charts below, Hall of Fame players are indicated in UPPER CASE. Currently active players are designated by "#". Data is current

through 1998. League averages exclude the individual player's data. POP Chart 1 shows some of the best batting seasons.

Perhaps the most startling POP results are the HR (home run) POPs. We all too often use just the absolute number of home runs to evaluate how well a batter hits home runs. There usually is less consideration of a batter's home run percentage and very little consideration of his league's average home run percentage. The HR POP allows us to incorporate these factors when we assess home run hitting abilities. POP Chart 2 shows the best season home run performances.

Babe Ruth had the six best home run seasons of all time. His best HR season was 54 homers in 1920, a greater accomplishment than his sixty home runs in 1927 because in 1920 he had a higher home run per-

POP chart 1

Best batting average seasons

	Player	YR	LG	BA POP	BA	H	AB	LG BA
1.	Tip O'Neill	1887	AA	15.21	.435	225	517	.270
2.	Fred Dunlap	1884	UA	14.70	.412	185	449	.242
3.	TY COBB	1911	AL	14.31	.420	248	591	.271
4.	NAP LAJOIE	1910	AL	14.09	.384	227	591	.241
5.	TY COBB	1912	AL	13.47	.410	227	553	.263
14.	ROGERS HORNSBY	1924	NL	11.91	.424	227	536	.281
16.	GEORGE SISLER	1920	AL	11.08	.407	257	631	.282
20.	ROD CAREW	1977	AL	10.67	.388	239	616	.265
22.	TED WILLIAMS	1941	AL	10.31	.406	185	456	.265
25.	HUGH DUFFY	1894	NL	10.08	.440	237	539	.308
39.	Wade Boggs #	1985	AL	8.96	.368	240	653	.260
49.	Tony Gwynn #	1987	NL	8.61	.370	218	589	.260
72.	GEORGE BRETT	1980	AL	7.82	.390	175	449	.268
77.	Kirby Puckett	1988	AL	7.70	.356	234	657	.258
87.	Larry Walker #	1997	NL	7.48	.366	208	568	.262

POP chart 2

Best home run seasons

	Player	YR	LG	HR POP	HR%	HR	AB	LG HR%
1.	RUTH	1920	AL	44.88	11.79	54	458	0.76
2.	RUTH	1927	AL	43.74	11.11	60	540	0.92
3.	RUTH	1921	AL	40.70	10.93	59	540	0.99
4.	RUTH	1928	AL	34.59	10.08	54	536	1.03
5.	RUTH	1926	AL	31.34	9.50	47	495	0.91
6.	RUTH	1924	AL	30.53	8.70	46	529	0.84
7.	FOXX	1932	AL	28.08	9.92	58	585	1.52
8.	GEHRIG	1927	AL	27.56	8.05	47	584	0.94
9.	McGwire #	1998	NL	26.54	13.75	70	509	2.83
10.	GREENBERG	1938	AL	24.16	10.43	58	556	1.92

POP chart 3

Career batting average leaders

	CAREER					BEST SEASON					
PLAYER	BA POP	BA	H	AB	YRS	BA POP	BA	H	AB	LG BA	YR
1. COBB	166.95	.367	4191	11429	24	14.31	.420	248	591	.271	1911
2. LAJOIE	100.09	.338	3244	9592	21	14.09	.384	227	591	.241	1910
3. SPEAKER	97.42	.345	3514	10197	22	12.43	.386	211	546	.247	1916
4. MUSIAL	90.54	.331	3630	10972	22	9.89	.376	230	611	.259	1948
5. WAGNER	84.46	.327	3418	10441	21	9.54	.354	201	568	.237	1908
6. HORNSBY	83.49	.358	2930	8173	23	11.91	.424	227	536	.281	1924
7. Gwynn #	83.28	.339	2928	8648	17	8.61	.370	218	589	.260	1987
8. T. WILLIAMS	80.42	.344	2654	7706	19	10.31	.406	185	456	.265	1941
9. CAREW	76.17	.328	3053	9315	19	10.67	.388	239	616	.265	1977
10. KEELER	75.84	.343	2945	8585	19	10.95	.424	239	564	.290	1897
11. ANSON	74.24	.329	3000	9108	22	9.07	.371	187	504	.249	1886
12. E. COLLINS	73.01	.333	3313	9951	25	7.78	.346	198	572	.242	1909
13. BROUTHERS	68.71	.342	2296	6711	19	8.71	.370	181	489	.249	1886
14. Rose	67.53	.303	4256	14053	24	7.59	.348	218	627	.249	1969
15. CLEMENTE	66.26	.317	3000	9454	18	8.61	.357	209	585	.248	1967
16. J. Jackson	65.19	.356	1774	4981	13	11.95	.408	233	571	.271	1911
17. BURKETT	64.66	.339	2853	8413	16	9.52	.382	228	597	.265	1901
18. DELAHANTY	64.04	.346	2597	7501	16	10.69	.410	238	581	.281	1899
19. Boggs #	63.42	.329	2922	8888	17	8.96	.368	240	653	.260	1985
20. AARON	61.67	.305	3771	12364	23	7.15	.355	223	629	.259	1959

POP chart 4

Career home run leaders

	CAREER					BEST SEASON					
PLAYER	HR POP	HR%	HR	AB	YR	HR POP	HR%	HR	AB	LG HR%	YR
1. RUTH	428.97	8.50	714	8399	22	44.88	11.79	54	458	0.76	1920
2. FOXX	190.02	6.57	534	8134	20	28.08	9.92	58	585	1.52	1932
3. GEHRIG	180.71	6.16	493	8001	17	27.56	8.05	47	584	0.94	1927
4. OTT	168.33	5.40	511	9456	22	15.10	7.71	42	545	1.68	1929
5. T. WILLIAMS	155.29	6.76	521	7706	19	15.90	6.90	36	522	1.20	1942
6. AARON	154.54	6.11	755	12364	23	17.14	9.50	47	495	2.04	1971
7. SCHMIDT	144.22	6.56	548	8352	18	17.98	8.76	48	548	1.82	1980
8. KILLEBREW	128.51	7.03	573	8147	22	12.73	8.04	44	547	2.15	1967
9. MCCOVEY	123.20	6.36	521	8197	22	14.79	9.17	45	491	2.18	1969
10. MAYS	122.77	6.07	660	10881	22	16.27	9.32	52	558	2.31	1965

centage in a league with a lower home run percentage.

For his sixty-one home runs in 1961, Roger Maris earned a season HR POP of 17.85. Sammy Sosa earned a 1998 HR POP of 18.09 for his sixty-six home runs, and Mark McGwire earned a 1998 HR POP of 26.54 for his seventy home runs, the best HR performance since 1932. Why are their home run achievements significantly less than Ruth's? The rate of home runs hit in the 1961 American League and in the 1998 National League was more than triple the home run rate in Ruth's 1920 American League. In 1998, McGwire would have had to hit ninety-three home runs in his 509 at bats (HR POP of 45.68) to beat Ruth's 1920 HR POP of 44.88.

Ruth, Williams, and Mantle had the three most outstanding on base seasons (see POP Chart 5).

Career POP—POP Chart 3 lists the twenty players with the best batting careers and includes each

POP chart 5

Career on-base leaders

	Player	CAREER					BEST SEASON					
		OB POP	OBP	OB	PA	YRs	OB POP	OBP	OB	PA	LG OBP	YR
1.	T. WILLIAMS	226.18	.481	4673	9725	19	25.97	.549	330	601	.337	1941
2.	RUTH	201.10	.471	4929	10455	22	26.06	.542	375	692	.343	1923
3.	COBB	171.27	.429	5440	12678	24	17.93	.479	326	681	.317	1915
4.	SPEAKER	131.62	.423	4895	11578	22	14.88	.467	293	628	.314	1916
5.	MUSIAL	128.48	.416	5229	12571	22	10.51	.448	303	676	.327	1951
6.	MANTLE	126.52	.422	4149	9836	18	22.58	.515	319	620	.322	1957
7.	E. COLLINS	124.40	.420	4816	11454	25	12.80	.456	292	640	.317	1915
8.	HORNSBY	122.47	.431	3968	9211	23	18.79	.506	316	625	.331	1924
9.	HAMILTON	111.26	.449	3347	7456	14	13.82	.516	346	670	.371	1894
10.	GEHRIG	108.32	.445	4229	9509	17	11.22	.472	327	693	.346	1927

player's best batting season. Seventh on the list, Tony Gwynn has a chance to achieve the second-best career batting career. Ty Cobb's career BA POP 166.95 seems unreachable. Pete Rose is ranked fourteenth by virtue of his record lifetime hit total. Shortstop Rabbit Maranville's career BA POP of 3.93 just edges catcher Ray Schalk's 4.01 as the worst batting career for a Hall of Fame position player.

POP Chart 4 lists the ten players with the best home run careers and includes each player's best home run season. Currently eleventh on the all-time home run list, Mark McGwire will move up at least 3 places after the 1999 season. Even with more home runs, Hank Aaron was not as good a home run hitter as Babe Ruth because Aaron had lower home run percentages while playing in an era of higher league average home run percentages. Nellie Fox is the only Hall of Fame position player to have a career HR POP of zero.

POP Chart 5 lists the ten players with the best on-base careers and includes each player's best on-base season. Wade Boggs is currently eleventh on the all-time list. Five batters who have distinguished themselves particularly as on-base artists are Billy Hamilton, Joe Morgan, Rickey Henderson, John McGraw, and Roy Thomas. Of all Hall of Fame position players, Joe Tinker (OB POP 4.75) edges fellow shortstop Rabbit Maranville (4.85) for the worst on base career.

Four players have career HR and OB POPs both greater than 100: Williams, Ruth, Mantle, and Gehrig. Barry Bonds has a reasonable chance to join this select group of players.

Nine outfielders of the '50s and '60s (Aaron, Kaline, Mantle, Mays, Musial, Robinson, Billy Williams, Ted Williams, Yastrzemski) had exceptional batting, home run, and on-base careers. Only four other hitters hit at least as well in all three career categories (BA, HR, and OB): Ruth, Gehrig, Foxx, and Hornsby.

Ted Williams is among the top eight hitters for each of the three career categories (BA, HR, OB). The other highest-ranking hitters are Hornsby (among the top twenty in each career category), Ruth (twenty-two), Mays (twenty-nine), Aaron (thirty), and Gehrig (thirty).

The all-time career hitters by position are shown in POP Chart 6. Williams and Hornsby are in the top two for their positions in each of the three statistics (BA, HR, OB). Other top hitters by position are Wagner and Aaron (both among the top four in each career category), Ruth (five), Mays (five), Gehrig (six), Lajoie (six), Mantle (six), Foxx (seven), Musial (ten), Frank Robinson (ten), and Dickey (ten). "All-Around" is defined as players with the highest minimum of all three career hitting POPs.

By using career POPs to profile players' performances, we have a new tools to evaluate players for the Hall of Fame. By POP analysis, some of the more overlooked players not yet selected for the Hall of Fame are Dick Allen, Pete Browning, Tony Oliva, Ron Santo, and Joe Torre.

POP chart 6

Career hitting leaders by position

POS.	BA	HR	OB	ALL-AROUND	POS.	BA	HR	OB	ALL-AROUND
catcher	J. Torre	J. BENCH	M. COCHRANE	M. Piazza #	shortstop	H. WAGNER	E. BANKS	H. WAGNER	H. WAGNER
	D. White*	G. HARTNETT	R. BRESNAHAN	B. DICKEY		L. APPLING	V. Stephens	A. VAUGHAN	J. CRONIN
	T. Simmons	Y. BERRA	J. Torre	J. Torre		A. VAUGHAN	R. Petrocelli	L. APPLING	C. Ripken #
	B. EWING*	G. Carter	G. Tenace	T. Simmons		J. Glasscock*	H. WAGNER	J. CRONIN	E. BANKS
	E. LOMBARDI	C. Fisk	W. Schang	M. C'CHRANE		G. DAVIS*	C. Ripken #	B. Larkin #	V. Stephens
	M. Piazza #	R. CAMPY	M. Piazza #	E. LOMBARDI		R. YOUNT	W. Held	P. REESE	B. Dahlen*
	B. DICKEY	E. LOMBARDI	B. DICKEY	B. EWING*		J. Larkin #	J. CRONIN	G. DAVIS*	G. DAVIS*
	M. Sanguillen	L. Parrish	G. HARTNETT	C. Fisk		J. Franco	H. Long*	J. Pesky	B. Larkin #
	S. Burgess	G. Tenace	S. Burgess	G. HARTNETT		H. JENNINGS*	B. Dahlen*	J. Franco	E. McKean*
	M. COCHRANE	B. DICKEY	B. EWING*	J. Clements*		J. Pesky	T. JACKSON	J. SEWELL	R. YOUNT
first base	R. CAREW	J. FOXX	L. GEHRIG	L. GEHRIG	left field	S. MUSIAL	T. WILLIAMS	T. WILLIAMS	T. WILLIAMS
	C. ANSON*	L. GEHRIG	C. ANSON*	J. FOXX		T. WILLIAMS	W. STARGELL	S. MUSIAL	S. MUSIAL
	D. BR'THERS*	H. KILLEBREW	D. BR'THERS*	R. CONNOR*		P. Rose	R. KINER	C. YAZ	C. YAZ
	G. SISLER	W. MCCOVEY	J. FOXX	J. MIZE		J. Jackson	F. Howard	J. BURKETT*	B. WILLIAMS
	R. CONNOR*	M. McGwire	R. CONNOR*	D. BR'THERS*		J. BURKETT*	B. Bonds #	B. Bonds #	A. SIMMONS
	L. GEHRIG	D. Kingman	R. CAREW	P. Guerrero		E. DEL'H'NTY*	K. Williams	R.Henderson#	G. GOSLIN
	J. FOXX	H. GR'NBERG	F. Thomas #	E. Murray		A. SIMMONS	G. Foster	P. Rose	J. MEDWICK
	B. TERRY	J. MIZE	W. MCCOVEY	D. Allen		Z. WHEAT	A. SIMMONS	E. DEL'H'NTY*	E. DEL'H'NTY*
	D. Orr*	D. Allen	H. KILLEBREW	W. Clark #		J. O'ROURKE*	B. Johnson	J. Jackson	R. Carty
	J. BECKLEY*	R. York	K. Hernandez	T. Perez		T. O'Neill*	S. MUSIAL	T. Raines #	S. Magee
second base	N. LAJOIE	R. HORNSBY	E. COLLINS	R. HORNSBY	center field	T. COBB	W. MAYS	T. COBB	W. MAYS
	R. HORNSBY	J. Gordon	R. HORNSBY	N. LAJOIE		T. SPEAKER	M. MANTLE	T. SPEAKER	M. MANTLE
	E. COLLINS	B. DOERR	J. MORGAN	R. Sandberg		P. Browning*	C. Williams	M. MANTLE	J. DIMAGGIO
	C. GEHRINGER	R. Sandberg	N. LAJOIE	J. MORGAN		W. MAYS	J. DIMAGGIO	B. HAMILTON*	T. COBB
	H. Richardson*	MORGAN	C. Childs*	C. G'HR'NGER		B. HAMILTON*	H. WILSON	W. MAYS	D. SNIDER
	N. FOX	N. LAJOIE	C. GEHRINGER	L. Doyle		M. MANTLE	D. Murphy	R. Thomas	T. SPEAKER
	F. FRISCH	F. Pfeffer*	E. Stanky	B. DOERR		R. ASHBURN	W. Berger	R. ASHBURN	J. Ryan*
	B. HERMAN	B. Grich	M. Bishop	H. Richardson*		K. Puckett	D. SNIDER	P. Browning*	E. AVERILL
	F. Dunlap*	L. Doyle	M. HUGGINS	F. Dunlap*		A. Oliver	A. Dawson	G. Gore*	F. Lynn
	J. ROBINSON	L. Whitaker	J. ROBINSON	L. Whitaker		J. DIMAGGIO	K. Griffey Jr. #	B. Butler	M. Donlin
third base	W. Boggs #	M. SCHMIDT	W. Boggs #	F. BAKER	right field	T. Gwynn #	B. RUTH	B. RUTH	H. AARON
	G. BRETT	E. MATHEWS	J. MCGRAW*	G. BRETT		W. KEELER*	M. OTT	M. OTT	B. RUTH
	P. Molitor	D. Evans	S. Hack	K. Boyer		R. CLEMENTE	H. AARON	P. WANER	F. ROBINSON
	B. Madlock	B. Horner	E. MATHEWS	R. Santo		H. AARON	R. JACKSON	H. AARON	A. KALINE
	G. KELL	M. Williams #	M. SCHMIDT	B. Bonilla #		B. RUTH	F. ROBINSON	F. ROBINSON	H. HEILMANN
	F. BAKER	G. Nettles	G. BRETT	D. Lyons*		S. CRAWFORD	D. Strawberry*	A. KALINE	C. KLEIN
	P. TRAYNOR	R. Cey	E. Martinez #	B. Elliot		P. WANER	J. Canseco #	T. Gwynn #	S. CRAWFORD
	L. Cross*	R. Santo	E. Yost	R. Hebner		H. HEILMANN	R. Colavito	H. HEILMANN	S. TH'MPS'N*
	E. Martinez #	A. Rosen	R. Santo	E. MATHEWS		A. KALINE	J. Clark	K. KELLY	M. OTT
	S. Hack	F. BAKER	P. Molitor	E. COLLINS		F. ROBINSON	G. Cravath	K. Singleton	R. Smith

Hall of famers in UPPER CASE.

Currently active players designated by #.

Primarily nineteenth-century players designated by *.

Was Joe Jackson's career good enough to be considered for the Hall of Fame? Jackson's BA POP of 65.19 ranks sixteenth all-time, and his OB POP of 62.60 is thirty-eighth best. Statistically, he is clearly good enough for the Hall of Fame, but statistics alone will not show that Shoeless Joe was "good" enough.

Statistical discussion—Because POP is a logarithmic form of the actual probability, it is useful to know what its different values mean. A BA POP of 0.3 represents an approximately average batting performance — an average player will have a 50 percent chance of doing at least as well. A POP of 1.00 signifies that an average player has a 10 percent chance of attaining this level of performance; a POP of 2.00 signifies a one percent chance; a POP of 3.00 signifies one chance in a thousand, and so on. Outstanding baseball performances by superstars are so unlikely to be attained by a league's average player that the probabilities of their performances are exceedingly small.

In 1971, Joe Torre batted .363 with 230 hits in 634 at bats in a league with an average league BA of .251. The probability of a league average player with a BA of .251 getting at least 230 hits in 634 at bats is 0.000000000252521, which equals $10^{(-9.60)}$, so Torre's season BA POP is 9.60. The average batter would have had less than one chance in a billion of achieving Torre's 1971 batting feat.

A necessary assumption for the calculation of POP is that the outcomes of a batter's discrete events (at-bats) are independent. Monaldo has shown this to be the case.[1] Another assumption is that the "average" players in different leagues are comparable, and that the major differences in league averages reflect differences in the game itself: liveliness of baseballs, characteristics of bats, distances of outfield fences, rules of pitching, definitions of strike zone, and strategies of the game.

A hitter's POP has been calculated with his individual data excluded from the league average. When a player is traded from one league to another during a season, his POP is calculated using a weighted league average, proportional to his at-bats in each league. Because the American League introduced the designated hitter in 1973, an appropriate adjustment would be to subtract all pitchers' hitting data (not readily available) from all league averages. What of park factor, pitching staff factor, etc? If relevant data were available, more specific POPs could be calculated by using appropriately weighted league averages.

Comparing individuals' batting averages between leagues has been done before, but these studies have not considered total production (hits) along with batting averages.[2,3] Moreover, when league averages vary greatly, Shoebotham's relative average method[2] does not produce realistic comparisons. For example, by using Shoebotham's form of relative means comparison, McGwire would have needed 176 home runs in 509 at-bats in 1998 to achieve Ruth's relative home run average of 12.19 earned by hitting sixty homers in 1927.

A player's cumulative career POP is the sum of his seasons' POPs, representing the probability of an average player achieving each year's performance. A career BA POP could be calculated instead by using the batter's lifetime hits and at-bats and a proportionate average of each of the league batting averages. But this different approach produces a less meaningful result because it blurs the improbabilities of more outstanding peak seasons with those of more probable seasons. A player's career POP as currently defined is clearly set in historical perspective and cannot decrease. Poor performances in later years will not decrease a career POP, but neither will they increase it. POP is a positive measure of achievement.

General relativity—Based on career HR POP and OB POP analyses, Barry Bonds is the greatest active hitter, Ted Williams is the greatest living hitter, and Babe Ruth is the greatest deceased hitter.

A less probable performance is a more outstanding achievement. Probability of performance (POP) provides more precise and comprehensive comparison of a player's performance to another player in the same league, to himself in a different year, or to another player in a different league in a different year.

Relativity is the sabermetric term for cross-era comparison. Probability of performance is the first relativity tool to incorporate all three basic components (amount of production, rate of production, and league average) in systematic comparisons of hitting across eras. POP provides improved and more general relativity for the baseball fan.

Notes:

1. Monaldo, Frank. "The Case for Independent At-Bats," *By the Numbers*, June, 1995, pp. 5-6.

2. Shoebotham, David. "Relative Batting Averages," *Baseball Research Journal*, 1976, vol. 5, pp. 37-42.

3. Yancey, George. "A Reexamination of Baseball's Greatest Single-Season Records." *Baseball Research Journal*, 1996, vol. 25, pp. 85-87.

Thanks to SABR's Alden Mead, Georjeanna Wilson-Doenges (Assistant Professor, University of Wisconsin-Green Bay), and Ray Sluss (my father) for reviewing this paper.

Baseball's Amateur Draft

A scouting department overview

David C. Thomas

Analysis of baseball's amateur draft is a laborious task for even the most dedicated draft follower or scouting guru. Unlike the NBA or NFL drafts, which are limited basically to college players, baseball's draft interjects a multitude of variables that can distort the hard-to-find facts even after they have been compiled and sorted.

This research does not attempt to analyze every round of every draft since 1965. Ninety percent of the players who make it to the majors are drafted in the first fifteen rounds, and the earlier decades of the draft had fewer teams and secondary phases. Therefore, this analysis focuses on the first fifteen rounds and covers the post-secondary draft period, which began in 1987. I used the 1994 draft as the cutoff point, because players drafted after that have not had enough time to make it to the majors.

Here is what I have discovered:

College players, regardless of position or geographic location, should be the primary focus for any organization. One in seven drafted Division 1 players makes it to the majors and one out of three of these players achieves 500 at-bats or 100 innings pitched in their major league career. On the other hand, only one in seventeen drafted high-school players makes it to the majors and only one in seven then reaches those longevity levels.

David C. Thomas *is vice-president of business development for Electrical South in Greensboro, North Carolina. He has published previous articles on the amateur draft in BRJ and has also published articles in SABR's Minor League History Journal.*

Within the college ranks, the PAC 10, SEC, Big Ten, Missouri Valley, and ACC should be the key conferences to scout, although all of the top twenty Division 1 conferences (see Tables # 3 and # 4) are fertile ground. For Division 1 college players, geographic location is far less important than it is in high schools (below). Collegians play longer seasons than high-school teams regardless of whether they are in the north or south.

The payback on small colleges and junior colleges is poor and should not consume significant scouting time. Over twenty percent of the small-college players who make it to the majors are from Florida schools. Over seventy-five percent of JUCO players making it to the majors come from colleges in California, Texas, Florida, South Carolina, Oklahoma, or Illinois, in that order.

While the high-school draft choice success rate is less than half that of college Division 1 players (14.4 percent to 31.3 percent), they don't take much longer to get there (4.50 years versus 3.29 years) despite their ages at the time of the draft (see table #1).

The real high-school focus should be on geographic regions—mainly warm-weather states. The best high-school players can be found in Alabama, Arizona, South Carolina, Virginia, Texas, California, North Carolina, Oklahoma, Florida, and Washington. There are exceptions to this rule. Indiana, New York, and Illinois. Pennsylvania, New Jersey, Tennessee, Arkansas and anywhere in the northern plains, upper Midwest, and Rockies are unlikely areas in which to find top players. Interestingly, Louisiana and Mississippi are also poor scouting grounds, and even Georgia sends a fairly low percentage of players to the majors (see Table # 2).

Regardless of region or playing level, infielders are most likely to make it to the majors, catchers least likely. The fact that fifty-three percent of all high-school infielders drafted were shortstops supports the perception that high-school shortstops may be the best athletes. In reality. only 15.9 percent of this group made it to the majors, while 16.1 percent of the other infield position players were chosen. (More college shortstops do make it to the majors than other college position players.) Overall, righthanders and lefthanders are equally likely to make it (14.4 percent to 14.6 percent). Oddly, righthanded high-school players make it sooner than lefties, while lefthanded collegians make it more quickly than righties (see Table # 1).

Details—Although drafted four-year college players are three to four years older than high-school players, their average time to reach the majors is only 1-1/4 years lower (3.29 years versus 4.5 years). The average eighteen-year-old high-school draftee who makes it to the majors will get there at age 22-1/4. The average twenty-one-year old Division 1 college player (drafted after his junior year) who makes it to the majors gets there at age 24-1/2.

Should a team go with high-school players because their average career would be roughly two years longer? No. College players are more than twice as likely to make it to the majors than high-school players (see Table #3). Junior college players are an even greater risk than high-school players since they are one to two years older when drafted, yet have only a slightly higherchance of reaching the majors. Small-college players have a similar success rate as junior college players, but they make it to the majors sooner than the JUCOs (3.68 years versus 4.05).

There are, however, significant differences even among the major and minor Division 1 conferences. Clearly the PAC 10, SEC, Big Ten, Missouri Valley, and ACC, top to bottom, are the conferences producing major league players. Other conferences have teams equal to these five, but on average don't yield the comparable percent of players-to-the-majors as these five conferences. More clearly stated, these five conferences have a 36.3% rate of drafted players making it to the majors, while the rest of the Division 1 conferences average 27.7%. They also arrive in the majors sooner (3.14 years versus 3.37 years).

Scouting Facts
- Although a much higher percent of college players were drafted from the larger southern and western college conferences, geographic region did not significantly affect future player performance of northern and eastern college conferences. Conferences such as the Big East and Atlantic Ten actually led all other conferences in average years to the majors of the players that did make it.
- Thirty-four percent of all Division 1 players drafted came from the PAC 10, SEC, and Big 12 conferences.
- The ACC had thirty-six percent fewer drafted players than the Big 12, yet had the same number of players make it to the majors.
- The PAC 10 had five teams out of 21 Division 1 teams with five or more players achieving either 500 ABs or 100 IP in the majors. The Big Ten had the highest percentage of players drafted make it to the majors (forty-three percent) and the second-highest percentage (fifty-nine percent) of players to make it and reach 500 career ABs or 100 IP.
- Stanford, LSU, Arizona State, UCLA, Florida State, and Kent had ten or more players make it to the majors. LSU (seventy-one percent), Florida State (sixty percent), and Stanford (fifty-eight percent) had the highest percentage of players making it to the majors with 500 AB's or 100 IP.
- 16.8 percent of high school righthanders and 17.1 percent of high school lefthanders make it to the majors.
- Fifty-eight percent of all drafted high school infielders are shortstops, but only 15.9 percent make it to the majors, while 16.1 percent of the.other infielders drafted make it. In Division 1 colleges, forty-four percent of infielders drafted are shortstops. 37.7 percent make it..
- More infielders (sixteen percent) make it to the majors than other position players. Catchers (12.6 percent) are at the bottom of the list.
- College catchers made it to the majors in less time (3.0 years) than all other college position players. Outfielders made it in 3.61 years, infielders in 3.25 years, righthanded pitchers 3.24 years, and lefthanded pitchers in 3.05.
- High-school outfielders made it to the majors in less time (4.19 years) than all other posi-

tion players except shortstops (4.15 years). Infielders as a whole took 4.73 years, catchers 4.31 years, righthanded pitchers 4.44 years, and lefthanded pitchers in 4.95 years.

References:

The Baseball Encyclopedia 18th Edition; 1998. St Martin's Press

Official Baseball Register; 1988 through 1998. The Sporting News

Baseball Almanac; 1991 through 1998. Baseball America

The Baseball Draft; The First 25 Years; 1965-1989, 1990. Baseball America

Baseball America, February 2-15, 1998. Baseball America

Table #1

Average Years-to-Majors / Percent of Players Drafted to Majors

	RHP	LHP	Catch.	IF	Short.	OF	Overall
High School							
Years to majors	4.44	4.95	4.31	4.73	4.15	4.19	4.50
% to majors	14.4	14.6	12.6	16.0	15.9	13.7	14.4
Division 1 Colleges							
Years to majors	3.31	3.06	3.00	3.28	3.40	3.59	3.29
% to majors	30.2	28.2	19.2	31.5	37.7	26.6	31.3
Small College							
Years to majors	4.07	3.25	3.00	3.60	3.17	3.43	3.68
% to majors	16.7	20.0	6.3	21.1	30.4	9.1	16.7
Junior College							
Years to majors	3.76	4.36	5.00	4.25	4.43	4.17	4.05
% to majors	16.2	20.0	6.3	21.1	30.4	9.1	16.7

Table # 2

Ranking of states: High School (numerals are rankings, not raw data)

	Players Drafted	Players to majors	% Drafted to majors	500 AB/ 100 IP	Ave. yrs. to majors	Overall
East*	5	4	4	4	3	4
Connecticut	34	15	1 (42.9)	15	27 (5.67)	22
Delaware	40	28	8 (20.0)	15	2 (3.00)	23
Maine	47	33	33	26	33	47
Massachusetts	24	15	6 (21.4)	26	1 (2.67)	15
New Hampshire	42	28	2 (33.3)	26	7 (4.00)	27
New Jersey	11	21	29 (7.7)	15	30 (6.00)	28
New York	9	4	4 (22.2)	4	22 (4.88)	4
Pennsylvania	11	21	29 (7.7)	15	7 (4.00)	17
Rhode Island	42	33	33	26	33	43
Vermont	47	33	33	26	33	47
West Virginia	34	33	33	26	3	37
Atlantic Coast*	6	6	1	4	5	5
Maryland	31	21	4 (22.2)	15	14 (4.50)	18
North Carolina	7	6	15 (16.67)	4	11 (4.14)	4
South Carolina	11	8	10 (19.2)	12	29 (5.80)	14
Virginia	18	10	11 (19.05)	6	12 (4.25)	9
South*	2	2	5	2	1	2
Alabama	14	8	7 (20.1)	12	21 (4.80)	13
Arkansas	27	28	28 (8.3)	26	7 (4.00)	30
Florida	2	2	17 (15.5)	2	6 (3.84)	1
Georgia	10	10	17 (12.1)	6	4 (3.50)	6
Kentucky	18	15	19 (14.3)	15	23 (5.00)	20
Louisiana	16	21	26 (9.1)	26	2 (3.00)	21
Mississippi	16	21	26 (9.1)	15	30 (6.00)	29
Tennessee	28	33	33	26	33	33
Midwest*	3	5	6	3	2	3
Illinois	5	4	13 (18.2)	6	20 (4.75)	7
Indiana	24	10	3 (28.6)	12	12 (4.25)	10
Iowa	40	33	33	26	33	42
Michigan	14	15	21 (12.5)	6	5 (3.75)	10
Minnesota	30	33	33	26	33	35
North Dakota	52	33	33	26	33	52
Ohio	6	10	25 (9.3)	6	14 (4.50)	10
South Dakota	52	33	33	26	33	52
Wisconsin	37	33	33	26	33	39
Plains*	4	3	3	6	6	5
Kansas	37	33	33	26	33	39
Missouri	28	33	33	26	33	34
Nebraska	37	33	33	26	33	39
Oklahoma	21	15	15 (16.67)	15	23 (5.00)	19
Texas	3	3	12 (19.0)	3	19 (4.74)	3
Rockies*	8	8	7	7	7	7
Colorado	22	28	33	26	30 (6.00)	32
Idaho	44	33	33	26	33	44
Montana	47	33	33	26	33	47

New Mexico	31	28	24 (11.1)	15	23 (5.00)	36	Oregon	24	21	19 (14.3)	15	14 (4.50)	23
Utah	31	33	33	26	33	36	Washington	8	7	18 (15.4)	26	18 (4.67)	16
Wyoming	47	33	33	26	33	47						

West*	**1**	**1**	**2**	**1**	**4**	**1**	**International***	**7**	**7**	**8**	**8**	**8**	**8**
Alaska	47	33	33	26	33	47	Canada	34	33	33	26	33	37
Arizona	20	10	8 (20.0)	6	7 (4.00)	8	Puerto Rico	4	15	32 (5.3)	26	27 (5.67)	26
California	1	1	14 (16.72)	1	17 (4.64)	2	Virgin Islands	44	33	33	26	33	44
Hawaii	44	33	33	26	33	44	All high school			14.4%		4.50 yes	
Nevada	23	21	21 (12.5)	15	23 (5.00)	25	*Ranked against each of the other regions						

Table # 3

Ranking of states: College (numerals are rankings, not raw data)

	Players Drafted	Players to majors	% Drafted to majors	500 AB/ 100 IP	Ave. yrs. to majors	Overall							
PAC 10	1	1	6 (35.7)	1	5 (2.97yrs)	1	Sun Belt	13	13	15 (27.5)	13	16 (3.72)	13
SEC	2	2	10 (31.7)	2	3 (2.87)	2	Colonial	14	14	11 (31.3)	16	15 (3.70)	13
Big Ten	6	3	2 (42.7)	3	12 (3.50)	3	West Coast	9	12	19 (21.8)	13	18 (4.08)	15
Missouri Valley	7	6	4 (38.4)	4	7 (3.04)	4	American East	19	18	13 (29.4)	16	6 (3.00)	16
ACC	5	3	5 (37.6)	5	13 (3.59)	5	Trans American	14	16	12 (29.6)	16	14 (3.63)	17
Big 12	3	3	18 (24.1)	5	4 (2.88)	6	Ohio Valley	20	17	1 (42.9)	20	20 (4.67)	18
Big West	8	8	7 (34.5)	8	8 (3.20)	7	Southern	16	20	20 (17.4)	16	9(3.33)	19
Big East	11	9	9 (31.9)	12	1 (2.73)	8	Southland	18	18	17 (26.3)	13	19 (4.40)	20
WAC	4	7	14 (27.9)	7	11 (3.42)	9	Other Division 1			23.8		3.04	
Atlantic 10	16	15	3 (39.1)	10	2 (2.78)	10	Total Division 1			31.3		3.26	
Mid-American	12	9	8 (32.6)	9	10 (3.40)	11	Small College			16.1		3.68	
Conference USA	10	11	16 (27.1)	10	17 (3.83)	12	Junior College			16.7		4.05	
							High School			14.4		4.50	

Table # 4

College Conference Team Performance

	Five or more players to majors	None or one player to majors
PAC 10	Stanford, Arizona St., UCLA, Arizona, USC, Washington St.	Oregon St., Portland St.
SEC	LSU, Florida	Vanderbilt, Alabama
Big Ten	Michigan, Minnesota	Penn St.
Missouri Valley	Witchita St., Creighton	Indiana St., N. Iowa, SW Missouri St., Illinois St.
ACC	Florida St., Clemson, Georgia Tech	Maryland, Virginia, Wake Forest
Big 12	Texas	Kansas St., Nebraska
Big West	Cal St. Fullerton, Long Beach St.	Pacific, New Mexico St., UC Santa Barbara
Big East	None	Providence, Boston College, Pittsburgh, Rutgers, Georgetown
WAC	Fresno St.	Utah, Air Force, Rice, New Mexico, San Jose St., Hawaii
Atlantic 10	None	All except Massachusetts, Fordham, Virginia Tech
Mid-American	Kent	All except Miami (Ohio)
Conference USA	None	All except Houston, S. Florida, Southern Miss, UNC Charlotte
Sun Belt	South Alabama	All except Lousiana Tech, New Orleans
Colonial	None	All except Vir. Comm., Old Dominion, James Madison
West Coast	None	All except Santa Clara, Pepperdine, Loyola (Cal)
American East	None	All except Maine
Trans American	None	All except Florida Int'l
Ohio Valley	None	All except Middle Tenn., Eastern Illinois
Southern	None	All except Georgia Southern
Southland	None	All teams
Other Division 1 Conferences and Independents Miami (Fla)		All except West Chester, Jackson St., Wright St.

The National Spit Tobacco Education Program

Joe Garagiola and baseball fight a deadly tradition

Leonard Koppett

The 1986 Surgeon General's report on the Health Consequences of Smokeless Tobacco Use focused attention on oral cancer and other diseases caused by "smokeless" or "spit" tobacco. At that time, the smokeless or "chewing" tobacco industry was in the midst of a campaign, begun in the late 1970s, to change attitudes toward its products while ramping up efforts to reach a more youthful audience. The industry, which used celebrity baseball players as models in its advertisements, attempted to convey a message that smokeless was synonymous with harmless.

The marketing strategy was successful. Sales of moist snuff—commonly referred to as "dip"—rose by 55 percent between 1978 and 1985. Baseball players, particularly, took to spit tobacco. A 1985 survey of male college baseball players found that 40 percent used spit tobacco regularly. A survey taken two years later revealed that over half of professional baseball players had a history of spit tobacco use and that 34 percent were current users.

As the result of a campaign led mainly by the National Cancer Institute, the NCAA in 1990 banned the use of tobacco in all tournament play. In 1992, spit tobacco was banned in Rookie and Class A leagues. The Los Angeles Dodgers banned players from carrying snuff or chewing tobacco while in uniform, and the Oakland A's banned tobacco advertising in its program.

At the same time, Joe Garagiola had been on a one-man crusade of his own against spit tobacco. In the fall of 1995, Garagiola, Oral Health America, and The Robert Wood Johnson Foundation developed the National Spit Tobacco Education Program (NSTEP). The initiative involved all twenty-eight major league teams. The Foundation's initial support of $800,000 was renewed for three years in 1997 to the tune of $3.5 million.

The cooperation of Major League Baseball can be attributed largely to Garagiola's passion and persistence. In this article, Leonard Koppett chronicles how Garagiola led an effort that changed the way Major League Baseball viewed and responded to the problems of spit tobacco. His particular brand of leadership may serve as a lesson for other public health campaigns.

As a boy in St. Louis, Joe Garagiola was the second-best baseball player on his block. The best was Larry Berra, also known as Yogi. After World War II, both Joe and Yogi became major league players, and Yogi went on to make it into the Hall of Fame. Yogi's malapropisms, many of them given circulation by Joe, have become a part of the language. "It ain't over till it's over" was one of Berra's maxims, and on another occasion he said, "It was deja vu all over again." When Garagiola's baseball career ended, his own wit

Leonard Koppett has been a sports journalist for fifty-five years, and has been named to the writers' wing of the Baseball Hall of Fame. He as worked for numerous newspapers, including the Herald Tribune, the New York Post, the New York Times, and The Sporting News as a contributing writer, columnist, and an editor. Koppett has taught journalism-related courses at Stanford University and San Jose State University. The author of twelve books, most of them about baseball, his most popular include A Thinking Man's Guide to Baseball, 24 Seconds to Shoot (An Informal History of the National Basketball Association), and Sports Illusion, Sports Reality, his most recent is Koppett's Concise History of Major League Baseball.

and way with words led him to a second career as a broadcaster and speaker. His work on nationally televised weekly broadcasts and World Series broadcasts gave his style a major showcase, and led to other broadcasting work.

Garagiola became a host on the Today show, wrote a couple of books, and in due course took a leadership position in the Baseball Assistance Team, or BAT, which is devoted to helping former players in need of financial aid and other help, especially those who did not enjoy the benefits of baseball's big-money era. It was through BAT that the scope of the tobacco problem involving ballplayers came to his attention.

"I can't really pinpoint the day that I started with this tobacco thing, any more than I can say that I had a plan to form a national group and do what is being done today," Garagiola said one day in Phoenix, where he now lives. "I'm very grateful for how it has evolved. But I'm not doing a humility act when I tell you that it just happened. I used to do my own little campaign, all by myself, when I was doing the Game of the Week. I'd have my scorebook with me all the time, and I always tried to find a newspaper clipping about oral cancer. I would paste it on the left-hand side of my scorebook so that when I wrote down the lineups it would be there."

Garagiola went on, "Well, you know how ball players are. They're going to come over to see what you're writing. So they would come over and see me writing the lineup—and one or two or more would wind up reading about chewing tobacco. It was always some simple headline, like 'Tobacco Causes Cancer,' and if we talked about it, it was always a one-on-one exchange. I would get on certain guys. One in particular who comes to mind is Bobby Cox. He was managing Toronto. I was sitting on the bench with him, and we talked about it. 'Bobby, that stuff is really bad,' I said. 'And I think you've got a sore in your mouth. You ought to let the trainer look at you.' One day he had the trainer look and found that he had a little sore there. The next time I saw him, he had switched to herbal, the nontobacco thing. I said, 'Bobby, that's great. But are you going to stand at home plate and tell kids who are watching you chew this stuff that it's herbal, that it really is not tobacco? It's just as important to get the message out that you're not using tobacco as it is to stop using it. Don't you see?' And he said, 'Well, what do you want me to do?' I told him, 'Use gum.' The last time I saw him, even before he said hello, he said, 'My jaws are about to fall off from chewing this gum,' and I said, 'Well, you're not going to die from tired jaws.' That's the way it went."

I would talk to these guys and kind of get on them, but that didn't do much. It was like trying to hit with a broken bat."

As a writer, I was around all the same people at the same time as Joe Garagiola. One of the first things you learned as a writer was where to put your feet so that the tobacco-chewing players wouldn't ruin your shoes when they spat. Nobody seemed to object to their chewing.

Three reasons why—"It was just so prevalent," Garagiola said. "I chewed when I played. I didn't know why. I thought it was part of being a ballplayer. Now I'm convinced guys chew, first of all, out of peer pressure; second, out of boredom; and third, to give off a macho image. I don't lean too much on the macho image part because I think a lot of guys get upset at that, but I do know about boredom. What happens is that you start to play games with the stuff. I spent enough time in the bullpen to know how bored you can get out there.

"In those days, there was none of this dip that you put next to your gums. It was all leaf tobacco, and you put the big chew in your mouth and kept it to one side and did a lot of spitting. So you think of games: who could spit the farthest, who could spit the straightest; hold out your foot, a dollar you can't hit it; there's an ant, let's see who can drown the ant. First guy to drown the ant wins the pot. So it was kind of like a fun thing, and yet it was becoming pretty addictive. That's why I don't minimize it. Guys tell me, 'I only chew when I come to the ball park. I never chew at home. I only chew when I play golf. I only use this stuff when I fish.' But that's not true, because the stuff is addictive. I know I wound up using it at home and thinking nothing of it. So what I was trying to do was simply to tell the other side of the story."

The other side of the story was never mentioned. Writers always write what the people they cover are talking about, and nobody ever talked against chewing. Smoking a cigarette in the dugout became unacceptable at some point, so a player—or the manager—would step down into the passageway to the clubhouse for a smoke. We wrote about that, taking it lightly or not, but that's what we do: reflect what's going on around us.

The word—"The tobacco companies have a word, and the guy who came up with that word should get a huge bonus, because with that one word they really put a whole new spin on this tobacco business, be it chew, be it snuff, be it dip," Garagiola went on. "The word is 'smokeless.' They refer to it as 'smokeless tobacco.' My big battle is to convince people that 'smokeless' is not 'harmless.' Now, 'smokeless' is a nice, fuzzy, protective kind of word, making you think it's a substitute for cigarettes—so go ahead and use it. I don't know how much stronger it is, but I've heard experts say that the nicotine from just one dip is the equivalent of what you can get from four cigarettes. Then how much is one can?

"Well, we did start to carry the message into the clubhouses, and they passed a rule against using tobacco in the minor leagues. There's a fine for doing it, and in the minors any fine is significant. But the policing is supposed to be done by managers and umpires, and they don't do it. They can't. So I don't think we can just ban tobacco use in the minors or the majors. There's no way to police it. That's why education is the key. When you finish a presentation, ballplayers will come up to you and say, 'Man, I really want to quit. What do I do?' Well, up to last year all we could do was give them a '1-800 FOR CANCER' number, and they could call and get some brochures. That was not really the answer."

Garagiola paused, and then said, "So what I was doing was a one-on-one thing. Wherever I went to make a speech, I would manage, somehow, to get the tobacco issue in there. Then a lot of guys would come up and say, 'Man, I'd like to help in your battle.' Well, that sounds good, but nobody was stepping up. Where it really kind of got started was here in Phoenix. I was doing a banquet, and my motivation had just been intensified by two statistics I saw. One was that in 1993, here in Arizona, 9.8 percent of the third- to sixth-graders were users. Now, I'm not a numbers guy, I'm a people guy, but this really got me. I thought, third- to sixth-graders? That's scary. Somebody has to say something. So I started talking about that, and people found it very hard to believe.

Getting some help—"Then I read a report that 20 percent of American high school boys, grades nine to twelve, are current spit tobacco users. Among white high school boys, it was 25 percent. Well, at this banquet in Phoenix, I was introduced to Don McKenzie, who was on the board of directors of Oral Health America. 'Don may be able to help you fight tobacco.'

"I said, 'If you can, good. But I've been getting nothing but lip service, I want you to know that. So if you're going to help, fine. If not, let's just say hello and I won't waste your time and you won't waste mine.' He looked at me and said, 'I've never been in-troduced to a guy like that before.' I said, 'Well, if we were just introduced to make friends, I'd be a little friendlier. But I get sick and tired of lip-service people.' He said, 'I think I can help you. I believe we're trying to do something. I'd like to talk to you about it.' So I said, 'Good, let's have a meeting.'"

Garagiola continued, "And he said, 'When can we do that?' I said, 'Any time. You want to do it after the banquet tonight?' He said, 'No, no really, because I have my wife with me and I really can't do it. How about tomorrow?' To myself I thought, I'll find out in a hurry if this guy is for real. 'O.K.,' I said. 'How about seven o'clock?' He said, 'Seven o'clock tomorrow night?' I said, 'No, no, tomorrow morning. I've got a very busy day.'"

"I didn't, but I figured that if this guy would meet me at seven o'clock in the morning, he's serious. Well, he did. We talked. He put me in touch with Oral Health America in Chicago. Their mission is to improve and promote the oral health of Americans. That was the beginning of an important contact."

By that time, Garagiola had collected some powerful real-life examples about tobacco use in baseball. There was the coach in the Cardinal organization known throughout the game for his baseball expertise. He blamed tobacco dip for the fact that a piece of his tongue had to be cut out. "Damn dipping," he said. "My doctor told me I'd better stop, but I had to lose part of my tongue to learn." Unable to speak clearly, he had to learn to speak all over again. Eleven months later, the coach died.

Then there was a young man from Montana who had lost half his face to cancer. Garagiola did a Today show spot with him. He was not a professional, just a guy who loved to play sports. He said that he had started dipping and chewing when he was twelve years old, because everybody else did it. The interview with the young pitcher revealed another aspect of the tragic consequences of tobacco-related disease. The young man talked about his operation, the pain, the inability to raise his arm above his head—and then he told a story about picking up his little boy at school. One day, the boy asked his father to park on the other side of the street. The father thought, He wants to show me how brave he is, that he can walk across the street. But that wasn't it at all. The other kids were teasing his son because of the way his father looked: most of the jaw on the right side of his face had been taken away, and the boy was ashamed of how his father looked.

"Now I'm emceeing the Golden Spikes dinner at the Waldorf in New York, where they honor the college baseball Player of the Year," Garagiola said in Phoenix. "I see all these young faces, and the tobacco thing keeps popping into my mind, and I say to myself, Oh, man, this isn't the spot to do it, but do it. Talk about it. Don't talk about it. I figure they're not paying me, so talking about spit tobacco would be my payday. So I went into my tobacco thing and directed it at these young guys. I gave it my best shot: smokeless is not harmless, the whole number. And the reaction from the audience was really good. In fact, it turns out that Alex Rodriquez, now with the Seattle Mariners, was on the dais at the time and heard me. He was one of the first players who wanted to help. He picked up the phone later, I didn't have to call him, and he said, 'What can I do?'

"Anyway, right after the awards dinner was over, Creighton Hale, the head of the Little League, who knew me, came up to me. 'I didn't realize you had such a passion against tobacco,' he said. I let loose.

"Oh, man, I just think we have to do something. We have an oral cancer epidemic on our hands. It's hidden. It's silent. Nobody's doing anything because smoking is getting all the publicity. Secondhand smoke and stop smoking here and no smoking on planes. And the tobacco companies are laughing. They're going to make their money by exporting the cigarettes, and what they will do is target the young people. You see it, the rodeos, the good-old-boys circuit with the Skoal-branded car, the country-western concerts and the rock concerts. And they give these free samples on the college breaks. You can see they're targeting the young people with this stuff and making it sound like a good alternative to cigarettes even though they put on the packages, 'This is not a safe alternative to cigarettes.' Then there's the whole insidious advertising campaign."

Garagiola went on, "I tell him about those little flavor packs, like little tea bags, which sting a little bit but taste like hard candy. That's how you start. And it says on there, 'Try Skoal flavor packs when you can't smoke,' although they don't actually say that. That's how they get you started. After you use that for a while, you want something stronger, and you go to the middle group, and then that buzz is not enough for you and you graduate to the top of the brand. Then they got you.

"At the time, I didn't know it would come out in the tobacco hearings that, yes, that's how they do it. They have a starter product and a graduation product. So Creighton Hale introduced me to Neil Romano. His company does educational programs, and they had done the anti-spit-tobacco campaign for the Little League. We put him in touch with Oral Health America. We got enough money to set up a press conference at the National Press Club in Washington, at which I would have Bill Tuttle tell his story."

Bill Tuttle—Bill Tuttle's story starts with a request to BAT—I had covered him when he played in the major leagues, but had lost touch with him after he retired. He was a first-rate outfielder with Detroit, Kansas City, and Minnesota for eleven years, ending in 1963—when pay scales were low and long before the players had an effective union. In 1993, his wife, Gloria, called BAT because Bill had to go to the hospital and they wouldn't admit him without a $5,000 down payment. She had noticed a big lump on the side of his jaw and thought he was still chewing in the house, but he said he wasn't. They went to a doctor, who took one look and said get him to a hospital immediately. In a thirteen-hour operation, they removed the biggest malignant tumor in the history of the University of Minnesota Hospital.

Gloria was all for going after the tobacco companies because they hadn't told the whole story about spit tobacco. Garagiola asked if they could come to a press conference in Washington. Gloria said sure, as Bill was going around to high schools and talking about it already.

"So Tuttle would be the story," Garagiola said. "But Bill Tuttle or Joe Garagiola was not going to attract a crowd to the National Press Club. So I called Mickey Mantle, asked him what his feelings were, and would he come? And he proceeded to tell me that he was anti-chewing tobacco. That was kind of interesting, because he said that when he came up to the Yankees, Casey Stengel, the manager, asked him if he had to chew that stuff. Mickey said he didn't have to, but he chewed it because he had done it back in Oklahoma. Anyhow, he said, 'Yeah, I'll come.'"

Garagiola went on, "The other player I wanted was Hank Aaron, because I'm a big Aaron fan. We all know what a great ballplayer he was and what he's done. I've always felt that when Henry Aaron has something to say and he believes it, he is going to say it and let the chips fall where they may. So I called Henry and he said, 'Yeah.' He told me a story about a high school kid he had tried to talk out of tobacco, a football player who eventually died. He told me how when he was running the minor league system for the Braves, he wouldn't even put pockets in the back of the players' pants so that they would have no place to put tobacco. Yes, he'd be happy to come.

"With Mickey Mantle and Hank Aaron as my

Bill Tuttle

Bill Tuttle was a fine ballplayer, an eleven-year big leaguer, and a nine-year regular, mostly with the Detroit Tigers and the Kansas City A's, almost entirely as a center fielder. He was a decent hitter (.259 lifetime, but .300 in 1959) with little power (67 career homers). Never a big name, he was known by his peers for his defense.

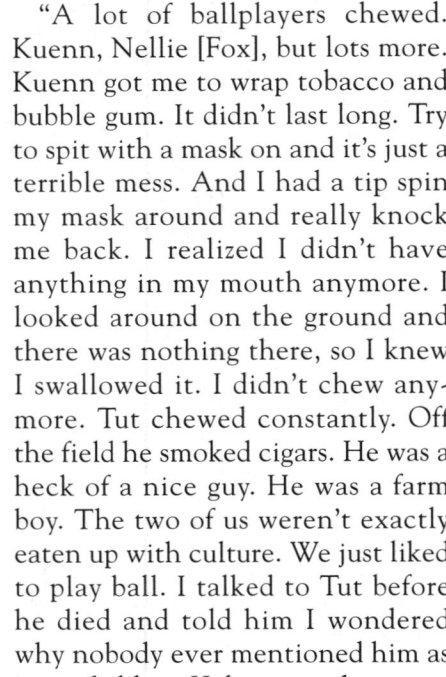

"He could catch anything out there, and he had a good arm," remembers catcher Frank House, his teammate at both Detroit and Kansas City, and his roommate with the Athletics. "He didn't have the speed of Mantle, but he caught everything. He'd run into fences, get knocked down.... He made a catch in deep left center in Yankee Stadium off Skowron. Mel Allen came into the clubhouse later and said it was the greatest catch he'd ever seen.

"I remember a game in Chicago. I hit a home run to put us ahead, and I'm squatting there behind the plate in the bottom of the ninth thinking, 'Man, I'm big print.' Then Lollar hits a shot, and I think, 'Oh, man, I'm small print.' But somehow Tut catches up with the ball. I don't know how.

"A lot of ballplayers chewed. Kuenn, Nellie [Fox], but lots more. Kuenn got me to wrap tobacco and bubble gum. It didn't last long. Try to spit with a mask on and it's just a terrible mess. And I had a tip spin my mask around and really knock me back. I realized I didn't have anything in my mouth anymore. I looked around on the ground and there was nothing there, so I knew I swallowed it. I didn't chew anymore. Tut chewed constantly. Off the field he smoked cigars. He was a heck of a nice guy. He was a farm boy. The two of us weren't exactly eaten up with culture. We just liked to play ball. I talked to Tut before he died and told him I wondered why nobody ever mentioned him as one of the great center fielders. Kaline was the greatest in right. Nobody better. With the Tigers people always said we were weak in left, but with Kaline and Tut out there we had nothing to worry about on that side.

—*Mark Alvarez*

headliners, and then Bill Tuttle and Leonard Coleman"—the president of the National League—"I knew that we would pack the place, because people would show up to at least try to get Mantle's and Aaron's autograph. And that's exactly what happened. It was a very successful press conference—so successful that Senator George Mitchell was having a press conference next door and nobody was showing up, so he came over to our room. So we had a big crowd, lots of cameras, a lot of publicity. Lo and behold, Mantle told a story. Aaron told a story. Coleman told a story, and Tuttle told his story—and Joycelyn Elders, the Surgeon General, was there to hear it. In fact, she even gave facts and figures on what spit tobacco did and was supportive. We got full coverage because the cameras and newspapers were there. That's when we started to develop a plan: we'd go to the major leaguers and tell our story.

The campaign—"The contact had been made with The Robert Wood Johnson Foundation because they had people who were interested. A proposal was made and they funded our effort, which we called The National Spit Tobacco Education Campaign. We started in the spring of 1996. Until Robert Wood Johnson came along, I was working with a broken bat—now I had a Louisville Slugger.

"When I'd go into a clubhouse, I could see the look on their faces that said, 'Oh, God, here comes another one of those sermons.' They get one from the FBI guy about unsavory characters and betting and all that, and then the insurance people come in. So I tell them right away that baseball did not pay our way. We're here because we believe in it and we thank the ball clubs for giving us the opportunity. But I'm also here to tell you we are going to talk about tobacco, but I'm not saying you should quit. I'm telling you it's a choice. Baseball is a game of choice. I chose to be a catcher. Some of you choose to be pitchers. Some choose to be infielders. I talk choice. You take a curve ball, you choose to hit a fast ball. That's the way it is with tobacco. We want you to make the right choice.

"Then Tuttle tells his story, and when he's finished, I say, 'You know, guys, now I want you to think about your wife or your father or your mother or your sister or brother or loved one, because you heard Bill Tuttle say that the doctor told him his operation was going to take two to two-and-a-half hours—and it took thirteen. Think of your wife or your loved one sitting in that waiting room thinking you're going to come out in two hours, and now it's hour five. It's hour seven.' And then I say, 'But I'm not going to tell you because I didn't live it. Gloria will tell you.'"

Garagiola continued, "And Gloria's even more powerful than Bill, because she doesn't have a script. But she also gets frustrated and angry. One time, she got angry and called me. 'Why don't you just write a letter, just to get it out,' I told her, 'and send it to me.' The letter was so powerful that I called USA Today and asked if they would print it. They did. The opening line was 'I'm watching the man I love die.' When I saw it in print, I thought, we have to get this into the hands of the wives. So I called Don Fehr, the head of the Players Association, and with his help we were able to get it to the wives. We got a big reaction from the wives.

"We also had a lot of help from the ballplayers themselves, and most were willing to help. The first players we approached to participate in the campaign were Jeff Bagwell, Frank Thomas, and Hank Aaron. Other players were volunteering to come up and help us. At a typical visit to the ballpark, players would walk up to me and say, 'how's the tobacco thing going? If there's anything I can do, let me know.' Now, because of The Robert Wood Johnson Foundation, we were able to do videos, posters, and all that good stuff. We were able to do things we couldn't do before. So we went to guys like Lenny Dykstra, Mike Piazza, Tino Martinez, Alex Rodriquez, and Paul Molitor, and they agreed to do television spots broadcast during major-league games. We did events in the stadiums and health and antitobacco people brought in kids from the community, and the ballplayers would join us after batting practice—on their own

time—to speak to the press and the young people and the Little Leaguers who were in the audience. And we'd hand out a poster featuring a player from every major-league team. Every town we went to, we got newspaper columns, we did interviews in the team's broadcast booth and we did radio and television shows. I also sent a letter and a brochure ('Talking About Spit Tobacco and Baseball with Joe Garagiola') to the networks and the baseball card companies. Fox, NBC, and others tried to keep the cameras away from players who were chewing and spitting. The trading card companies stopped photographing players with a big wad in their cheek. We had our ads in team magazines and other publications. The Seattle Mariners, for one, even made the decision to ban tobacco advertising in all of its publications and in the stadium. And Major League Baseball gave us full-page ads in the World Series and All Star Games programs.

"More help came from Charles Schulz—Sparky—who does the 'Peanuts' comic strip. He not only did a cartoon, he did it on a Sunday, the day before the All-Star Game in 1996. The coverage on that was tremendous. Not only that, he used his own money to do an animation piece for us. It's used by most ball clubs. It's a very powerful one.

"I told my story to President Clinton and urged him not to refer to it as smokeless tobacco but as 'spit tobacco.' I told him why, and he agreed, and he used that in an announcement he made in the East Room of the White House about their effort to keep tobacco away from kids. That was the beginning of getting really big support, because the President talking about not only cigarettes but also spit tobacco brought this subject to the forefront.

"We were doing our spring training tour, and the President wanted to single us out. He called a press conference, and two young women from the Olympic soccer team were to be singled out for their battle against tobacco. Gloria and Bill Tuttle were there with me, and the President singled us out, so that was a sign of approval. Before such a press conference, you get a chance to talk to the President. I asked him if he was going to throw out the first ball at Baltimore—after the strike—and he said yes.

"'If you would just issue another statement,' I said, 'or even have a press conference, which would be great, I think—I'm sure—I could get Bud Selig and Don Fehr to be there. That would be the first time that these guys had been together and able to agree on anything, and you would be the guy who brought them together.'"

Bud Selig, owner of the Milwaukee Brewers and the acting commissioner of baseball, and Don Fehr had been the principal opposing figures in the strike that led to cancellation of the 1994 World Series and was settled only after most of the 1995 spring training session had been wiped out. They stood at the opposite poles of the labor war. An earlier attempt by President Clinton to mediate the strike had failed. Garagiola's suggestion had many positive overtones.

Garagiola went on, "The President said, 'I'll talk to my scheduling people.' Well, it worked out. We had the press conference, we went to the ball game with the President, were seen with him, and that really gave us the Good Housekeeping Seal of Approval. Now we were really off and running.

"We got even more funding from The Robert Wood Johnson Foundation in 1997—for three years—to try and get the final piece: cessation programs. We've talked to Major League Baseball and the Players Association and they've agreed to do a cessation program—the job now is to make sure it gets put in place. We can't just do it with brochures. Players have to have experts to help them quit. Guys would walk up to me in the clubhouse after our presentation and say, 'Man, I want to quit.' We want to get to a point where the team doctors and dentists can provide the help. Rather than the players coming up to me for advice ... that wasn't cutting it. I'd feel inadequate giving a brochure. So now the players can get checked regularly for signs of oral cancer at spring training and the cessation specialists will be there to help the players who want to quit.

"We'll start to work on the rural areas with rodeo, 4-H kids, colleges, baseball coaches, and the NCAA. That's how we'll spread the word and get the message out. When I spoke to two thousand coaches of the ABCA (that's the American Baseball Coaches Association) in Dallas, I couldn't believe the number of coaches and managers that were using spit tobacco even though they have a big campaign on: 'If you spit, you sit.' I also spoke at the Little League Congress twice trying to get coaches to spread the word. I want these coaches to be ambassadors. It's like throwing a rock out on the lake and getting the ripple effect. I'm deputizing these guys to go back to their towns and carry out the NSTEP, or National Spit Tobacco Education Program, campaign. But when I did a gig for the Arizona State University baseball team, I asked how strongly it was enforced. 'One of the first things the umpires say,' a coach told me, 'is "look, if you're going to use the stuff, try not to use it in the open, okay?"' So they're not encouraging it, but they certainly are condoning it, because they don't want to be watchdogs.

"On the other hand," Garagiola said, "the trainers have been terrifically supportive—minor league, major league, colleges, all of them. Supportive from day one had been Fehr and Gene Orza of the Players Association; Len Coleman and Gene Budig, the major league presidents; and Bud Selig. In one sense, baseball gets a bad rap. People say, 'Look at the big leaguers who use it.' But now we're getting kids into the system who use it in high school and college, as if the big leaguers made them do it. Somehow, baseball has got the reputation that tobacco—chew and dip—are part of baseball tradition. Well, as I tell everybody, cancer has never been a tradition.

"More and more prominent players are speaking out for us. Our poster shows one star from every team. Mark McGwire, whose father is a dentist, told a St. Louis audience recently, 'You know how I feel about spit tobacco. It doesn't help you hit. Don't do it. Don't start.' Major league baseball has been most supportive, and many big stars are speaking up for us. And I'll never forget what Mantle and Aaron did for us."

Listening to Garagiola's account, I was struck by two things in particular. One was the possibility suggested by the incident of spreading the word to the wives. Perhaps the best targets for this education campaign are girls and young women. They have the most direct effect on the behavior of boys and men in the same age group. If girls can be persuaded to show boys that they, the girls, find spit tobacco use disgusting, a powerful force against its use might be generated. The other was how much could be accomplished by one determined and talented person who could continue to be motivated through long periods of little visible result.

Of course, Joe had certain advantages that most people don't. The breadth of his contacts and friendships throughout the baseball world, along with his degree of celebrity, gave him access to people who were also notables in this field. It also gave his message credibility. As an ultimate insider, he had an opportunity outsiders can't match. The steps by which Garagiola moved to develop a wider level of support—his persistence and creative use of publicity when the right circumstances presented themselves—can guide all sorts of health education projects.

From a Researcher's Notebook

Al Kermisch

"Hit 'em Where They Ain't" was Answer to Letter from Fan

Willie Keeler's "Hit 'em where they ain't" is part of baseball lore, but the origin of the famous remark has never been pinned down. It appears that Keeler brought it up in an article in the Brooklyn *Daily Eagle* on August 7, 1901. During a rainout, a few Brooklyn players, among them Keeler, were chatting with an *Eagle* reporter. The main topic of conversation was betting on where the clubs would finish at the season's end:

"Early in the season, when the New Yorks were ten games in front of the Brooklyns, and looked like sure pennant winners, there was supposed to be a lot of money going begging that the Giants would beat out the champions.

"Keeler was there with the coin and got down $125 at even money that Brooklyn would finish in front of New York when the curtain fell. He also sent out a commissioner with $500 to bet on the same proposition but there was no more money in sight. A well known clubman offered a bonus of $100 to anybody who could get down $1,000 in the same way. No one could be found to take the New York end.

"'I guess I lose that $100 and a quarter,' said Willie with his infectious laugh as he looked over the record and saw the New Yorks ten games behind. 'I don't

think it'll be long before I cash in.'

"'Lucky Willie,' remarked a bystander.

"'Lucky nothing,' said Wee Willie, 'It's the great people I am, why, they're all looking to me for information. Here's one of the few communications that I've received this year. I'll have to hire a secretary if this thing keeps up.'

"And Keeler produced a letter from far away in Littleton, N.C., which read:

"'Mr. William Keeler: Dear Sir—Have you any treatise on the art of batting written by yourself? If so, please inform me where I can obtain such and the price thereof. I enclose stamp for reply.

"'I have always considered you the best batter in the country and from your work this year I am thoroughly satisfied that you are. Hence, wishing to become a batter myself, you can readily see why I wish to obtain information from the country's best batter.'

"'Wouldn't that make you chesty,' remarked Keeler. 'I've already written that treatise and it reads like this: 'Keep your eyes clear and hit 'em where they ain't.' That's all.'"

Yankees Perfect in "8" Years

Of the ten years ending with the number "8" in the twentieth century, the New York Yankees were in the World Series five times and won all five times with

---

Al Kermisch *coached army baseball teams in New Cumberland, Pennsylvania, 1941-42; HQ, VIII Corps, Texas, 1943, and HQ, Eighth Army, Korea, 1953.*

three of the victories ending in four-game sweeps. In 1928, the Yanks defeated the St. Louis Cardinals in four straight, with Babe Ruth hitting three home runs in the fourth game, the second time he had hit a trio of homers in a Series game. In 1938, the Chicago Cubs were the victims of a four-game sweep. In 1958, New York won over Milwaukee in seven games after losing three of the first four. In 1978, the Yankees lost the first two games to the Los Angeles Dodgers, then won four in a row. And in 1998, New York ended a spectacular season by sweeping San Diego.

Five different clubs won the Series in the other five years ending in "8." The Cubs beat the Detroit Tigers four games to one in 1908. The Boston Red Sox won over the Cubs four games to two in 1918. In 1948, the Cleveland Indians beat the Boston Braves four games to two. The Tigers defeated the Cardinals in seven games in 1968, and the Dodgers downed the Oakland Athletics four games to one in 1988.

Youngs, at 16, Played Game in '13

Ross "Pep" Youngs, who died of Bright's disease in 1927 after a ten-year major league career, was elected to baseball's Hall of Fame by the Veterans Committee in 1972. Youngs was the right fielder for the John McGraw's New York Giants when they won four straight pennants from 1921 through 1924, including World Series victories over the Yankees in 1921 and 1922. Although he was able to play in only 95 games in his final season of 1926, he still managed to hit .306, and his career average was .322.

Youngs got an early start in Organized Baseball when he played one game for his hometown San Antonio team of the South Texas League on August 26, 1913. The local paper stated: "The locals used a 16-year-old lad from the local High School at second base and he did well." Ross went 0-for-3 and had three putouts, two assists, and one error in the field.

Cy Young Not Proud of First No-Hitter

Cy Young was credited with a perfect game and two no-hitters in his Hall of Fame career, but his first no-hitter for Cleveland on September 17, 1897, only the second in the majors at 60 feet, 6 inches, was tainted. The game took place in Cleveland and was the first game of a twin bill with Cincinnati.

Early in the game third baseman Bobby Wallace fumbled a shot off the bat of Bug Holliday, which was scored as a hit. After the eighth inning, Wallace sent this note to the press box: "I should have an error on that boot in the third. No hits off Cy so far." The hit was changed to an error and Cy had a no-hit game.

In an article that appeared in the Cleveland *Plain Dealer* on June 1, 1904, Young was quoted as follows:

"The no-hit game I was credited with having pitched on September 17, 1897, was really a one-hit game," said modest Cy Young Wednesday. "In the fifth or sixth inning a ball was hit down to Wallace that was too warm for Bobby to handle. It looked like a hit off me more than it did an error for Bobby, but he sent a note to the scorer's box begging to be given an error in order to allow me a no-hit game. This was done and I got credit for letting the Reds down without a hit. I've never forgiven him for that, but it was only one instance of the good fellowship prevailing in the old Cleveland club."

Joe DiMaggio Played Only Game at First in Washington

Joe DiMaggio was one of the most graceful outfielders in major league history. During his Hall of Fame career the Yankee Clipper played 1,721 games in the outfield and just one game at first base—at Washington in 1950. The Yankees had used three men at first base that season—Tommy Henrich and Johnny Mize, both thirty-seven, and Joe Collins, twenty-eight. All three were lefthanded batters. With Henrich ailing, manager Casey Stengel announced after a game in Boston on July 2 that DiMaggio would play first base the next day in Washington. Stengel also stated that first base had been a sore spot all season and decided to use DiMaggio there until Henrich returned to the lineup. DiMaggio started at first base on July 3, with Cliff Mapes in center and Hank Bauer in right field. In the seventh inning Bauer opened with a single and slid into second when Bud Stewart fumbled the ball. Bauer hurt his ankle on the play, but stayed in the game long enough to score on a single by Bill Johnson. He then left the game. The Senators defeated the Yanks, 7-2, before a gathering of 2,653. DiMaggio went 0-for-4 against Al Sima and Mickey Harris. He handled thirteen chances without an error.

A relieved DiMaggio went back to center field the next day. In the first of two games the Yanks thumped the Nats, 16-9. Joe was 2-for-6 with a double, triple, and three RBIs. The second game ended in a 3-3 tie, called after nine innings because of darkness. Joe had one hit in three at bats. After his one game experiment at first base, DiMaggio admitted he was too green. "If I'm going to play first base, I ought to be learning in spring training, not now."

Arlett's Assault on HR Record in 1932 Stymied by Injury

In 1932, Buzz Arlett, switch-hitting outfielder of the International League Baltimore Orioles, started the season at such a fast pace it appeared he was on his way to breaking all existing home run records. On July 4, Arlett had hit forty-one home runs in just eighty-two games, including four in a game twice in a period of five weeks. Two years earlier another Oriole, Joe Hauser, had hit sixty-three home runs to set a new record. On July 4, 1930, Hauser had hit twenty-six home runs in eighty games, and did not hit his forty-first circuit clout until August 1 in his 114th game. As a comparison, in the great home run duel between Mark McGwire and Sammy Sosa in 1998, Mark had his forty-first circuit clout on July 17 in his ninety-fifth contest, while Sammy smashed his forty-first on July 28 in his 107th game.

Both McGwire and Sosa stayed healthy for the season, the Cardinal slugger playing in 155 games and Sosa in 159. Arlett was not so fortunate. On August 1, 1932, in the sixth inning of a game against Newark, Arlett caught his spikes while coming in full tilt to get under Red Rolfe's short fly and fell heavily on his shoulder. He missed a total of twenty-one games and never regained his early season form. He finished with fifty-four home runs, but still led the league, seventeen homers ahead of his teammate Frank McGowan.

Connolly Apologized to Fans

Tommy Connolly umpired in the American League from 1901 to 1931, when he retired from active service and was appointed Umpire in Chief of the AL, a position he held for another twenty-three years. He umpired the first American League game after the league attained major league status, in Chicago on April 24, 1901, with the White Sox defeating Cleveland, 8-2. Connolly and Bill Klem were the first umpires elected to the Hall of Fame by the Committee of Veterans in 1953.

Connolly was a good diplomat. He hated to throw a player out of the game and once went ten years without putting a player off the field. In a game in New York on June 16, 1905, the Highlanders defeated the White Sox, 3-0, with Al Orth besting Nick Altrock. In this game Connolly actually apologized to the fans. The following item appeared in the New York *Times* on June 17, 1905:

"Another incident, one rarely observed on the field, was an open apology by Umpire Connolly for an omission in calling either a ball or strike on one of Orth's deliveries. The matter probably would have been allowed to pass but for the urgent demands of the spectators to know what kind of pitch it was. Connolly, facing the grandstand, said that for some reason or other, he did not see the ball properly. 'It was purely an accident,' he continued, 'and would not hurt either pitcher nor batsman.'"

True Birth Date Saved Larry Doyle from Service in WW I

Larry Doyle, who played in the majors for fourteen years with the New York Giants and the Chicago Cubs, and who led the National League in batting in 1915 with a .320 average, had an unusual experience with the Army draft board in 1918. When Doyle entered the baseball ranks he listed his birth date as July 31, 1886. This made him eligible for the draft in the summer of 1918. When his birthday came around on July 31, 1918, Doyle "discovered" that he was born a year earlier, on July 31, 1885, which made him thirty-three instead of thirty-two and not eligible for the Army draft. Doyle obtained an affidavit from the priest who christened him at the time of his birth in Caseyville, Illinois, and the document was filed with his draft board.

Streaks of Hubbell and Clemens Ended by NY Clubs

Carl Hubbell's major league record of twenty-four consecutive victories for the New York Giants in 1936-37, and Roger Clemens' American League record of twenty for the Blue Jays and Yankees in 1998-99, were both stopped by New York clubs.

Hubbell's downfall came in the first game of a doubleheader at the Polo Grounds on May 31, 1937. The Brooklyn Dodgers, a sixth-place club, knocked the screwball king out of the box on seven hits in three and one-third innings, winning easily by a score of 10-2. Clemens' skein came to an end on the night of June 6, 1999, in an interleague game at Yankee Stadium. The Mets, losers of eight straight games, got to Roger for eight hits and seven runs in two and two-third innings and went on to win, 7-2.

Research in Baseball Index (RBI)

An Electronic Index to Baseball Literature

www.sabr.org/rbicdrom.shtml

What is RBI?

RBI is an electronic index to baseball literature encompassing books, pamphlets, magazine and feature newspaper articles, recordings, scores, films - in other words, nearly *everything* - about baseball. Currently, we have cataloged over 127,000 items (over 17,000 books, 97,000 articles, and 12,000 book sections) and are adding thousands more each year.

RBI is now by far the largest resource available on baseball literature and provides an excellent starting point for any baseball research project.

- *Are you writing a book about Cal Ripken?*
- *Are you interested in the Black Sox Scandal?*
- *Are you looking for some books on how to throw a curveball?*
- *Are you working on a bibliography to baseball poetry?*
- *Are you researching aluminum vs. wood bats?*

RBI will list many sources on these subjects.

Individual records include:

- Author
- Title
- Copyright date
- Statistical and graphical information
- Material type
- Named persons (significant detail)
- Topics
- Full bibliographic data

All types of information are searchable.

How can I get it?

RBI is available to anyone as a data file on CD-ROM. A free **demo download** is available at:

www.sabr.org/merchandise/ rbi.shtml

The CD-ROM includes the **RBI** database, a subject term directory, an index to RBI's Bibliographic Coding system, and a printed manual with searching tips (manual and coding system are included as electronic text files).

Available formats are:

- **MS Access 97+**
- **Paradox 5.0+**
- **dBase**
- **MS FoxPro**
- **MS Excel 97**
- **Lotus 1-2-3**
- **Lotus Approach**
- **FileMaker Pro 3.0+ (only Mac format available)**

Minimum Requirements:

- **Pentium 75, 16mbs RAM or higher (PC)**
- **68040, 8mbs RAM of higher (Mac)**
- **50 mbs of hard disc space**

Simply copy the RBI database to your computer's hard disc and search it the way you would any other file using your computer's commercial database program (see available formats listed above).

When placing your order, be sure to include the computer and software types you require.

RBI on CD-ROM

(Full Database)
Includes Manual and Coding Key

	One-Time Purchase	One-Year* Subscription
SABR members	$70	$90
Non-Members	$105	$130

Note: Institutional and Network orders are available. Please contact us at the one of the addresses below.

* - Includes first copy plus two updates (one every six months). Subscriptions are renewable at half the first year price.

International customers, please pay in US dollars.

Payment can be made with check, money order, or Visa/ Master Card payable to SABR. Institutions: Please include purchase order number.

Orders are filled within 2 weeks upon receipt of payment or purchase order.

Mail or phone in your order to:

**SABR
812 Huron Rd. #719
Cleveland, OH 44115
Ph: (216) 575-0500
Fax: (216) 575-0502**

Questions? Please write to us at the address above or at:

sabrrbi@baldeagle.com